The Large Group Re-Visited

The International Library of Group Analysis

Edited by Malcolm Pines, Institute of Group Analysis, London

The aim of this series is to represent innovative work in group psychotherapy, particularly but not exclusively group analysis. Group analysis, taught and practised widely in Europe, derives from the work of SH Foulkes.

other titles in the series

The Social Unconscious
Selected Papers
Earl Hopper
ISBN 1 84310 088 6
International Library of Group Analysis 22

Traumatic Experience in the Unconscious Life of Groups
The Fourth Basic Assumption: Incohesion: Aggregation/Massification or (ba) I:A/M
Earl Hopper
ISBN 1 84310 087 8
International Library of Group Analysis 23

Operative Groups
The Latin-American Approach to Group Analysis
Juan Tubert-Oklander and Reyna Hernández de Tubert
ISBN 1 84310 094 0
International Library of Group Analysis 24

Building on Bion: Roots
Origins and Context of Bion's Contributions to Theory and Practice
Edited by Robert M. Lipgar and Malcolm Pines
ISBN 1 84310 710 4
International Library of Group Analysis 20

Building on Bion: Branches
Contemporary Developments and Applications
of Bion's Contributions to Theory and Practice
Edited by Robert M. Lipgar and Malcolm Pines
ISBN 1 84310 711 2
International Library of Group Analysis 21

Relational Group Psychotherapy
From Basic Assumptions to Passion
Richard M. Billow
ISBN 1 84310 739 2 pb
ISBN 1 84310 738 4 hb
International Library of Group Analysis 26

Dreams in Group Psychotherapy
Theory and Technique
Claudio Neri, Malcolm Pines and Robi Friedman
ISBN 1 85302 923 8
International Library of Group Analysis 18

Rediscovering Groups
A Psychoanalyst's Journey Beyond Individual Psychology
Marshall Edelson and David N. Berg
ISBN 1 85302 726 X pb
ISBN 1 85302 725 1 hb
Internal Library of Group analysis 9

INTERNATIONAL LIBRARY OF GROUP ANALYSIS 25

The Large Group Re-Visited
The Herd, Primal Horde, Crowds and Masses

Edited by Stanley Schneider and Haim Weinberg

Foreword by Malcolm Pines

Jessica Kingsley Publishers
London and Philadelphia

First published in the United Kingdom in 2003
by Jessica Kingsley Publishers
116 Pentonville Road
London N1 9JB, UK
and
400 Market Street, Suite 400
Philadelphia, PA 19106, USA

www.jkp.com

Copyright © 2003 Jessica Kingsley Publishers
Printed digitally since 2005

Library of Congress Cataloging in Publication Data
A CIP catalog record for this book is available from the Library of Congress

British Library Cataloguing in Publication Data
A CIP catalogue record for this book is available from the British Library

ISBN-13: 978 1 84310 099 7 hb
ISBN-10: 1 84310 099 1 hb

ISBN-13: 978 1 84310 097 3 pb
ISBN-10: 1 84310 097 5 pb

For
Adele, our children and grandchildren
Martha for being my soul-mate

Contents

Foreword

As I write this in April 2003 the media are full of the war in Iraq, the downfall of the cities, the breakdown of civil society, the fear of continuing chaos and anarchy. Since the first large group book appeared in 1975, we have witnessed or participated in huge political and social changes such as the fall of the Iron Curtain, the disintegration of former Yugoslavia, the overthrow of tyrannical regimes in the Balkan countries. Political scientists have used the insights of psychoanalysts and group analysts to grasp more deeply the nature of these conflicts, to see how some repair work can be done as the map of the world is ripped up and new geographies are formed.

The Large Group Re-Visited: The Herd, Primal Horde, Crowds and Masses refers back to *Large Group*, which Kreeger edited in 1975. That pioneering book had a direct historical link to therapeutic community rehabilitation pioneered during World War II: Bion, Foulkes, Main, Bridger and de Maré were cited. The flow of ideas from war-time psychiatry led to reforms in large psychiatric institutions: the dawning awareness of the exploratory power of large groups was pioneered by British and American psychiatrists and significant thoughtful exploration of this work appeared in Kreeger's *Large Group*. Since then, the median and large group movement has rippled out across much of the world, principally Western Europe, the United States and parts of the former Soviet Union. In my own contribution, I report some traveller's tales from the many parts of the world that I have visited and where I have taken part in large group experiences.

During a lengthy career in psychiatry, psychoanalysis and group analysis, I have met and worked with the great majority of contributors to this new book. Having looked for some years for editors of a new large group book, I was pleased and fortunate that two Israeli group analysts,

Haim Weinberg and Stanley Schneider, picked up the baton and ran with it efficiently, so that this book has been completed in good time. I will allow myself to celebrate my connection with Tom Main, with whom I worked for more than a decade at the Cassel Hospital, Lamis Jarrar, who I first met at the Washington School of Psychiatry and then saw at work in the large group meeting in Jerusalem at the International Congress of Group Psychotherapy, with Earl Hopper, whose two books appear in this series, with the editors, whom I have met both in Israel and at international conferences, with Gerhard Wilke, who trained with us at the Institute of Group Analysis in London, with Robert Lipgar, with whom I have toiled fruitfully to produce the two Bion monographs in this series, with Jo Berke whose work at the Arbours Foundation I have known and admired for many years.

I was privileged to be invited as a visitor and consultant to Otto Kernberg's hospital in White Plains, New York, where Howard Kibel was introducing and coordinating small and large group work. I well remember an occasion when I was chairing the final plenary session of the International Congress of Group Psychotherapy in Copenhagen, 1980, when a political movement broke through the container of the large group, threatening to subvert the meeting for its own ends. I well remember telling the plenary that I would use the authority that had been bestowed upon me as the Chair of that meeting to bring it back to its work task, with Otto sitting beside me and I think very much supporting my leadership. His deeply thought-through contribution to this volume is vital to our understanding of the phenomenon of terrorism, its ideology and the terribly dangerous splits it causes in society. This is a theme that Earl Hopper has also clarified for us and I empathise with and appreciate what he writes about character-assassination and attacks on leadership. When such situations arise, it is helpful to see them not only on the surface, but explore them in depth.

I was glad to be able to introduce Rolf Schmidt's work to the editors, having accepted an invitation to a meeting in Munich extended to me by the members of Gunther Ammon's enterprising movement. Ammon had brought back from his years at Menninger ideas that initiated significant changes in German psychiatry and psychoanalytic psychotherapy. The only contributor to this book who I have not met or sat with in a large group is Joseph Triest, and I have appreciated meeting him through the pages of this book.

Finally, I come to two people whom I feel personally enriched by through my work with them over many years. S. H. Foulkes was my own analyst, though he should not have to take responsibility for all that I have done since that experience of 50 years ago. Foulkes gave us a theoretical framework upon which our work stands, a matrix of thought and practice. We still know too little about some aspects of Foulkes's mentality and personality and Gerhard Wilke sheds some interesting light upon these areas. Next, to Pat de Maré, always a man ahead of his times. Pat is a man of great psychological, social and philosophical vision: so often what I regarded in him as a too narrowly focused perspective has turned out to be illuminating a pathway that, years later, we find ourselves following. His thoughts and practice with median and large groups make possible this volume. In the 1930s, de Maré was a frontrunner in thinking deeply about social, political and psychological issues. He was enthusiastic about the economic ideas of Major Douglas, the originator of the Social Credit movement that had some considerable following and practical success in Canada. Only very recently did I see in a current journal that there was a revival of interest in the ideas of Social Credit. Group analytic theory and some aspects of economic theory have begun to be interwoven, as exemplified by the European Symposium of 2002 in Bologna entitled 'The Economy of the Group'.

I warmly congratulate the editors for bringing together this most significant volume.

Malcolm Pines,
Institute of Group Analysis, London

Background, Structure and Dynamics of the Large Group

Haim Weinberg and Stanley Schneider

Historical background

The impetus for this book arose out of the burgeoning interest in recent years in the large group. In the early 1970s, studying the large group became part of the educational curriculum in some training programs in group analysis. But it was only in 1972 that the Institute of Group Analysis and the Group Analytic Society (London) formally included the large group experience as an experiential part of their conferences. Many international and local group conferences (e.g. those run by the American Group Psychotherapy Association, the International Group Psychotherapy Association, the Eastern Group Psychotherapy Association, Israel Group Psychotherapy Association, and others) followed suit and now include the large group experience as part of their programs. In addition, therapeutic communities and psychiatric facilities make use of the large group in unit and ward meetings. A collection of papers on the large group (Kreeger 1975) and a special issue of the journal *Group* appeared in order to meet the need for understanding of large group processes; however, what is still lacking is a clear exposition and description of the theoretical, technical and practical aspects of technique with regard to the large group. This book attempts to fill that vacuum.

What we should be noting now is the date or period of time that large groups have been in vogue, but we find it is very difficult to pinpoint a time

period when group psychotherapists began to focus on the dynamics and
theoretical underpinnings of the large group.

We could look at Le Bon's (1952; originally published in 1896) classic
work, *The Crowd*, as a philosophical beginning in studying the psychology
of large numbers of people who come together – or, as Le Bon subtitled his
work: 'A Study of the Popular Mind.' Le Bon felt that individuals who join
a crowd subjugate their individual self, unique personality traits and moral
values in order to be part of a large amorphous whole and this releases the
'wild' part of one's personality. The individual in the crowd operates on a
lower ethical and personality level, losing individuality and revealing
'quasi-psychopathic leanings' with weaker superego functions and with
reduced feelings of guilt and anxiety. The reason for the behavioral change
is due to the fact that the crowd gives to the individual a feeling of power
while at the same time diffusing power and responsibility – which paradoxically transforms the individual from part of a crowd to an anonymous
individual within the crowd. The crowd has tremendous power over the
individual and has a contagious effect. We only have to look at political
and sporting events around the world in order to be able to see the effects
of a crowd.

Or possibly we should look to Bion's (1961) book *Experiences in
Groups* as a starting point since this work serves as a basic guideline for
Tavistock, A. K. Rice Group Relations Conferences and the Leicester Conferences; Bion led groups at Tavistock, and Rice was one of his group
members (cf. Rioch 1981). As an aside, it's important to note that Rice
(1965) viewed the large group in leader-centered terms, and even called
his text *Learning for Leadership*. While this is not exactly what we have in
mind with regard to large group dynamics, we can nonetheless see how
influential large group theory can be with regard to practical applications.

The concept of the large group was applied in another direction by
Main (1946), who began to view the therapeutic institution, in this case
the psychiatric hospital, as a large therapeutic group. Main's experience
came from the Second Northfield Experiment where a cadre of pioneering
intellectuals advanced the idea of a therapeutic community and therapeutic
milieu (Harrison 2000). However, the real pioneer in advancing the
concept of the large group to the sphere of therapeutic communities was
Maxwell Jones (1953). For the first time, psychiatry became cognizant of

the importance of social factors in treating larger numbers of patients (Schneider 1978).

From a theoretical vantage point, Marshall Edelson (1970) was instrumental in applying large group theory and principles in understanding how socio-therapy can deal with inter- and intra-group tensions. While Edelson viewed therapeutic community meetings as task-oriented (shades of Bion's concepts), Foulkes (1964, 1975) utilized group analytic principles with larger groups that were not necessarily task-oriented.

With this as a backdrop, de Maré (1972, 1985, 1989, de Maré *et al.* 1991) entered the fray. De Maré, coined the phrase 'the larger group,' to refer to groups that had numbers above the usual and traditional amount. For the first time we had a theoretical framework that distinguished between small groups, 'regular' groups, median groups and large groups. De Maré feels that 'the capacity for change in the large group is immense' (Whiteley and Gordon 1979, p.128). We now began to appreciate the importance of larger groups in terms of a capacity for change, as well as for understanding culture and society.

In 1975 Kreeger edited a volume entitled *The Large Group: Dynamics and Therapy*. For the first time, a collection of papers centering around the theme of the large group attempted to quantify and qualify the concept. Some of the original papers (by Foulkes, Main, Turquet, de Maré, Hopper and Weyman, and Pines) have become classics. This book appears over 25 years later, and shows how large group theory has evolved and helps explain culture, institutions, organizations and…even individuals. We have experts, clinicians and theoreticians from seven countries (Austria, Germany, Israel, Italy, Norway, the United Kingdom and the United States) who, in 14 papers, guide us through the intricate web of large group theory and practice.

Definition of terms

We now need to define our terms. What should be the size of a group, and what constitutes a large group? As de Maré, (1972) writes: 'The problem for the member of the small group is how to feel spontaneously…whereas for the large group it is primarily how to think' (p.106). Small groups optimally have between 7 and 12 members, with some theoreticians allowing for up to 15. Gosling (1981) even writes about very small groups of five members. The median group, as defined by de Maré *et al.* (1991), note 'that the figure of 18–20 members appears to be the appropriate size for…median groups' (p.16). Others (Storck 2002) note the more accepted standard of 15–30. In order to obviate the need for a precise categorization, de Maré's terms: 'the larger group' (1991, p.15) and 'the larger-sized-group approach' (1990, p.115), counts 20 and upwards. We generally count large group membership as anything above 30–35. Turquet (1975) addresses himself to large groups of 40–80 (p.87). However, large groups can include many hundreds of participants, or even more if we include societal groups: ethnic, cultural, political, etc. (Volkan 2001).

Not only do numbers change the physical characteristics of a group, but the dynamics and character of the group also change with the numbers of group members. As Turquet (1975) notes: '…with such numbers the group can no longer be face to face' (p.88). This, in effect, categorizes the dynamic understanding of the large group: such large numbers do not allow for intimacy but rather can engender feelings of difference and alienation. This raises a technical issue that has psychological importance: how to plan the seating arrangements. Having only one large circle doesn't allow the conductor(s) to recognize those sitting at the other end of a large room. It creates a feeling of a large cavernous body without the ability to contain; metaphorically a womb that is unable to be fertile. What has proved to be more efficacious (although not without drawbacks) are 'three to five concentric circles' (Turquet 1975, p.88) that enable group participants to be closer to one another. However, this gives rise to a situation where some participants are facing the backs of others and this can foster paranoid thoughts, as well as a dizzy, convoluted feeling. Add to this the common practice that more seasoned veterans of large group experiences usually sit within the 'inner' circle and/or close to the conductor(s), and we *de facto* awaken feelings of superiority and inferiority.

Purpose

What is the purpose of the large group? This can be viewed as a 'trick' question because large groups, as societal, educational and political structures, exist anyhow. But we do artificially create large group settings in order for participants to learn experientially what large group processes actually are. In general the consensus holds that large group experiences are not, in or of themselves, psychotherapy. A notable exception is Springmann (1975), who discusses the large ward meeting on a psychiatric ward. Today, we would refer to this type of 'psychotherapy' more as a large therapeutic community, and not psychotherapy proper.

We utilize the large group experience as a laboratory in which to study large group processes, both conscious and unconscious, as a way of understanding their impact and influence upon social, organizational and systemic thinking, feelings and actions. The large group is not capable of dealing with the specific feelings and pains of the individual and can often intensify feelings of aloneness. It cannot function as a form or type of psychotherapy, although, in some participants, it may engender feelings of containment. The large group is, however, an important tool in understanding social interactive processes and interrelationships within society. As de Maré writes: 'The large group…offers us a context and a possible tool for exploring the interface between the polarised and split areas of psychotherapy and sociotherapy. This is the area of the inter-group and of the transdisciplinary…' (1975, p.146).

Foulkes (1964) delineated multiple dimensions that operate within the group. He wrote that we could discern four levels 'from surface to deeper and hidden aspects' (p.114). The last level, 'the primordial level' (p.115), corresponds to the deepest unconscious level of Freud and the collective unconscious level of Jung. Powell (1994, p.16) wonders ('wishful thinking') how Foulkes attributed primordial images to Freud. In Foulkes' own words: 'it is always the transpersonal network which is sensitized and gives utterance, or responds. In this sense we can postulate the existence of a group "mind"…' (1964, p.118). We can see from the spiralic transvergencies that arise within the large group the parallelisms that occur within the social interactional environment known as the societal microcosm. The large group reflects not only what is occurring in the here-and-now, but also relates on a transferential level what is occurring in the organization, conference, political climate, etc.

The participant in the large group learns how to be a good 'citizen' in the group and/or society. As de Maré et al. note: 'large groups are tilted towards socio-cultural awareness. Citizenship is only adequately observable in a larger setting…' (1991, p.11). As a citizen one learns how to influence others and also how impotent we all may be. The large group

participant develops connections and feelings of belonging to society –
the large whole – and not to a specific subgroup. This enables participants
to take a more active role (emotionally if not actually physically) and to
'take in other people's points of view' (James 1994, p.60). This is
'important to the development of citizenship' (James 1994, p.60).

The large group helps in role differentiation and integration in
developing both individual and group identity. These identities can
include gender, political, religious, ethnic, etc. As these individual identity
traits emerge, they are always in the context of the large group: for
comparison, to accentuate difference, or to imitate.

The large group is an ideal venue for investigating issues of leadership
and authority. The Tavistock Conferences explore these issues within
clearly defined boundaries, which is often perceived as engendering
feelings of alienation and loneliness. In organizational consultation, the
large group is also used in order to explore conflicts and tensions within
organizational structures. As de Maré et al. (1991) write: 'large groups
provide a setting in which we can explore our social myths (the social
unconscious) and where we can begin to bridge the gap between ourselves
and our socio-cultural environment…' (p.10).

The large group participant is the 'individual' within the 'crowd.' This
is, generally, an uncomfortable feeling. The individual feels like a cog in a
wheel, losing part of his individuality and being pulled by regressive large
group dynamics. One feels in limbo between conscious and unconscious
dynamics, with the collective unconscious adding its weight to the
regressive phenomena. And there is a regressive pull in the area of
separation–individuation, between self and other. On the one hand there is
the need to belong and feel part of and contained, and on the other hand,
an opposing pull towards separation and individuation. It's very hard to
maintain one's sense of self against the onslaught of large group/crowd
dynamics.

Dynamic processes

The dynamic processes, specifically the projective processes, are different
in the large group from what we find in other, smaller group constellations.
The large group awakens feelings of anxiety much sooner than we find in
smaller groups. This is probably due to the weaker container function of

the large group, fluidity of boundaries, and the seemingly chaotic structure which awakens regressed, primary anxiety formations of feelings of fragmentation, disintegration and loss of reality. 'In a Large Group the single member feels threatened and isolated and a sense of helplessness in the face of chaos is dominant' (Ricciardi von Platen 1996, p.486). Group participants try to find order and make sense of the chaos so as not to feel lost, alone, isolated, and possibly have 'a fear of breakdown' (Winnicott 1974, p.87) and disappear. They feel 'a *threat of annihilation...* a very real primitive anxiety' (Winnicott 1956, p.303) or, as Kohut described it, disintegration anxiety: 'The core of disintegration anxiety is the anticipation of the breakup of the self...' (1977, p.104). Some large group participants may sense the increasing anxiety and sit next to someone they know, or within a subgroup structure which may separate according to nationality, religion, gender, socio-economic divisions, etc. And then there is the individual who protects the self by staying a 'singleton' (Turquet 1975), the one who is alone within the crowd.

It is not easy to talk in the large group. There are some participants who feel that if they talk even only once, they have broken the ice and achieved something major. This risking of self may also enable them to try again. And there are others who are silent for the entire large group experience, because the anxiety associated with attempting to talk and then to deal with whether what they say is accepted, or mocked, etc. is too much for them to handle.

Another important 'technical' factor that has importance for the large group experience is the ability to hear what is being said. We refer to hearing both as sensory auditory input and auditory perception. While the former relates more to physiology and acoustic structure, the latter includes emotional auditory perception. We often observe in large groups the difficulty participants have with 'hearing' – obviously an important part of the large group process. Both aspects, physical and emotional, need to be taken into account by conductors of large groups. An interesting phenomenon that occurs in the large group experience that is spread over several sessions, is that the group participants in the first or earlier sessions complain that they cannot 'hear.' Miraculously, after this initial auditory 'blockage,' group members do hear and recall what they didn't hear earlier on. We clearly see how emotions, especially anxiety, can block even abstract thinking processes and regress participants to a more concrete mode of understanding (Schneider 1987). This shift from flexible feeling and thinking to a more inflexible mode is a predictable part of the psychodynamic process in large groups.

Feelings of alienation are most prominent in the individual who has become part of a crowd, or large group. This is because in the large group there is a feeling of being alone among a large mass of people, not connected to anyone, feeling very alone and isolated. The fact that important visual and other perceptual cues are either absent or lost in the crowd, prevents the individual from gauging the body language of others. The intersubjective experience is missing. For those who are used to more fulfilling experiences in smaller group situations, the large group is an initially jolting experience. The expectation of containment, warmth and acceptance is experienced differently in the large group. Sometimes the 'wandering participant' phenomenon occurs. This is where a large-group participant feels alone and without any grounding and moves to another part of the large group in order to try and receive warmth and holding from others. This wandering often brings with it a response opposite to that expected. Often the participants who feel intruded upon react with anger and rejection. Instead of finding acceptance, holding and empathy, the 'wandering participant' feels even more isolated and alienated.

Individual identity undergoes a type of transformation. Those who are strongly identified with their own self are able to accept the rollercoaster effect that the large group has on their individual identity. However, there are those who feel lost when exposed to a large group experience. These individuals feel that their basic coping skills are deficient, and are not able to separate their own self from the others in the large group. One feels a regressive pull towards joining and merger and now seeks out the other in order to form an identity. This blurring of identity and boundaries is a distinct possibility in the large group. In order to re-assert control over one's own identity, there is the possibility of acting out in order to create a strong statement of 'here I am.' This can be expressed verbally as the participant blurts out something to the large group that is not in line with what would normally be expected. However, this 'statement' is necessary in order for the group participant to assert his or her identity.

At times the group participant feels the unconscious need to assert oneself and defend 'the flag.' When one feels attacked and identity is shaky, the counter-phobic reaction is to overextend and bend over backwards in order to reinforce and strengthen one's identity. This arises out of a fear of losing one's identity.

Main (1975), in a pioneering paper, discusses projective processes and reality-testing in the large group. Main tries to explain why the participant in the large group may often have the feeling of unreality – a type of divorce from reality. This is not a psychotic split but rather a protective mechanism allowing the participant to 'float' above what is going on so as eventually to find a comfortable level of containment and functioning. As Main (1975) writes: 'In malignant projective identification…with the ego impoverished by loss of a major part of the self, reality-testing becomes defective' (p.63). If one projects into another, there is something missing in oneself – this is the feeling of unreality: '…many individuals because of projective loss now become "not themselves"' (p.69). This feeling of unreality mixes with feelings of 'depersonalization and personality invasion…accompanied by bizarre object-relations…' (Main 1975, p.64).

Due to the frustration that may arise in the large-group participant, anger and hate may erupt in potentially uncontrollable ways. De Maré describes this as a necessity in understanding and accepting the importance of the 'larger-sized-group approach' (1990, p.115). One needs to have 'an appreciation of the significant relationship of hate as the driving power of mind and mental energy' (de Maré 2002, p.205). We see polarization of feelings and affects in the large group: splitting, extremism, prejudice and stereotypical thoughts, feelings and behaviors in the large group. A knowledge and awareness of projective processes can help the conductor(s) be better able to understand the group process and judiciously know when, and when not, to intervene.

Outline of the book

We have divided the book into two main sections: 'The Large Group: Theory and Technique,' which contains seven chapters and 'The Large Group: Application to Society,' which contains six chapters. The book ends with an Epilogue.

The first section of our book opens with an interesting contribution from Lamis Jarrar (USA). Jarrar, who leads workshops in the Tavistock and A. K. Rice traditions, writes from the perspective of a consultant, clinician and trainer who is attempting to analyze the large group unconscious.

Equally adept at object relations and Kleinian theory, Jarrar looks at how polarizations need to, and can, be bridged in order to reach the 'other,' while taking into account the consultant's biases and prejudices. Large group participants and the conductor's identities interact with each other, as the large group venue enables transforming and transformative dialogues to take place.

Malcolm Pines (UK) gives a comprehensive description of the history of the large group and its various appearances in different cultures, starting with Trigant Burrow's pioneering yet forgotten research in America in the second decade of the twentieth century. Pines' rich experience with groups around the world allows him to recount the story of the large group in countries such as France, Argentina and South Africa. Pines has been a pioneer in the study of group process in general and large group process in particular, especially in the context of transcultural understanding.

Earl Hopper (UK) outlines several propositions about aggression in the large group, leaning on his fourth basic assumption of 'Incohesion: Aggregation/Massification.' He starts with the intriguing idea that not all social systems are groups, specifies the targets, functions and forms of aggressive feelings in the large group, and explains assassination, character assassination and scapegoating in the light of the fourth basic assumption. A true trailblazer in the theoretical and philosophical understanding of group process, in developing the fourth basic assumption Hopper took great courage and put himself on the firing line against many old-time hardliners who were resistant to new understandings and interpretations. This chapter also includes some of his ideas about leaders and their vulnerabilities.

In recent years we have witnessed a proliferation of studies on the dynamic unconscious and intersubjectivity operating in all psychotherapeutic encounters. In the large group the potential for strong underlying unconscious processes is greater than in any other therapeutic context. Stanley Schneider (Israel) looks at the mystical and spiritual dimensions of the large group experience. His chapter also looks at Kabbalistic and Buddhistic understandings of mystical awareness and unconscious communication.

Chaos and order are themes that predominate in the large group experience. In attempting to inject some order into understanding the large group, Gerhard Wilke (UK) points out that although group analysts, following Foulkes, understood how the group matrix could have a healing power, widening and deepening the communication among its members, they failed to transfer this optimistic attitude from the small into the large group setting. He analyzes three generations of group therapists, starting from Bion and Foulkes, and concludes that we now have the chance to integrate the work of the 'grandparents' and the 'parents' into preventative and curative models in large group work.

No study on large group processes could be complete without a theoretical understanding of Bion's contributions, and Robert Lipgar (USA), who has recently produced two books on Bion and group process, does justice to the task. Lipgar, building on Bion, describes his own experience with starting a large group in the Manteno Mental Health Hospital in Illinois, USA, in the early 1960s. It is interesting to follow the difficulties he encountered in starting a large group experience on the psychiatric ward. His persistence and consistency, in true Bionic tradition, were the main reasons why this adventure had positive outcomes. Lipgar summarizes aspects of Bion's thinking that influenced his work and concludes that 'large group meetings work best when leadership is able to bring to the meeting a clear understanding of the distinctive purpose of the gathering.'

Projective processes are the 'bread-and-butter' of large groups. Joseph Berke (UK) has worked with Maxwell Jones and R. D. Laing and has learned through these associations how malignant projective processes can be crucial in developing therapeutic community programs. Berke, one of the founders of the Arbours programs in London, a pioneer program in the containment and treatment of persons in emotional distress, describes the power of projective processes in the large group. Berke's mixture of clinical, theoretical and anecdotal material makes for an interesting read from a gifted theoretician and clinician.

Otto Kernberg (USA) opens our second section of the book with a comprehensive paper on socially sanctioned violence from a psychodynamic viewpoint. Today we note a major increase in violence and terror, and Kernberg feels that society sanctions the use of violence. His paper reviews psychodynamic group psychology, ideological beliefs in violence and terror, and the effects of the mass media, and ends with an investigation into fundamentalism with its narcissistic and paranoid parts. Ending on an optimistic note, Kernberg writes: 'In so far as psychological factors, however, influence conflicts and violence both at individual, group, and national levels, and provide understanding for the structural analyses of ideological systems as well as leadership, hopefully, they will become part of our social armamentarium to reduce, if not eliminate, the terrible problem of violence in our human reality.'

The jump from society-as-a-whole to political process is a short one. Josef Shaked (Austria) muses about the way the large group reflects political processes. He brings examples from large groups in Austria, the Ukraine and Israel, describing how political events and processes such as the end of the Cold War, German – Jewish memories of the Holocaust, and the Israeli–Arab conflict impact upon what is going on in the large group and are reflected in it. The large group becomes a remarkable transcultural meeting, where confrontation with the stranger offers an understanding of the stranger within us.

Joseph Triest's (Israel) chapter returns us to the old debate between Le Bon and McDougall about the differentiation between the mob and the organization. His original conclusion is that 'an organization traps the "group spirit," like a genie in a bottle, and by so doing in fact preserves an eternal tension.' The meaning here is that the dialogue between order and chaos continues even when the large group is apparently tamed into being part of the organizational setting. Nonetheless, 'the large group will always threaten the setting imposed upon it by the organization.' Triest's training as both psychoanalyst and organizational consultant pairs the theoretical and clinical in an interesting and unique way.

Many of the original early experiences with large groups took place in institutional settings. Rolf Schmidts (Germany) describes in detail in-patient large group meetings at the Clinic Menterschwaige in Munich, Germany. He addresses technical questions such as the large group's venue and seating arrangements, the director's tasks, subgrouping and absences of staff members. His chapter clarifies how an in-patient large group develops a therapeutic culture. A fascinating treatment of a complex subject.

Haim Weinberg (Israel) introduces us to the new, innovative world of the large group in cyberspace. He compares the large group attributes in face-to-face settings to those in the virtual environment. It is surprising to find many similar features in both environments. Expressions of alienation, aggression, being lost in the crowd and losing one's voice appear also on the Internet. What is quite different is the strong tendency for idealization of the group leader on the Internet. Weinberg coins a new term, 'the Internet unconscious' which is related to the social unconscious.

Thor Kristian Island (Norway) focuses on a different setting in describing the large group experience in a group analytic training program in Norway. This context of the large group is seldom written about. One of its important aspects is the integrating function as the training community 'city square.' This unique setting implies that the large group is led by a team of conductors, and raises questions about collective leadership. It seems that group-analytic candidates attribute much of their personal and professional development to the large group, and this paper offers us some insight as to why it is so important in the training program.

Our book ends with an epilogue written by Pat de Maré (UK) and Roberto Schöllberger (Italy). In this final chapter de Maré and Schöllberger muse philosophically about the Larger Group as a meeting of minds – a fitting conclusion by one of the more original thinkers in group analysis and the median group, Pat de Maré.

References

Bion, W. (1961) *Experiences in Groups*. London: Tavistock Publications.

de Maré, P. (1972) 'Large group psychotherapy: a suggested technique.' *Group Analysis 5*, 106–108.

de Maré, P. (1975) 'The politics of large groups.' In L. Kreeger (ed) *The Large Group: Dynamics and Therapy*. London: Constable.

de Maré, P. (1985) 'Large group perspectives.' *Group Analysis 18*, 78–92.

de Maré, P. (1989) *The History of Large Group Phenomena*. New York: Brunner/Mazel.

de Maré, P. (1990) 'The development of the median group.' *Group Analysis 23*, 113–127.

de Maré, P. (2002) 'The millennium and the median group.' *Group Analysis 35*, 195–208.

de Maré, P., Piper, R. and Thompson, S. (1991) *Koinonia: From Hate, through Dialogue, to Culture in the Large Group*. London: Karnac Books.

Edelson, M. (1970) *Sociotherapy and Psychotherapy*. Chicago: University of Chicago Press.

Foulkes, S. H. (1964) *Therapeutic Group Analysis*. London: Karnac Books, 1984.

Foulkes, S. H. (1975) *Group Analytic Psychotherapy: Methods and Principles*. London: Karnac Books, 1986.

Gosling, R. (1981) 'A study of very small groups.' In J. S. Grotstein (ed) *Do I Dare Disturb the Universe?* London: Karnac Books, 1983.

Harrison, T. (2000) *Bion, Rickman, Foulkes and the Northfield Experiments*. London: Jessica Kingsley Publishers.

James, D.C. (1994) '"Holding" and "containing" in the group and society.' In D. Brown and L. Zinkin (eds) *The Psyche and the Social World.* London: Routledge.

Jones, M. (1953) *The Therapeutic Community.* New York: Basic Books.

Kohut, H. (1977) *The Restoration of the Self.* New York: International Universities Press.

Kreeger, L. (1975) (ed) *The Large Group: Dynamics and Therapy.* London: Constable.

Le Bon, G. (1952) *The Crowd.* London: Ernest Benn, 1952. First published as *La Psychologie des Foules.* Paris, 1896.

Main, T. F. (1946) 'The hospital as a therapeutic institution.' *Bulletin of the Menninger Clinic 10,* 66–70.

Main, T. F. (1975) 'Some psychodynamics of large groups.' In L. Kreeger (ed) *The Large Group: Dynamics and Therapy.* London: Constable.

Powell, A. (1994) 'Towards a unifying concept of the group matrix.' In D. Brown and L. Zinkin (eds) *The Psyche and the Social World.* London: Routledge.

Ricciardi von Platen, A. (1996) 'Thoughts on the setting of the large analytic group.' *Group Analysis 29,* 485–489.

Rice, A. K. (1965) *Learning for Leadership: Interpersonal and Intergroup Relations.* London: Tavistock Publications.

Rioch, M. (1981) 'The influence of Wilfred Bion on the A. K. Rice Group Relations Conferences.' In J. S. Grotstein (ed) *Do I Dare Disturb the Universe?* London: Karnac Books, 1988.

Schneider, S. (1978) 'A model for an alternative educational/treatment program for adolescents.' *Israel Annals of Psychiatry 16,* 1–20.

Schneider, S. (1987) 'Psychotherapy and social work training: individual differences.' *Jewish Social Work Forum 23,* 38–48.

Springmann, R. (1975) 'Psychotherapy in the large group.' In L. Kreeger (ed) *The Large Group: Dynamics and Therapy.* London: Constable.

Storck, L. (2002) '"Reality" or "illusion"? Things of interest about social class as a large group.' *Group Analysis 35,* 351–366.

Turquet, P. (1975) 'Threats to identity in the large group.' In L. Kreeger (ed) *The Large Group: Dynamics and Therapy.* London: Constable.

Volkan, V. (2001) 'Transgenerational transmissions and chosen traumas: an aspect of large group identity.' *Group Analysis 34,* 79–97.

Whiteley, J. S. and Gordon, J. (1979) *Group Approaches in Psychiatry.* London: Routledge and Kegan Paul.

Winnicott, D. W. (1956) 'Primary maternal preoccupation.' In *Through Paediatrics to Psycho-Analysis.* London: Hogarth Press, 1982.

Winnicott, D. W. (1974) 'Fear of breakdown.' In C. Winnicott, R. Shepherd and M. Davis (eds) *Psycho-Analytic Explorations.* Cambridge: Harvard University Press, 1989.

Part I

The Large Group

Theory and Technique

CHAPTER 1

A Consultant's Journey into the Large Group Unconscious

Principles and Techniques

Lamis K. Jarrar

The other within

'The unconscious is the discourse of the other,' Lacan tells us (1977, p.439). His voice is one of many within the relational and intersubjective perspectives, in which the other is accorded a prominent and central position. Unlike traditional psychoanalytic thinking and its emphasis on individual wholeness, separateness and integrity, in these postmodern perspectives the boundaries between the self and other are quite fluid and permeable, if not messy, and there is 'no neat line between the two – because otherness inhabit and constitute the individual' (Sampson 1993a, p.52). Similarly, Verhaeghe explains the meaning of Lacan's position as 'Identity is always outside with the Other or, more precisely, in the particular relation to this Other' (1997, p.99).

I would like to demonstrate my subjective understanding of this theoretical position by sharing my reactions and fantasies about writing this piece; after all, writing can be construed as participation in a large group experience with members in the mind. I recall very vividly my passionate internal response to the two male Israeli editors, Professor Schneider and Dr Weinberg, who dared to ask me to contribute a chapter to this book. I was furious with both of them because I was convinced that they were going through the motions, and could not possibly be genuine and sincere about their request. Furthermore, since the whole world knows about my writing inhibitions, they expected me to say no, and then would feel morally superior for having considered a Palestinian woman for such a task. I was almost certain that Malcolm Pines was the mastermind behind this request and that they were unable to refuse him. After the dust settled, I realized that I had had a similar set of reactions to writing an article for the Washington School of Psychiatry newsletter about co-leading the large group in Jerusalem 2000. In that article, I wrote: 'My initial response was a mixture of excitement and trepidation, hopeful irony and suspicion, caution and courage. Many questions, however, came to mind, among them: what was the underlying motivation behind pairing a Palestinian Israeli American woman with a Jewish American man? Was this choice indicative of a superficial and politically correct showcasing of triumphant diversity or was it a genuine and authentic attempt for collaborative and equal partnership? What are the inter-/intra-organizational political dynamics surrounding such a decision? Am I going to be truly authorized, or am I going to be used as a token so the school will look good? And most important, would it be at all possible for me to follow Bion's golden rule of entering every group without memory or desire while working in Jerusalem at this particular time with its intense symbolic representations in the minds of many?' (Jarrar 2001, p.1)

Voice and visibility

How are these thoughts relevant to our subject matter? Is there wisdom in disclosing such intimate details? What are the possible dangers of doing so? Apparently there is a parallel between my experience and that of group members and consultants as they consider self-revelation or hiding in silence in the group. Members and consultants alike do indeed struggle with what and how much to say to whom, and when. If they reveal too much, they may risk exposure, humiliation and shame. If they remain withdrawn and silent, they may risk becoming isolated, marginalized, paralyzed and uninvolved. Ultimately, to what extent is one capable of intimate engagement and connection with others in a rather public setting and why is that so troublesome to us in our times? The Greek conscious-ness of self, Bakhtin (1981) informs us, was not bound with artificial dichotomies of private and public, internal and external; that is, 'There is no mute or invisible core to the individual himself; he is entirely visible and audible…a mute internal life, a mute grief, mute thought, were completely foreign to the Greek' (p.134). Bakhtin concludes that essentially a 'conversation with one's own self turns directly into a conversation with someone else, without a hint of any necessary boundaries between the two' (p.134). To some extent, the proliferations of TV and radio talk shows in America and other parts of the world may be indicative of our wish to bridge the gap between our private and public worlds.

How these conflicts between self-revelation and silence are resolved by the membership has direct bearing on the pace and rhythms of the group. Undoubtedly, the attitude and comfort level of the consultants with self-disclosure affects the depth and breadth of members' experience. If the consultant does not model being an 'Individual Member,' using Turquet's (1975) term, it is unlikely that members will self-actualize and realize their own specific subjectivity as they also acknowledge their intersubjective experience. Therefore, my self-revealing is used to illustrate not only the prominence of the Kleinian schizoid-paranoid position when genuine dialogue is absent, but also the centrality of identity politics and the importance of its exploration in the large group. My desire as a large group consultant is to help members to become aware of their internal dialogues with the imagined other and transform them into an external and authentic dialogue with the real other. I strongly believe that it is through rigorous and painstaking engagement that the possibility of knowing, understanding and recognizing the specificity, particularity and uniqueness of both the self and the other emerges. This is, in my view, the essence of large group work. The large group provides members with opportunities to explore and learn about the difficulties we all have, as subjects, in recognizing other subjects as 'equivalent centers of experience' and enabling a move towards enhancing capacities for mutual recognition in the group. The daunting task of the consultant is to create a culture such that 'Where objects were, subjects must be' (Benjamin 1999, p.184).

Identity and diversity

Examination of one's group identities in relation to others' group identities is anxiety-provoking and threatening, particularly in a large group setting which is a close approximation to the world we live in. I believe that the consultant's willingness and capacity to enter the large group experience aware of different aspects of the self, making them available for use in service of the task, furthers the development of dialogue. Understanding the psychological impact of nationality, gender, race, culture, religion, history, biases, allegiances, ideology, political positions, on the way she assumes her role is essential. Flexibility, elasticity and transparency influence our reading of the group and our capacity to work with the tension, uncertainty, dialectic and contradictions. It is also important to register the theories she uses to inform her work, as well as our idiosyn-cratic ways of internalizing, modifying and transforming such influences.

Our suspicion, ambivalence and reluctance to show our vulnerable, unstable and shifting identities is quite understandable, knowing that primitive group defenses are used to manage anxieties and inadequacies. Such mechanisms of denial, avoidance, splitting, projective and introjective identifications abound. The evil, ugly, oppressive, weak, powerless characterize the Not Me Group or the other, while the good, healthy, beautiful, powerful, sane describe the Me Group. Clearly, locating and purging the repugnant and unacceptable parts of the group self into and onto the other has been very costly; the license we have used to justify and legitimize the many dreadful atrocities we commit. It is not surprising that de Maré (1975, 1991) views the function of the large group as an effort at humanizing society.

Morrison (1992) captures the very essence of how one group, in this case white Americans, has used another, African Americans, as a container for all the disavowed parts of the group self. She refers to this process as 'Africanism.' She writes, 'Africanism is the vehicle by which the American self knows itself as not enslaved, but free; not repulsive, but desirable; not helpless, but licensed and powerful; not history-less, but historical; not damned, but innocent; not a blind accident of evolution, but a progressive fulfillment of destiny' (p.52). Similar dynamics are present between men and women; Palestinians and Israelis; colonized and colonizers; heterosex-uals and homosexuals – and the list goes on.

Another problem that we may encounter in naming and working diversity and identity dynamics is the question of voice and visibility of oppressed minority subgroups and their individual members, and their relation to the mainstream dominant group. What voices are permitted/excluded, and on behalf of which group? Can minority members express their subjective life experiences without the dominant group silencing their presence? O'Leary argues that 'The highest moral value of postmodernism lies in its quest to give expression to the disempowered' (2001, p.479). However, Sampson cautions us about the limitation of accommodating such voices since they do not bring fundamental and transformative changes in the existing arrangements of power. He states: '…Merely to have a speaking part is still not to have one's own group's interests, point of view, or specificity represented in a genuine dialogue. If, in order to be heard, I must speak in ways that you have proposed, then I can be heard only if I speak like you, not like me. Rather than being an equal contributor, I remain enclosed in a discursive game that ensures your continuing advantage…this condition does not reflect mere chance but rather reflects the operation of the power of those in charge to dictate the terms by which psychological and social reality will be encountered' (1993b, p.1220).

These are precisely the challenges we have to deal with in the large group. Holding and containing all voices, central and marginal alike, is an art. However, sustainable development of an authentic dialogue may be impeded by subtle and insidious attempts at denigrating and negating the 'different inferior other.' As has been indicated by Skolnick, 'While group membership is essential to a viable self, group processes continually present threats to the experience of a stable positive identity' (2000, p.135). I take Turquet's (1975) views one step further by suggesting that threats to group identity as well as individual identity are at stake in the large group. I enter the group with multiple group identities, in which I am simultaneously female, American, Israeli, Palestinian, Arab, Muslim, psychologist, consultant, victim, victimizer, etc., with some aspects of my identity in the foreground and others in the background. I must be aware and reflective of my internal space in which the different parts co-exist side by side or on top of each other, available to be pulled or pushed by group pressures. This is also true for the members, who bring in their multiple selves with all their inherent complexity. The different parts of the group self are not necessarily in a harmonious relationship with each other and at times conflicts and tensions may be present. One dimension or another may take center stage in our relatedness to others and will 'hijack' all other aspects of the self. Maalouf, an eminent Lebanese-French novelist, posits that there is always some sort of hierarchy among the elements that constitutes individual identities, yet that hierarchy is not immutable, and it changes with time. He also stresses that identity is made up of a number of allegiances and affiliations. He argues that the allegiance under attack invades the person's whole identity and eclipses all other aspects of the self. He says: 'but whether he accepts or conceals it, proclaims it discretely or flaunts it, it is with that allegiance that the person concerned identifies…other people who share the same allegiance sympathise; they all gather together, join forces, encourage one another, challenge the other side. For them, asserting their identity inevitably becomes an act of courage, of liberation' (2000, p.26). These are the struggles of individuals and identity subgroups as they face the desirable and undesirable elements of themselves and each other. How do they order these elements? What aspects of identity and which subgroups assume prominent positions, and why, become fertile ground for generating hypotheses about what is happening in the group and in society.

It is noteworthy that privileging identity politics in large group discourse might be surprising, unfamiliar and, to some, simply irrelevant, particularly to members representing dominant and mainstream subgroups, i.e. white American heterosexual males. Yet, those who have suffered from marginalization, oppression, disenfranchisement, and exploitation, the voiceless ones, tend to be hyper-aware and at one with those very dimensions of their identity as primary constituents of the self and their impact on every aspect of their being. Consequently and ironically, different members of the latter group can emerge as visible leaders and exert noticeable influence as their voices become distinct, loud and clear. However, a significant difficulty is that members of oppressed groups may feel the pressure and burden of representation. Therefore, it is important to investigate group differences and sanction and affirm differentiation from one's own subgroup. While this experience might be enriching and a cause for celebration to some, for many others it can be disorienting at best and terrifying at worst. In fact, the large group becomes the arena for each subgroup to highlight, work through and repair transgenerational traumas suffered by its members, such as slavery, holocaust, colonization, immigration, etc. Competition for who has been most oppressed is a central part of the dialogue. In fact, it tends to be delivered in the form of monologues, particularly in the beginning stages of the group. The main challenge then is to transform monologues into dialogical encounters.

Developing dialogue

The use of the concept 'dialogue' in contrast to 'study' in describing the task of the large group demonstrates a significant shift in conceptualizing the primary purpose of the large group. While the focus is still on experiential learning, there is an explicit message suggesting the importance of engaging across various boundaries as a desirable way to learn and understand the self and its relation to the other. Clearly, in order to have a conversation that can possibly lead to mutual understanding, we assume the presence of 'at least "different other"' who is equally interested in talking and listening and possibly learning about differences. Sampson affirms that what is most essential about human nature is its 'dialogic quality.' He states that 'people's lives are characterized by the ongoing conversations and dialogues they carry out in the course of their everyday activities, and therefore the most important thing about people is not what is contained within them, but what transpires between them' (1993a, p.20). It is safe to assume that he favors the interpersonal, intersubjective and relational perspective with its emphasis on conversation, and rejects what he terms the 'self-celebratory monologic' (p.4) view that dominates Western theories about human nature. The prevalence of inter-group conflict, both nationally and internationally, has contributed to the emergence of dialogue as the buzzword of the 90s. The message suggests the importance of active engagement across various boundaries as a desirable vehicle for learning and understanding more about the self in relation to the other. Without doubt, learning through dialogue is most difficult. It entails making ourselves available to genuine and authentic dialogue with each other in the here and now, rather than the there and then. To do so, members are asked to look at themselves and their relationships to other fellow members, up close and personal. It is the primary responsibility of the consulting team, therefore, to provide a safe and good enough container within which members are free to explore, play, and learn about the world within, the world outside and the world between the self and the other as it emerges in the group.

Through our dialogical encounters, we may discover our own subjectivity and the subjectivities of those whom we objectify and denigrate by our biases, prejudices and projections. The value and universal usefulness of this method of learning is endorsed by modern philosophers of education, such as Paulo Freire. In his seminal book, *Pedagogy of the Oppressed*, he asserts 'every human being…is capable of looking critically at the world in dialogical encounters with others' (1970, p.14). He also states, 'man's ontological vocation…is to be a Subject who acts upon and transforms the world, and in so doing moves towards ever new possibilities of fuller and richer life individually and collectively' (pp.12–13). Freire understood the value and power of speech. As we engage in a conversation, 'the word takes on new power. It is no longer an abstraction or magic but a means by which man discovers himself and his potential as he gives names to things around him…each man wins back his right to *say his own word, to name the world*' (p.13).

The task of the consulting team is to create and foster an atmosphere that facilitates and encourages sustainable and active development of dialogue between and among individuals and subgroups. Widening the circle of particpation and inclusion of diverse voices is a desirable and worthy goal. The emphasis is on dialogical encounters, in which participants discover their own unique subjectivities and in turn discover that of the 'others'.

Large groups in context

In the Group Relations tradition, a brochure describes the task of each event offered, including the large group. The large group task is generally defined as the study of its own behavior in the here and now in a setting where group size reduces the opportunities for face-to-face interaction. Rioch (1970) explained that the large group provides members with possibilities to experience and deal with 'situations in which sides are taken spontaneously, existing subgroups adhere and split, other factions are formed for apparently rational reasons, and the individual can suddenly feel bereft of support' (p.348).

More recently, trainees receive a brief description of the task of the large group, which reads as follows: 'The large group is composed of all conference members. Its stated task is to develop a dialogue that illuminates group process as it happens and to identify covert barriers to communication. Its aim is to increase understanding of the impact of societal and subgroup dynamics, such as race, gender, age, sexual orientation, class, professional discipline and status on the process of the small and large study groups and the conference as a whole. The large group provides an opportunity to give voice to the kind of contextual forces that most often exert a strong but silent influence on our psychotherapy groups'.

In conferences that feature the large group as part of the program, it is important to adapt the task of the large group to the theme of the conference as a whole. By so doing, the contextual framework and the theme of the conference are highlighted as an immediate experience, which influences the shared narrative the membership and consulting team co-create. I believe that this method gives participants a chance to relate more closely to the theoretical material presented so they may become more vital and connected with themselves and each other.

For example, I began the first large group session at a conference entitled 'Women's Power – Women's Passion: from Accommodation to Agency' by reading the primary task of the large group, followed by a few suggestive remarks about the nature of participation in large groups. I explained that this experience might be unfamiliar to many, and in general it is quite a challenge for each individual member to find their own unique voice and still be in contact with another member and the group as a whole. I asked that the members be available and in tune with what they were experiencing from moment to moment, both internally and in relation to others, and find a way to speak to it, regardless of the imperfection of the formulation. Participants were also invited to incorporate the theme of the conference and notice where they positioned themselves in relation to it. I believe that this gentle introduction of the task to the members had a significant impact on group development and set the stage for broader and deeper levels of relatedness and interaction among participants. The task was stated as follows: 'Under-representation of women in positions of power and authority is quite evident throughout our local, national and international organizations. This experiential workshop will engage participants in an authentic dialogue with each other in a large group. It will focus on the unique challenges and dilemmas women encounter in claiming their power and authority, the fantasies, myths and unconscious fears about women's power and influence, and the internal and external barriers to assuming visible leadership roles in our organizations and communities. We will also highlight the hidden and contextual forces underlying women's inhibitions in exercising authority, including real and imagined threats.'

The question arises as to why I am dwelling on the detailed description of the task and setting in which the large group takes place. The short answer is, because the task might be viewed as a condensation of the theoretical and practical principles involved in conducting large groups. It also reflects my biases, assumptions, and desires as I take up this particular role. Furthermore, I am attempting to highlight the shifts that occur in conducting such groups. I will say a few words about these developments. First, context is a key element in understanding what goes on in the group. I acknowledge the importance of socio-political and cultural forces in shaping my subjective experience and its interaction with the subjectivities of other members, and how it guides and informs my understanding and interpretation of group dynamics (see de Maré 1975; Foulkes 1975). I have embraced the intersubjective theory outlined by Stolorow, Brandshaft and Atwood (1987) and more recently by Orange, Atwood and Stolorow (1997). This perspective and its emphasis on working contextually is particularly relevant to the large group, where the contextual forces are inherently under microscopic examination. Interpretations are geared towards linking the material emerging in the group with what might be going on in society, at both micro and macro levels. Focusing on socio-political and cultural context can be jarring to those who tend to look solely at intra- and inter-psychic processes. However, this approach is in keeping with the statement by Orange et al.: 'Thinking contextually means ongoing sensitivity and relentless attention to a multiplicity of contexts – developmental, relational, gender-related, cultural and so on' (1997, p.476). This contextual field is composed of our multiplicity of selves, history, personality, and the imprints of the various theories we have internalized over the years. Now more than ever before we recognize the importance of deliberate and intentional exploration of the different dimensions of our group identities. Those aspects of the social self that stem from our belonging to various groupings take a prominent position in the analysis of the unconscious group processes (Skolnick and Green 1993; Reed and Noumair 2000). The consultant must help participants explore and understand:

1. unconscious and irrational forces underlying their fears of difference

2. assumptions, myths and prejudices about difference that invoke divisiveness, marginality and alienation

3. conscious and unconscious uses and misuses of difference that may lead to destruction and annihilation of the other

4. how, when and why they are internally or externally pressed to claim only a single aspect of their multiple identities while relegating the remaining parts of the self to the background?

5. what are some of the processes involved in defining and redefining who we are, our perception of ourselves and others' perception of us?

The location and / or dislocation of the self in the group and the group in the self becomes the fabric and texture of large group experience. Ettin's succinct assertion regarding the 'inherent relationship between "persons in group" and "groups in persons," that is, the intersect of personal and collective identity' becomes the thematic focus of large group sessions (2000, p.239). Similarly, Pines points to the organic linkage between the self and the group and what may appear as an illusory boundary between the two. He affirms group analysis views regarding the 'essential element of "group" in the constitution of the individual…the individual is conceived of as being born into and constituted out of a network of other persons, who gain a sense of personal identity from the possibilities offered by the nature of their network: the horizontal or lateral dimension of social organizations, therefore – notions of culture, politics, religion, economical and historical circumstances – have to be considered as con-stituents of the individual self' (1998, p.24).

The role of the consultant

Interventions and interpretations of large group process are informed and colored not only by the multiple group identities, but also the multiple conscious and unconscious roles held by consultants. Discourse is shaped and determined largely by the consultant as a combination of consultant, facilitator, manager, therapist, comedian, sociopolitical commentator, alternating between participant-observer and participant-leader. I would like to emphasize that the boundaries between these roles are artificial at best. Moreover, because of the complex nature of the large group we must draw upon every conceivable resource at our disposal to formulate hypotheses, hoping that they will resonate with members' experiences and will advance the work of the group. Making rigid distinctions between person and role and acting on it destroys the endeavor. Holding on to a traditional analytic stance characterized by anonymity, neutrality and objective distance is not useful or relevant to our purposes, depriving ourselves and the members of the richness of our internal dialogue. However, it is crucial to maintain a delicate balance between making oneself available as an object to be used as a repository for members' projections, and emerging as a potentially known and knowable subject. This implies seeing the consultant as more than just essentially holding and containing the group (Blackwell 2000), but as an active participant in guiding, shaping and influencing its developing dialogue.

Wright discusses the use and misuse of the self in the group from a relational perspective. He explains Hoffman's dialectic relation in therapy between a 'personal-egalitarian aspect which allows for spontaneity, creativity, freedom and self expression and a role-defined hierarchical aspect which requires ritual, constraint, role determined behavior and adherence to institutionalized givens' (2000, p.192). I believe that our capacity to hold the tension between these two dimensions and intervene from the 'in-between-space' is what is most challenging.

I would like to clarify my position on participatory leadership in this context. As a leader of such an enterprise, I wish to influence the flow of communication and the direction and movement of the group. My vision is, that at a minimal level we move from hatred to impersonal fellowship (de Maré 1991) and at a maximal and more ambitious level there be moments of grace and transcendence (Lawrence 1993). In order to accomplish these goals, the consultant must assist in taming and managing the passionate and regressive pulls of the group. Movement from the paranoid-schizoid position to the depressive position requires noting, naming, working through and deconstructing pronounced dichotomies. The consultant must be hyper-vigilant yet empathic to group members' tendencies to avoid and resist dealing with taboo subjects. However, naming the unspeakable is an act of courage that is necessary for the group to develop. Deconstruction of polarizations by dialogue may lead to members becoming both known and knowable entities, rather than alienated and isolated, caricature representatives of their subgroups. The consultant's interpretation of projective and introjective identification is central in helping members understand their functioning in the group. She must first tolerate and track what group members do with their destructive impulses such as aggression, hatred, greed and envy, then help them to restore and recover the split-off pieces by reconstructing an integrative and meaningful narrative. To get to these points members and consultants must move from the paranoid-schizoid position to the depressive position; from envy and hatred to gratitude; from monologic to dialogic engagement; and from negation to mutual recognition of both self and other as subjects. As this is established, members may move from dealing with visible and not so visible dynamics of power, control and dominance, to revealing their vulnerabilities and their life stories. By so doing, the possibilities for intimate connections increase and the large group starts to look more like the small group with its hallmark of familiarity, cohesion and intimacy (Agazarian and Carter 1993; Segalla 1996).

Transforming and transformative dialogues in the large group may become the most promising avenue for changing the geography of group relations.

Acknowledgement

I wish to express my deep gratitude and appreciation to Dr Rosemary Segalla for her thoughtful editorial remarks.

References

Agazarian, Y. and Carter, F. (1993) 'Discussions on the large group.' *Group 17*, 4, 210–234.

Bakhtin, M. M. (1981) *The Dialogic Imagination*. Austin, Texas: University of Texas Press.

Benjamin, J. (1999) 'Recognition and destruction: an outline of intersubjectivity.' In S. Mitchell and L. Aron (eds) *Relational Psychoanalysis: The Emergence of a Tradition*. Hillsdale, NJ: The Analytic Press.

Blackwell, D. (2000) 'The politicisation of group analysis in the 21st century.' *Group 24*, 1, 65–73.

de Maré, P. B. (1975) 'The politics of large groups.' In L. Kreeger (ed) *The Large Group: Dynamics and Therapy*. London: Karnac Books.

de Maré, P. B. (1991) *Koinonia: From Hate, through Dialogue, to Culture in the Large Group*. London and New York: Karnac Books.

Ettin, M. F. (2000) 'Fostering a "group ethos": truth or dare.' *Group 24*, 2/3, 229–240.

Foulkes, S. H. (1975) 'Problems of the large group from a group-analytic point of view.' In L. Kreeger (ed) *The Large Group: Dynamics and Therapy*. London: Karnac Books.

Freire, P. (1970) *Pedagogy of the Oppressed*. New York: The Seabury Press.

Jarrar, L. K. (2001) 'WSP faculty leads event at group conference in Jerusalem: one person's account of a rare experience.' Washington School of Psychiatry News, Winter, pp.1 and 6.

Lacan, J. (1977) É crits New York: W.W. Norton and Co.

Lawrence, W. G. (1993) 'Signals of transcendence in large groups as systems.' *Group 17*, 4, 254–266.

Maalouf, A. (2000) *In the Name of Identity: Violence and the Need to Belong*. New York: Arcade Publishing.

Morrison, T. (1992) *Playing in the Dark: Whiteness and the Literary Imagination*. Cambridge, MA: Harvard University Press.

O'Leary, J. V. (2001) 'The postmodern turn in group therapy.' *International Journal of Group Psychotherapy 51*, 4, 473–487.

Orange, D. M., Atwood, G. E. and Stolorow, R. D. (1997) *Working Intersubjectively: Contextualism in Psychoanalytic Practice*. Hillsdale, NJ and London: The Analytic Press.

Pines, M. (1998) 'The self as a group: the group as self.' In I. N. H. Harwood and M. Pines (eds) *Self Experiences in Group: Intersubjective and Self Psychological Pathways to Human Understanding*. London and Philadelphia: Jesseca Kingsley Publishers.

Reed, G. M. and Noumair, D. A. (2000) 'The tiller of authority in a sea of diversity: empowerment, disempowerment, and the politics of identity.' In E. B. Klein, F. Gabelnick and P. Herr (eds) *Dynamic Consultation in a Changing Workplace*. Madison, Connecticut: Psychosocial Press.

Rioch, M. J. (1970) 'Group relations: rationale and technique.' *International Journal of Group Psychotherapy 20*, 340–355.

Sampson, E. E. (1993a) *Celebrating the Other: A Dialogic Account of Human Nature.* Boulder. San Francisco: Westview Press.

Sampson, E. E (1993b) 'Identity politics: challenges to psychology's understanding.' *American Psychologist 48*, 12, 1219–1230.

Segalla, R. A. (1996) '"The unbearable embeddedness of being": self psychology, intersubjectivity and large group experiences.' *Group 20*, 4, 257–271.

Skolnick, M. (2000) 'Microcosm–macrocosm.' *Group 24*, 2/3, 133–145.

Skolnick, M. and Green, Z. (1993) 'Diversity, group relations and the denigrated other.' In S. Cytrynbaum and S. Lee (eds) *Transformations in Global and Organizational Systems: Changing Boundaries in the 90s. Proceedings of the Tenth Scientific Meeting of the A. K. Rice Institute.* Jupiter, FL: A. K. Rice Institute.

Stolorow, R. D., Brandshaft, B. and Atwood, G. (1987) *Psychoanalytic Treatment: An Intersubjective Approach.* Hillsdale, NJ: Analytic Press.

Turquet, P. (1975) 'Threats to identity in the large group.' In L. Kreeger (ed) *The Large Group: Dynamics and Therapy.* London: Karnac Books.

Verhaeghe, P. (1997) *Does Woman Exist? From Freud's Hysteric to Lacan's Feminine.* New York: Other Press.

Wright, F. (2000) 'The use of the self in group.' *International Journal of Group Psychotherapy 50*, 2, 181–198.

CHAPTER 2

Large Groups and Culture

Malcolm Pines

First, I shall consider the sociocultural framework from which the large group concept emerged and was then applied. I will then describe some of my large group experiences in different settings, and finally see what conclusions can be arrived at when considering large group and culture.

The setting for assembling large groups has mostly been made within institutions; treatment-directed psychiatric institutions such as mental hospitals; therapeutic communities; training programmes in group analysis and therapeutic community work. However, prior to these better-known, more recent experiences, there had been a lengthy gestation in lesser-known situations. I have outlined this history in my paper 'Forgotten pioneers: the unwritten history of the therapeutic community movement' (Pines 1999).

I will focus on two factors:

1. the innovative work of Trigant Burrow in the United States in the 1920s and 30s (Pertegato 1999)

2. experiences in educational settings of the same time period.

Trigant Burrow

Burrow was one of the first psychoanalysts in the United States of America. In his earlier writings, Burrow described a pre-oedipal phase of primary identification of infant with mother, a developmental phase that remains pre-conscious, i.e. before consciousness. He theorised that, as a species, man's (and woman's) organism is forever deeply connected with its maternal source; mankind is ever in infancy and ever achieving new maturity.

Man suffers from a universal neurosis; health lies in overcoming distorted, prejudiced, self-centred thought and behaviour. Burrow had moved from psychoanalysis to phylo-analysis (Riese 1963). This can only be explored and understood through intensive study in and of groups. Burrow's theories and methods had in the eyes of his fellow psychoanalysts moved far beyond them – and he continued to remind them that psychoanalysis 'in its present, unconscious, social involvement is not a study of neurosis: it *is* a neurosis'. Burrow had been a founder member and a past president of the American Psychoanalytic Association. When, in 1933, this association was dissolved and reformed, Burrow was not invited to rejoin as a member.

He began his researches into 'the group method of analysis' after personal experiences impressed on him the power of social forces inherent in the dyadic psychoanalytic situation. He described these psychoanalytic meetings as 'secret conferences'. In 1927, he asserted before an audience of psychoanalysts that 'the fact that we all disguise is that neurosis is social and that a social neurosis can be met only through a social analysis'.

Burrow organised residential camps where in daily meetings each person's self-image was religiously exposed under the scrutiny of others. Each had to recognise how (s)he enacts a social role; the aim of the group is to enable the individual to express him/herself as (s)he is – as (s)he thinks and feels when divorced from and unsupported by the social image of the self. His radically new concept of the group as a whole was expressed as 'under no circumstances is the reaction of anyone regarded as isolated or separated' (1927). Burrow's concerns were to explore the here and now of the whole group, including the conductor. His work presaged that of the later generation who created the group-analytic and therapeutic community movements from the 1940s onwards: S. H. Foulkes, Bion and Rickman, de Maré, Kreeger, Turquet and Main. I know that S. H. Foulkes had read and been impressed by Burrow's writings. Bion wrote, from his own experience, that the mystic or genius, bearer of a new idea, is always disruptive to the establishment, those who exercise power and responsibility within the social group. The psychoanalytic establishment expelled Burrow in 1933, but his ideas have endured.

Between World War I and World War II

Tom Harrison has provided an excellent account of the context of psychiatry and psychology in the decade before World War II, which led up to the Northfield experiments (Harrison 2000).

Wilfred Bion and John Rickman pioneered large group meetings in the setting of the military psychiatry hospital at Northfield. It is clear that Rickman was the driving force. During World War I, Rickman, as a Quaker, had served in one of their units in Russian Siberia. It was there that he came into contact with the social forces within a village and observed how the community dealt with their internal and external conflicts. This was before Rickman trained as a psychiatrist and psychoanalyst. Rickman, more than any other psychoanalyst in pre-World War II days, sought to integrate social issues with a psychoanalytic outlook. His very interesting and significant papers have remained unpublished until now, but will soon make an appearance under the editorship of Pearl King, a British psychoanalyst who shares this viewpoint.

Progressive education

While still a medical student, already intending a career in psychiatry and psychoanalysis, I paid a visit to A. S. Neil at his famous Summerhill School. Neil, a disciple of Wilhelm Reich, was a radical reforming educator who introduced large group culture to his school. I sat in on such a meeting and was impressed by the respect Neil paid to the pupils' discussions and decisions. He was one of several reforming educators whose innovations laid a groundwork for the Northfield experiments of World War II. School work had extended into work with maladjusted adolescents and young adults. Later Maxwell Jones was to use similar methods at Henderson Hospital. It is interesting that though the British Therapeutic Community movement was adopted by North American psychiatry, there had earlier been a significant influence from North America to British progressive education, which had introduced self-government into schools.

August Aichorn pioneered work with delinquents and his example influenced Maxwell Jones in his methods at Henderson Hospital. Anna Freud admired Aichorn and was another channel from psychoanalysis to progressive education.

The North American experiments in progressive education, influenced by the theories of the educator John Dewey, were brought to Britain in 1913 by Homer Lane. He founded 'The Little Commonwealth', in which any meeting of the whole school was an occasion for searching group analysis. Lane, an amateur psychotherapist, fell into disrepute following charges of sexual impropriety. However, Lane was admired by other educators. David Wills has written about the Q Camp Experiment where psychoanalysis was introduced into residential treatment for maladjusted youths (Pines 1999). This work was sponsored and supported by the psychoanalysts Marjorie Franklin and Dennis Carroll. Franklin, a pioneer of psychoanalytic insights into delinquency, had trained with Ferenczi. Dennis Carroll, a brilliant scientist who trained as a psychoanalyst in the 1930s, was Edward Glover's right-hand man. Together with Glover, he pioneered psychoanalytic work with delinquents and criminals and was a co-founder of the Psychopathic Clinic, later the Portman Clinic. Interestingly, Bion was a staff member of the Psychopathic Clinic before the war, therefore had contact with Carroll, who went on to be Commanding Officer at Northfield, though not at the same time as when Bion and Rickman were there. Could Bion have known about the methods of therapeutic community in progressive education?

There were many experiments in social living in the 1920s and 30s, which involved an exploration of large group dynamics: kibbutzim in Palestine, Burrow's Camp in America, the Peckham Experiment in London, which was an important centre of research into the nature of physical and mental health, taking the family as a basic unit of human life, and the small community as the next stage beyond the family. The Peckham Experiment strongly influenced Harold Bridger's organisation of social living at Northfield (Bridger 1985, p.99).

Large groups in psychiatry

P. B. de Maré is the acknowledged pioneer. In the 1970s, excited by his enthusiasm for large group meetings, we introduced such meetings into the new trainings offered by the Institute of Group Analysis (IGA), London, founded in 1971. At that time, we had over 100 persons a year in our trainings. We dedicated the lecture sessions of the third terms of a three-term programme to large group meetings. We experienced the

excitement, confusion, anxiety of these meetings and despite a considerable number of non-attenders in those earlier meetings, we have
maintained the large group component of group-analytic trainings and
conferences. Then I worked at the Cassel Hospital under the charismatic
directorship of Tom Main. Under Main, the Cassel Hospital was a leading
centre for in-patient psychodynamic therapy. Main (see references) insisted
on maintaining a clear boundary between individual therapy offered to
patients and the exploration and clinical use of the group dynamics of the
hospital. He maintained that this was the domain of nurses and of the
designated community doctor who conducted large group meetings.
When I left the Cassel for St George's Hospital, Professor Arthur Crisp
invited me to introduce a therapeutic milieu approach into what had been
previously a fairly traditional in-patient psychiatric setting, where the
dynamics of the community were not addressed.

I instituted thrice weekly meetings of a whole community of over 80
patients and 40 or more staff. The patient population included individuals
with both acute and chronic psychoses, severe neuroses, borderline
disorders, severe eating disorders and a research sample of patients
receiving stereo-tactic leucotomy operations for severe chronic neuroses. It
was a constant struggle to maintain a therapeutic culture, to introduce
psychodynamic concepts to staff who were used to a hierarchical structure
with clear definitions of the role of patient and staff.

We gained experience and confidence in the containing capacity of the
large group to accommodate the extremes of acute psychosis, chronic
depression and personality disorders. The personal factor in maintaining
the large group culture became clear after I had left and the enthusiasm for
large group meetings somewhat declined (Pines 1975).

In the 1970s, the culture of large groups was spread through the Association of Therapeutic Communities, which brought about meetings
between the scattered and beleaguered units which needed mutual support
and stimulation. David Clark, a leading figure of the movement to
modernise psychiatric hospitals by introducing group methods, has
vividly described his own experiences at Fulbourn Hospital, Cambridge
(Clark 1996).

Group analytic experiences outside the United Kingdom

As the influence of group analysis extended into continental Europe, British group analysts began to meet their confrères and to exchange experiences. In France, Anzieu (1984) had studied large training groups and his approach had a powerful influence. On account of this, group analysis has had less acceptance in France than in other European countries. Group-analytic training programmes were instituted first in Denmark, later in Norway; in Spain (Bilbao and Barcelona) and in Israel and Russia. In Greece, the Institute of Group Analysis, Athens, was soon established and therefore did not have to rely on visitors from Britain. What follows are my own memories and impressions of the large group experiences in different cultures.

The Danes initially tended to be conservative, respectful of the authority of group conductors, who were also their small-group conductors and teachers. In Norway, there was more questioning of the conductor's role and challenging of their authority. Large groups in Mediterranean cultures were less prone to use defences of silence; indeed, I vividly recall a large group in Spain whose communications resembled those of a lively community meeting in a village square, exchanging comments and gossip, choosing to ignore interpretations of manic flight.

Encounters with French colleagues were problematic. Though both sides wanted to get to know and to appreciate the other's theory and practice, after initial enthusiastic exploration we ran into difficulties centering on the power of language, English v. French, and the authority that the use of language conveyed. The British group-analytic style of conductor or conductors facilitating group communication contrasted with the French approach, which focused more on interpretation of unconscious anxieties and conflicts. British empiricism met with French intellectual purity!

The European Association of Transcultural Group Analysis

The meeting of different nationalities led to the formation of EATGA, in which group analysts from several European countries take part in three-day meetings. There is a large experiential component to these meetings, in which participants are free to use their own languages. As a consequence, there were battles over not using English as a lingua franca.

French and English predominated and the use of German came only later, after issues to do with German cultural history, specifically the horror of the holocaust, had been voiced. Eventually German group analysts recovered the freedom to own their own history and to use their own tongue.

Large groups, freedom to think, freedom to speak out

Psychodynamic psychotherapy is driven underground under totalitarian regimes which set out to impose an authoritarian ideology on men's and women's minds. Bakhtin, who wrote under Stalinism, described this well, contrasting the authoritarian and persuasive voices (Bakhtin 1981). Psychodynamic thought and practice flourishes only in the daylight of liberal democratic cultures.

I hold an unforgettable, vivid picture in my mind from a large group meeting in Buenos Aires, shortly after the conclusion of the Falklands-Malvinas war. It was part of a conference called 'The first encounter of psychoanalysis, psychodrama and group psychotherapy'. The large group meeting was allocated a room that could seat some 30 to 40 persons. As more and more people flooded the room to bursting, Gerald Wooster and I led the delegates in search of a bigger room. There being none to be had, we simply sat on a staircase with our more than 60 persons who were bursting with eagerness to speak out and be heard.

My only comparable experience occurred on the second day of the First Psychoanalytic Conference held in South Africa (1998). The programme had not included small or large group meetings; eventually the pressure for free speech and for exploration of conference dynamics was recognised by the conference organisers. There was a sense of the South African delegates' domination by the visitors, several of whom were themselves of South African origin and who had trained abroad as psychoanalysts. Asked to convene a large group meeting, we improvised a setting in the main conference hall, which gave expression to the suppressed voice of the majority. The 'equivalence' (Hopper 2002) of the conference dynamics to those of the South African experience of apartheid could be recognised and voiced. After this large group meeting the constructive work for which the conference had been organised progressed in a freer and friendlier manner.

The Second Psychoanalytic Conference built large group meetings into the programme which were conducted by IGA members. These made a significant contribution to the work of the second conference.

Large group and the survivor syndrome

In 1979, a survivor syndrome workshop was organised by the Group Analytic Society, London. These were early days for large group ventures; we believed it possible that the large group on the course would expose survivors to regressive experiences and, hopefully, facilitate emergence strengthened through these experiences. The workshop participants included survivors, Germans, other Europeans and Britons.

The three sessions were an arena of very powerful experiences, helplessness, persecution. The large group served and survived as a container for the intense feelings that emerged as the victim-and-perpetrator relationship was replayed. The experience of the workshop has been sensitively described in the proceedings of the survivor syndrome workshop (Garland 1980).

Large groups and politics

When large groups are held in countries where there are turbulent political relations, such as Israel and South Africa, there are constraints on the emergence of the socio-political context. Eruption of these issues which carry such dark forces can overwhelm the containing capacity of the setting. De Maré et al. (1991) have shown how hatred can energise the emergence of dialogue in median groups, a process which the large group may not accomplish since the large numbers can quickly lead to massive splits and projections. These are new areas for large group meetings, which developed from work in institutional and training settings.

Pichon-Rivière and large groups

Contemporary with, but independent from Foulkes' group analysis was the work and teaching of the Swiss-born Argentine psychoanalyst Enrique Pichon-Rivière. Pichon studied learning, training and discussion groups, then applied the principles he had developed for them to group therapy. He believed in the essential identity between the processes of teaching and learning on the one hand, and of therapy on the other. The term 'operative groups' points to the aim of group work: to make effective changes.

Pichon's work has received little attention in the English-speaking countries, as so little of his work has been translated. This situation will soon be put right by the publication of a book on Pichon-Rivière by the Mexican psychoanalyst and group analyst Juan Tubert-Oklander (2003). From this book I cite the section dealing with the Rosario Experience, an attempt to apply operative group work to a whole city – Rosario, which was the third largest city in Argentina. This took place in 1958, organised and conducted by Pichon-Rivière and his team from the Argentine Institute for Social Studies, which he had founded in 1953.

The Rosario experience began with a lecture by Pichon-Rivière. The audience was then divided into small heterogeneous discussion groups conducted by analysts. This was followed by a meeting of all group conductors with Pichon as the general coordinator, then the second session of the heterogeneous groups and another meeting of the team. Pichon-Rivière followed that with a new plenary address, now with a larger attendance. His intention was to bring back to the large group what had been discussed in the small groups, to help their members to see themselves in a wider perspective. The effect of this was to change the audience from passive spectators to behaving as members of a large discussion group. Homogeneous groups were formed: psychosomatic medicine, psychology, statistics, one of painters, one of boxers, and one of insurance salesmen. There was a final plenary meeting with members of both the homogeneous and heterogeneous groups.

Following this experience, several new groups began to work on some of the city's problems under the supervision of the Institute for Social Studies. So the experiment was an attempt to turn a focal group experience into a community process.

The fascinating life and career of Pichon-Rivière deserves to be much more widely known outside the Latin countries, where his work has received much attention and has formed the basis for a great deal of subsequent group work.

Introducing large group culture into organisations

Here I draw upon my experiences of introducing large group meetings into the North American group therapy organisations, American Group Psychotherapy Association (AGPA) and the North-Eastern Group Psychotherapy Society. I was partnered in these experiences by Meg Sharpe. We proposed large group meetings to the Program Committee of AGPA for at least two years before we were accepted. Given the Early Bird Slot at 7.30am, we expected a low attendance, but in the event each of three hour-long sessions was well attended and membership grew in subsequent years.

Delegates were attracted to a situation which encouraged free speech, discussion of conference dynamics and the exploration of what, for the majority of attendees, was a new dimension of group experience. The sustained popularity of these events has led to AGPA instituting a large, median and group analytic section to their organisation (Storck SIG).

Large group in the European Symposia for Group Analysis

Large group meetings are an established part of the culture of these meetings. The organisers in Heidelberg, Copenhagen, Budapest and Bologna have devised settings in which upwards of 200 persons can see and hear each other, using tiered seatings. Pat de Maré once held a Foulkes lecture in a circular room in London, which was the ideal setting for a large group. Nowadays we are accustomed to the high levels of anxiety, expression of experiences of helplessness, of chaos and confusion, which eventually lead on to acceptance of the situation. Large group dynamics can be explored and new dimensions encountered and understood. The fact that many participants have met more than once over the years brings a sense of history and continuity, a formation of the large group matrix.

As I write this section, I have in mind the large group at the Bologna 12th Symposium in Group Analysis. This follows the sequence of large group meetings in these symposia, where there have been over 200 persons and as many as 400 present. In these meetings group analysts and interested persons from diverse group-analytic communities and cultures meet for several days in unstructured meetings, where the least and the most prestigious, the least and the most experienced, seasoned and unseasoned individuals are face-to-face: each and everyone may speak, be heard, ignored, responded to. Remarkable occasions with remarkable experiences. Remembering that Elias's concepts for socio-genesis and psycho-genesis are at the heart of group-analytic theory, I wish to apply the sociological concept of social capital to this large group situation. The idea of social capital, which originated in the eighteenth century through the famous economist Adam Smith, is to count all the acquired and useful abilities of labourers as part of the capital in any country. Marx's economic analysis of capital, based on class structure, has evolved into what is called the neoclassical theory, which includes human capital, cultural capital and social capital as sources of capital.

A gathering of so many group analysts in the Symposium's large group represents a huge potential for exploring what may be available as social capital of the group-analytic movement. Social capital is captured through social relations – 'investment in social relations with expected returns in the market-place' (Lin 2001). The marketplace is the group-analytic community. Potential social assets lie in the connection between partici-pant actors, and in access to resources in the network.

The Symposium's large group is a non-hierarchical setting. Formal structures of power and authority are abrogated. A cat may talk with the king and queen. The Emperor's new clothes are visible to those with eyes to see. Social structure is undone and all may participate in evolving a new structure. Social networks, which are characterised by fluidity and persuasion instead of compliance, where reciprocity and empathy are a social currency, replace hierarchically organised social systems. These social networks emerge gradually in the course of the events and thereby become social resources for the members' sense of identity, which has been threatened by the size and anonymity of the large group.

People relate more easily to others who are 'like me' ('homophily' is the term for relations between actors with single resources), whereas relating to actors with dissimilar resources (heterophily) demands more effort, as the actors are aware of their inequalities: what they have to gain, or risk losing, in their interaction. Position, prestige, reputation can be lost, but there are also possibilities of new relations, new insides and outside, new resources. The greater efforts, if rewarded, can lead to the increased sense of personal agency.

The dark side of the large group

The French sociologist Bordieu (Lin 2001, p.15) asserts that 'symbolic violence' exists when a dominant class legitimises its culture and values as the 'objective' culture and values of that society; unseen, they are transmitted through pedagogic action, 'misrecognised' as being the culture and values of the whole society, whereas they derive from the dominant class. (Here we can recognise the influence of Norbert Elias on Bordieu.)

Bordieu also makes much use of the term 'habitus' to define the internalised durable training in the reproduction of the culture. This is a term already much used by Norbert Elias, and before him by other sociologists, to represent the 'second nature' that we accept without recognising its socio-genic origins (Krieken 1998).

Large group meetings are becoming 'second nature' in the group-analytic movement. Is this reproducing a dominant culture, or is it, as we hope, exposing the 'invisible hand' of 'habitus' in our group-analytic culture?

Theories of cultural and social capital provide perspectives that have not yet, to my knowledge, been used in the understanding of large group phenomena. They can help to bridge the processes of sociogenesis and psychogenesis, which are at the heart of group analysis.

Large group and time

Large groups in institutions and conferences always have a time for beginning and a time for ending, usually between 60 and 90 minutes. However, the group-analytic meeting to explore the theme of 'time', held in Greenwich at the time of the millennium, included a large group session without a fixed finishing time. I was the group conductor. Members had the novel experience of deciding for themselves if and when to leave the group. These experiences have yet to be fully described, including responses to questionnaires, but many issues encountered in the exploration of time were significant. It is clear that the 'hidden dimension' of time came to the fore and evoked powerful experiences. The only comparable experience to this that I recall is when we introduced the theme of religious upbringing into an EATGA meeting. This also evoked powerful affects relating to experiences which had long been put aside. Papers on time, based on this experience, will eventually appear in *Group Analysis*.

Conclusion

The culture of the large group is an innovation within group psychotherapy which is by now well-established. Large groups allow the exploration of hidden dimensions which do not appear in small group settings.
They provide opportunities for understanding powerful social constraints
relating to authority, organisational dynamics, personal responsibility.
Large group meetings lead to an understanding of fellowship and citizenship.

I have not had the opportunity to work with large groups in Norway,
Finland, Ireland, Israel or Hungary, with the exception of the large group
of the meeting of the Group-Analytic Society held in Koszek. My
experience there was that the cultural barriers between Hungarian and
other European colleagues became evident. The significance of Koszek as
the last bastion of defence against the Mongol invasion of Europe was part
of the fantasy structure of that workshop. The fantasy structures of these
different nations resemble what Bion called the 'selected fact', the
bringing together of underlying fantasy structures that creates coherence.
In different cultures, folk history, folktales, mythology, add unique features
to the psychological make-up of both the individuals and the groups.
These selected facts become more apparent in large groups than in small
groups. Their manifestations of the social unconscious in these cultures are
not present both as necessary features, but can also represent defences
against what may be felt to be an invasion or take-over by group
conductors who come from outside the culture. I have been told that these
features are particularly apparent in cultures which are undergoing rapid
transitions from longstanding and traditional forms of organisation to
contemporary ones, which makes it important to hold on to cultural
features which formerly unified people. Group conductors from other
cultures have needed to familiarise themselves with these folk ways, in
order to appreciate them and be able to recognise the deeper meanings of
what is being said, and also the better to appreciate when these cultural
motifs are being used defensively.

Theory of large groups

This will be dealt with fully in other contributions to this volume, so I will not address it here. The impact of culture on the large group has been well described in an issue of *Group* devoted to group psychotherapy in Israel (*Group* 26.1.2002).

References

Anzieu, D. (1984) *The Group and the Unconscious.* London: Routledge.

Bakhtin, M. (1981) (ed. M. Holquist) *The Dialogic Imagination. Four Essays by M. M. Bakhtin.* Austin, Texas: University of Texas Press.

Bridger, H. (1985) 'Northfield revisited.' In M. Pines (ed) *Bion and Group Psychotherapy.* London: Routledge and Kegan Paul. Reprinted London: Jessica Kingsley Publishers, 2000.

Burrow, T. (1927) 'The group method of analysis.' *Psychoanalytic Review 14*, 268–280.

Clark, D. (1996) *The Story of a Mental Hospital, Fulbourn 1858–1983.* London: Process Press.

de Maré, P., Piper, R. and Thompson, S. (1991) Koinonina: *From Hate, Through Dialogue, to Culture in the Large Group.* London: Karnac Books.

Garland, C. (ed) (1980) 'Proceedings of the survivor syndrome workshop' (1979). *Group Analysis,* special edition, November, 67–81.

Harrison, T. (2000) *Bion, Rickman, Foulkes and the Northfield Experiment: Advancing on a Different Front.* London: Jessica Kingsley Publishers.

Hopper, E. (2002) *The Social Unconscious.* London: Jessica Kingsley Publishers.

Krieken, R. (1998) *Norbert Elias.* London: Routledge.

Lin, N. (2001) *Social Capital, a Theory of Social Structure in Action.* Cambridge: Cambridge University Press.

Main, T. F. (1989) *The Ailment and other Psychoanalytic Essays.* London: Free Association Books.

Pertegato, E. G. (1994) 'Researching the matrix of group analysis.' *Rivista Italiana di Gruppo Analisi 9*, 1.

Pertegato, E. G. (1999) 'Trigant Burrow and unearthing the origin of group analysis.' *Group Analysis 32*, 2, 269–284.

Pines, M. (1975) 'Overview.' In L. Kreeger (ed) *The Large Group: Dynamics and Therapy.* London: Constable.

Pines, M. (1999) 'Forgotten pioneers: the unwritten history of the therapeutic community movement.' *Therapeutic Communities 20*, 1, 23–42.

Riese, W. (1963) 'Phylo analysis (Burrow) – its historical and philosophical implications.' *Acta. Psychother., Suppl. Ad. 11*, 5–36.

Storck, L. lauren_storck@hms.harvard.edu

Tubert-Oklander, J. and Hernandez de Tubert, R. (2003) *Operative Groups.* London: Jessica Kingsley Publishers.

CHAPTER 3

Aspects of Aggression in Large Groups Characterised by (ba) I:A/M

Earl Hopper

In this article I will outline several propositions about aggressive feelings and aggression within groups characterised by 'Incohesion: Aggregation/Massification' or (ba) I:A/M, the fourth basic assumption in the unconscious life of groups and group-like social systems. Incohesion is especially prevalent and intense in social systems that have been traumatised and/or in social systems whose members have been traumatised.

Thus aggression and (ba) I:A/M are particularly pertinent to the study of large groups, because participation in large groups is associated with traumatic experience: stimulus bombardment, threats to identity and to the boundaries of the self, narcissistic injury, affronts to self-esteem, confusion, and failed dependency. My theory of Incohesion is developed in *The Social Unconscious: Selected Papers* (Hopper 2003a), and in *Traumatic Experience in the Unconscious Life of Groups: The Fourth Basic Assumption: Incohesion: Aggregation/Massification or (ba) I:A/M* (Hopper 2003b), which include detailed clinical illustrations, empirical data, and extensive bibliography.

In the first instance it is necessary to stress several points:

1. Although many psychoanalysts and group analysts assume that all social systems are groups, in fact this is not true. Societies and their geographical parts, like cities, towns and villages, and organisations and families are social systems, but they are not actually groups. The value of inferences from the study of groups to more complex social systems, and vice versa, depends on the degree to which the social systems are isomorphic in structure and kind. However, when a social system is traumatised, it is likely to regress, e.g. traumatised societies become like groups, and traumatised groups become like people, and our knowledge of one becomes applicable to the others.

2. Most of what has been written about large groups is based on large groups as training events, or in professional conferences. Such large groups are especially vulnerable to traumatic experience, because usually they are juxtaposed with more intimate small groups, in comparison with which they are strange and overwhelming. Participants come into these groups feeling manipulated and resentful, somewhat bewildered and lost. Obviously, the findings from the study of large groups as training events within organisational settings should be referred to other kinds of large group with caution.

3. The constraints of the social unconscious are especially important in the development and maintenance of processes of incohesion in large groups, because large groups are so open to the constraints of their social context.

4. Large group processes are highly amplified and magnified and liable to sudden inflammations and conflagrations. This may be based on the inevitability that in large groups no one member can at any one time take account of each of the other members in the group, and that inevitably participation will be characterised by intense splitting and projective and introjective communications of various kinds. With respect to aggression, the large group is like dry tinder: a slight spark can create a full fire very quickly.

5. It is sometimes assumed that Foulkesian group analysts eschew an interest in aggression in groups, whereas, in contrast, those who

work within the Group Relations tradition are especially interested in this phenomenon. However, more detailed study suggests that ironically it may be the other way around. Foulkes did attend to aggression in groups, as I know from personal experience and as can be gleaned from his written work, e.g. Foulkes (1968), whereas in contrast, Bion (1961) implied that aggressive feelings and aggression occur only in the context of (ba) Fight/Flight; and in his theory of the fourth basic assumption of Oneness, Turquet (1975) argued that the aggression associated with extreme regression is actually eradicated through 'homogenisation' processes.

6. Aggression depends both on the strength of aggressive feelings, and on the normative controls over the expression of feelings in general and aggressive feelings in particular. The suppression of aggressive feelings is often associated with covert aggression. Aggressive feelings and aggression may be unconscious.

7. The targets, functions and forms of aggressive feelings and aggression should be distinguished:

   (a) *targets:* aggressive feelings and aggression can be displaced from the body to parts of the body, states of mind, reputation, objects of collective identification, others within the groups with which a person identifies and is seen to be identified, such as family, ethnic group, and nation. Aggressive feelings may be diffuse, and, therefore, detached from any particular object, in which case these feelings are liable to be mobilised towards a variety of targets.

   (b) *functions:* the functions of aggression are numerous and various. However, in this context it should be emphasised that aggression is often used to maintain pressure on people and subgroups to comply with and conform to various moral norms which are central to the identity of the group, especially when the survival of the group is threatened. General processes of social control become a form of punishment, and vice versa.

(c) *forms:* aggression can involve either verbal or nonverbal attacks, or both. It can involve actions that are immoral rather than illegal, marked by boundary breaking, exploitation, deception, corruption, seduction and complicity. Gossip can become grotesquely distorted into forms of lying, rumour-mongering, ridicule and other kinds of denigration.

The fate of aggression in the context of Incohesion: Aggregation/Massification

1. In the context of aggregation which develops as a consequence of traumatogenic processes, aggressive feelings are prevalent, ranging from indifference, hostility and withdrawal from relationships to the more open hatred and conflict of a 'free-for-all', in which each person is against each person, and each subgroup is against each subgroup, or in effect each subgroup becomes a contra-group. In contrast, in the context of massification, which develops as a defence against the psychotic anxieties associated with aggregation, it is essential to eliminate all parts of the group 'mother' (Schindler 1966) that may prevent a merger with 'her' (Chasseguet-Smirgel 1985). It is also important to eliminate the group father and 'his' parts that are perceived to block access to merger. Thus, in the first instance, the group engages in processes of pseudo-speciation, that is, targets of aggression are displaced from objects within the group into objects within the group's environment, especially into 'other' groups and their members, who are defined as pseudo-species (Erikson 1968), and then perceived to be a source of pollution, denigrated as 'different', 'strange', and 'inferior', and, therefore, repudiated. However, pseudo-speciation depends on the development and maintenance of massification, in the same way that massification depends on the development and main-tenance of pseudo-speciation.

Pseudo-speciation and massification depend, in turn, on the develop-ment and maintenance of two fundamental, intertwined processes:

(a) *the development of a ritualised way of life,* both in private and in public domains. Daily life becomes an expression of moral and religious perfection and purification. The pressures to conform and to comply are immense. The boundaries of a group are marked continuously, and personal identity is asserted in terms of membership of the group, i.e. the members of the group become 'membership individuals'.

(b) *the 'sexualisation' of aggressive feelings.* Aggressive feelings are diluted and made more manageable through their sexualisation or libidinalisation. Ligatures are transformed into ligaments, and bonds into bondage, and vice versa (which in extreme form is the basis of sadism in which hate masquerades as love, and pain becomes inseparable from pleasure) – e.g. competition among men is converted into banding, as seen in a so-called 'band of brothers', in which homosexuality becomes problematic.

2. Patterns of ritualisation and the sexualisation of aggression are rarely completely effective. Thus, pseudo-speciation, on which massification depends, and vice versa, is highly unstable. It is, therefore, necessary to ask: what happens when these prophylactics against aggressive feelings and aggression within the group prove to be inadequate? In general terms, the answer is that aggressive feelings and aggression towards targets within the group are likely to become more acute: on the one hand, aggression becomes more essential to the maintenance of massification; and, on the other, in so far as massification gives way to aggregation, aggression erupts in connection with contra-grouping and isolation. More specifically, four interrelated forms of aggression become ubiquitous:

(a) *the development and maintenance of an attitude of 'moral superiority'* by those who are at the core or centre of the group towards those who are at the periphery of it (Hopper 1981): the development and maintenance of an attitude of moral superiority is based on manipulation of the norms that regulate moral judgements so as to ensure that the targets of aggressive feelings are defined as deviant, immoral and criminal. These judgements are then used to justify and to mobilise pressure to conform, participate in various public rituals, and comply with the expectations of those in authority.

(b) *the development and maintenance of processes of 'anonymisation'* (Main 1975): the essence of anonymisation is an attack on the personal identity of each individual member of a group. Anonymisation reduces the sense of personal responsibility for thought, feeling and deed, because action is felt to originate in a specific role and not in the mind of a unique person who interprets the role. Anonymisation also eliminates the possibility of giving credit to individuals for their contributions. Paradoxically, although anonymisation is a form of aggression towards individuals, it also functions to reduce the envy of individuality and hence it helps to dilute aggressive feelings and aggression towards people who are able to retain their 'names'. Thus, people who feel frightened and helpless tend to anonymise themselves in order to pre-empt envy from others (Kreeger 1992).

(c) *shunning:* people who are defined as deviant, immoral and criminal are likely to be shunned, that is, marginalised, peripheralised and ignored in order to deprive them of social and cultural sustenance. At one extreme, the shunned are merely ignored and deprived of a sense of being recognised; at the other, they are deprived of help and support.

(d) *banishment:* in the last resort, shunning gives way to banishing, sending a person beyond the pale. This may even involve regarding him as 'dead', and as the object of rituals of mourning. Banishment is the ultimate expression of social and cultural purification.

3. Based on the development and maintenance of moral superiority, anonymisation, shunning and banishment, two additional and interrelated forms of aggression are especially prominent in groups who are attempting to maintain a state of Massification, and are used both against targets within the group and in the service of pseudo-speciation:

(a) *scapegoating* (Cartwright and Zander 1953; Lewin 1948;
     Scheidlinger 1982): in scapegoating, the members of a
     group purge themselves of unacceptable and dangerous
     feelings, ideas, attributes and qualities by projecting them
     into particular people and subgroups, who are then judged
     very stringently, and in absolute rather than relative terms,
     and perceived to be guilty. They are punished by being
     peripheralised, marginalised, shunned and even banished.

     Scapegoating may involve an unconscious attack on the
     Father (Money-Kyrle 1929), who is perceived to have failed
     the group and/or to have stopped access to the Mother.
     People and subgroups who are perceived to be either
     obstacles to merger with a perfect group and/or as impurities
     within the hallucination of perfection (Chasseguet-Smirgel
     1985) are displacements from the Father.

     Scapegoating also stems from helplessness and envy of
     the Mother and the mother-group, on the basis of which 'she'
     is split into good and bad objects. The 'bad' target is attacked,
     and ultimately banished. However, the 'good' target is killed
     and eaten, or at least incorporated symbolically, thus
     initiating a process of atonement (Cohen and Schermer 2002;
     Maccoby 1982).

     A target of scapegoating may be more or less deserving of
     the projections. He may even possess desirable and highly
     valued qualities or attributes, in which case the motive for the
     attack may be envy and/or punishment for acting as though
     he were a God or a special kind of human being, for example,
     for being too intelligent or for assuming that he does not need
     natural protection, such as the foreskin. Moreover, the
     scapegoat '…may respond *antagonistically*, by condemning or
     withdrawing from the community while, in contrast, exalting
     (himself)'; 'or *agonistically*, by joining with the community in
     both its condemnation of the scapegoat and exaltation of
     (himself)' (Cohen and Schermer 2002, p.93).

     Although it has been observed that in small groups
     scapegoats are drawn from the ranks of singletons or isolates

(Roth 1980), scapegoats are always likely to be central persons who carry the group's thoughts and feelings. Although the process may be unconscious, it is always political. The dilemma is how to banish a person or a subgroup without losing useful qualities and attributes.

The scapegoating process is rarely self-contained and self-limiting. Those who actively personify and lead the scapegoating process are likely to become passive personifiers and victims of later scapegoating processes connected with guilt and blame for the aggression that was inherent in previous scapegoating processes, which spans the generations.

(b) the *assassination* of people and their characters: obviously, actual assassinations occur less often than character assassinations, and actual assassinations are unlikely to occur within the context and frame of reference of organisations and groups (no matter how some of us who are active in the politics of our professional organisations might wish). Nonetheless, groups who meet more than once do provide time and space outside their meetings for interactions between individual participants, subgroups and contra-groups. Character assassinations occur between meetings of the group. All members of a group may be subjected to character assassination, especially the central persons of the basic assumption processes, and the leader of the work group.

Although mainly used in attempts to purge a group of obstacles to massification and in the service of pseudo-speciation, assassination can be used in order to provoke aggregation. Within a stable society governed by the rule of law, an assassination of a leader violates expectations about personal and public life, and it becomes extremely difficult to maintain the morale of the work group. The loss of a leader involves a loss of social glue, and anomie of norms that govern both social goals and the means for achieving them is likely to arise. Isolation, subgrouping and contra-grouping become ubiquitous. An assassination is likely to delay the natural shift from aggregation to massification. Moreover, an assassination is very difficult to mourn.

Some types of actual assassination and character assassination are associated with scapegoating. Both the target of the assassination and the assassin are the recipients of projections of repudiated qualities and characteristics, not only in their own right but also on behalf of the groups they represent. Moreover, the subsequent suicide, murder, execution or incarceration of the assassin, which almost always occurs, can be seen in terms of the two-stage process of scapegoating. Similarly, it is often said that eventually gossips and mongers of rumour ruin their own reputations.

The personification of aggressive feelings and aggression by the central persons of Incohesion: Aggregation/Massification

Crustacean, contact-shunning and amoeboid, merger-hungry characters are especially likely to personify the malignant and malevolent forms of social control associated with Incohesion. They are highly susceptible to the suction of roles that characterise aggregation and massification, which provide them with self-definition, protection, and normative support for their feelings. This is especially important because they have great difficulty in acknowledging and experiencing aggressive feelings, both in themselves and in others. However, when crustaceans become angry, they become cold and over-contained; and when amoeboids become angry, they become intrusive and engulfing, based on their tendencies towards vacuole incorporation.

Crustacean and amoeboid characters are unconsciously compelled to try to communicate the story of their traumatic experience. Other people are forced to collude with both the narrative and the narrator. However, when the narrator is unable to tell his story in a particular way, or when he has no one to listen to it, he attempts unconsciously to communicate through enactments.

1. Within the context of Incohesion in general, crustaceans and amoeboids are likely to be both perpetrators and victims of aggression. They acquire identity both through attack and through being attacked. This involves contradictory processes, some of which occur simultaneously, and some at different phases of the oscillation between aggregation and massification:

   (a) within the context of aggregation, crustaceans, who are prone to assert their identities as singletons and isolates, are likely to attack the group and its members by withdrawing their affect and involvement from them. They repudiate the group, and they refuse to 'join in'. However, amoeboids, who are prone to assert their identities as membership individuals, are likely to regard crustaceans as responsible for the group's inability to 'come together', for the common experience of empty, silent and cold meaninglessness and for other anxieties associated with aggregation. Hence, amoeboids are likely to attack crustaceans.

   (b) within the context of the early phases of massification, when the compulsion to protect against the psychotic anxieties associated with fission and fragmentation, and hence with aggregation, is most intense, the people and subgroups who are perceived as having maintained the idiosyncrasies of identity, and who therefore stand out from the crowd, are likely to be regarded as 'mavericks', and 'loose cannons'. They must be shunned, and even banished. Hence, amoeboids are likely to attack crustaceans.

   (c) within the context of the later phases of massification, when the psychotic anxieties associated with fusion and confusion are most intense, the people and subgroups who are perceived as responsible for the loss of autonomy, freedom and individuality, the experience of cultural suffocation, and various other anxieties associated with massification, are likely to be regarded as 'conformists', who must be replaced. Hence, crustaceans are likely to attack amoeboids.

Charismatic-amoeboid characters are especially vulnerable to attack, because they are highly unusual objects of envy (the desire to spoil the valued objects of another person or group). As a defence against the full recognition that they have suffered special predicaments and catastrophes, they both perceive themselves and are perceived by others as having special contact with God or the sacred in general, as being touched by grace, and as having been given a unique 'blessing', which excuses them from ordinary social and cultural constraints, and from the need for ordinary protections. They have been 'chosen' for special treatments and special dispensations. They are beyond cause and effect, which technically is what 'charisma' means. Thus, they both perceive themselves and are perceived by others as able to violate 'natural' laws and 'get away with it', for example: to evince a surfeit of bisexuality; to be unnaturally self-sufficient in general; to contain their own parentage, and, in effect, to have given birth to themselves specifically; and to be unnaturally youthful or in possession of a charmed combination of youth and maturity which is not subject to the normal processes of ageing. The son or daughter part of these parent–child combined and amalgamated objects is denigrated, and the father or mother part or parts is idealised, and/or vice versa. Other combinations of gender and generation may also be denigrated and idealised simultaneously in terms of judgements such as competent/incompetent, intelligent/stupid, feared/fearful and worshipped/worshipful, or in other words, in terms of a 'magician' and a 'Mario', the two archetypical figures in *Mario and the Magician*, the famous short story by Thomas Mann (1930). Moreover, even if the illusion of being 'special' and 'chosen' is supported through collusion, it is experienced as exceptionally arrogant, which magnifies the envy aroused by the illusion in the first place, and more or less ensures that the people and subgroups who maintain this illusion will be chosen for special 'treatment'.

2. Within the context of Incohesion in general, the leaders of the work group and the subgroups associated with the realities of structure and hierarchy and of positional and relational goods are especially vulnerable to attack, for several reasons:

(a) leaders are expected to be perfect. A kind of 'Rebecca myth' almost always constrains the group's valuation of them in terms of an idealisation of previous social and political arrangements that have been lost but unmourned (Gouldner 1955). When dependency fails, leaders are likely to be perceived as responsible for the woes of the group, to have betrayed the people, and to be singularly responsible for their feelings of group disgrace. Hence, it is dangerous to be a bad leader.

(b) leaders must make people conscious of the need to make choices within the context of scarce resources, the inevitability of partial failure, the need for realism, and the constraints of various kinds of social dilemma. Very few decisions can ever be made and realised without some degree of tension and conflict. Moreover, all leaders must have a degree of detachment and aloofness which allows them to resist the romantic idealisation of power, which makes them obstacles to the harmony, enchantment, and magic of massification, which has been collusively promised and expected. It is ironic that when massification prevails, the better the leadership of the work group, the greater is the desire for its elimination. Hence, it is dangerous to be a good leader.

(c) male leaders tend to be perceived as fathers (or parts of them) who are adored by the mother group, and therefore as an obstacle to 'her'. Consequently, a good leader may be experienced as a 'bad father' who prevents merger with a 'good mother' group (Ruiz 1972; Gibbard et al. 1974). Similarly, female leaders tend to be perceived as mothers (or parts of them) who are adored by the father group, and therefore as an obstacle to 'him'. This might apply to both male and female leaders, because in all relationships in which transference predominates, a female may be experienced as a man and a father, and a male as a woman and a mother, so that the actual sex of the leader may not determine the configuration of Oedipal fantasies about the group and its leaders, especially in the context of compulsions to merge with the perfect mother-group. However, authoritarian leaders use a scapegoating process in order to displace aggression directed towards themselves onto more vulnerable targets (Scheidlinger 1952), so that the propensity to attack the 'bad' father and the 'bad' mother leaders is not always apparent.

(d) people want to be close to a powerful leader, and attacking a leader offers a way of doing this. Such attacks may be associated with homosexual feelings and the paranoid dread of them, which are then blamed on the object, who is regarded as responsible for having created the desire. The victim becomes 'bad', and the perpetrator 'good' through eliminating the offending homosexuality both from the victim and himself (Socarides 1979). However, the desire to attack the leader may arouse an erotic defence, that is, a desire to be close to the object of hatred. Again, the homosexual transference to a female leader may involve very similar feelings and defences against her. The powerful leader who appears to be bisexual is especially at risk.

3. A leader of the work group who is also charismatic, or in other words, who is both a leader of the work group and a personifier of the massification process, is especially vulnerable to attack. Historically, very few people have been able to fulfil the requirements of these combined roles, at least not for very long. Usually, these roles are shared between either a leader and a central person, two leaders with complementary skills and qualities, or among a group of leaders and central persons. Such relationships are difficult, because they are subjected to splitting attacks, and the leader of the work group becomes envious of the admiration and adoration directed towards the charismatic personifier of the massification process, and/or vice versa.

The loss of a leader and transgenerational failed dependency

The loss of a leader is almost always associated with failed dependency, which is experienced as traumatic. Consequently, following the loss of a leader, social systems tend towards aggregation, whether primary or secondary, because the loss of a leader is analogous to a person's losing his head. Panic is likely to ensue but this is likely to be followed by massification. Within this context people are unable and unwilling to mourn. Traumatogenic processes become attached to chosen trauma (Volkan 1991), and are transmitted across the generations.

Summary

Within the context of the fourth basic assumption of Incohesion: Aggregation/Massification, which is characteristic of large groups and traumatised social systems in general, aggressive feelings and aggression take particular forms. Although they are the essence of aggregation, they are essential for the development and the maintenance of massification processes. Of particular importance are the development and maintenance of moral superiority, anonymisation, shunning, and banishment, especially as seen in processes of scapegoating and assassination. Within the roles offered by the processes of Incohesion, crustacean and amoeboid characters are likely to be both perpetrators of aggression and the victims of aggression from others. Within the context of massification processes, the work group leader is always vulnerable, especially when he is charismatic. Processes in Incohesion are transgenerational.

References

Bion, W. R. (1961) *Experiences in Groups.* London: Tavistock Publications.

Cartwright, D. and Zander, A. (eds) (1953) *Group Dynamics: Research and Theory.* Evanston, IL: Row.

Chasseguet-Smirgel, J. (1985) *Creativity and the Perversions.* London: Free Association Books.

Cohen, B. D. and Schermer, V. L. (2002) 'On scapegoating in therapy groups: A social constructivist and intersubjective outlook.' *International Journal of Group Psychotherapy* 52, 1, 89–110.

Erikson, E. (1968) *Identity, Youth and Crisis.* New York: Norton.

Foulkes, S. H. (1968) 'On interpretation in group analysis.' *International Journal of Group Psychotherapy 18, 4*, 432–444.

Gibbard, G., Hartman, J. and Mann, R. (eds) (1974) *Analysis in Groups*. MD: Jossey-Bass.

Gouldner, A. W. (1955) *Wildcat Strike: A Study of an Unofficial Strike*. London: Routledge & Kegan Paul.

Hopper, E. (1981) *Social Mobility: A Study of Social Control and Insatiability*. Oxford: Blackwell.

Hopper, E. (2001) 'On the nature of hope in psychoanalysis and group analysis.' *British Journal of Psychotherapy 18, 2*, 205–226. Re-published in E. Hopper (2003a).

Hopper, E. (2003a) *The Social Unconscious: Selected Papers*. London: Jessica Kingsley Publishers.

Hopper, E. (2003b) *Traumatic Experience in the Unconscious Life of Groups: The Fourth Basic Assumption: Incohesion: Aggregation/Massification or (ba) I:A/M*. London: Jessica Kingsley Publishers (in press).

Kreeger, L. (1992) 'Envy pre-emption in small and large groups.' *Group Analysis 25, 4*, 391–408.

Lewin, K. (1948) *Resolving Social Conflicts*. New York: Harper & Row.

Maccoby, H. (1982) *The Sacred Executioner*. London: Thames & Hudson.

Main, T. (1975) 'Some psychodynamics of large groups.' In L. Kreeger (ed) *The Large Group: Dynamics and Therapy*. London: Karnac Books. Reprinted in 1994.

Mann, T. (1930) (1996) *Mario and the Magician*. London: Random House. (Original work published in German in 1930.)

Money-Kyrle, R. (1929) *The Meaning of Sacrifice*. London: Hogarth Press and the Institute of Psychoanalysis.

Roth, B. (1980) 'Understanding the development of a homogenous identity impaired group through countertransference phenomena.' *International Journal of Group Psychotherapy 30*, 405–426.

Ruiz, J. (1972) 'On the perception of the 'mother group' in T-groups.' *International Journal of Group Psychotherapy 22*, 488–491.

Scheidlinger, S. (1952) *Psychoanalysis and Group Behavior*. New York: Norton.

Scheidlinger, S. (1982) 'On scapegoating in group psychotherapy.' *International Journal of Group Psychotherapy 32*, 131–143.

Schindler, W. (1966) 'The role of the mother in group psychotherapy.' *International Journal of Group Psychotherapy 16*, 198–200.

Socarides, C. (1979) 'Why Sirhan killed Kennedy: Psychoanalytical speculations on an assassination.' *Journal of Psycho-history 6*, 447–460.

Turquet, P. (1975) 'Threats to identity in the large group.' In L. Kreeger (ed) *The Large Group: Dynamics and Therapy*. London: Karnac Books. Reprinted in 1994.

Volkan, V. (1991) 'On chosen traumas.' *Mind and Human Interactions 3*, 13.

CHAPTER 4

The Mystical and the Spiritual in the Large Group

Stanley Schneider

Introduction

I have always been fascinated by the ability of the large group to elicit emotions, feelings and even activity on the part of its participants – even those who 'swore' they would only be spectators and would never allow themselves to be involved! What unconscious processes are operating that compel one to be both passively and actively involved?

Le Bon (1896) hinted at one possibility: 'I allude to that suggestibility of which, moreover, the contagion…is neither more nor less than an effect… Such also is approximately the state of the individual forming part of a psychological crowd. He is no longer conscious of his acts' (pp.30–31). The crowd, or large group, through an electrifying suggestibility, seemingly plants within the individual's psyche an unconscious identification with the surrounding crowd. No longer is one an individual, but rather a part of a large whole through a process known as contagion. Just as a contagious disease infects those in proximity to it, so too the emotional contagion spreads to all those who are part of the crowd or large group. Freud (1889) noted that the '…physician…retains a directing power over the sleeping brain in its artificial sleep' (p.94). Somehow, in the psychotherapeutic interaction, there is an underlying influence that is unconsciously felt and transmitted.

I would like to try and understand how unconscious thoughts and feelings become aroused and evoked in the large group experience. I don't think it is just by happenstance that the large group propels itself. True, the conductor has to create the atmosphere that allows the cultural and societal unconscious processes to emerge. But it is the individual participants, guided by the unconscious collective, who set the tone, affect and content of the large group experience. The large group is a symbolic container for all of society's feelings and experiences. As Rollo May (1969) interestingly notes: 'Satan, or the devil, comes from the Greek word *diabolos*; "diabolic" is the term in contemporary English. *Diabolos*...literally means "to tear apart." ...Now it is fascinating to note that this "diabolic" is the antonym to "symbolic." The latter comes from *sym-bollein*, and means "to throw together," to unite...the *symbolic* is that which draws together, ties, integrates the individual in himself and with his group...' (p.137).

In order to try and 'experience' the large group, we need to explore what I would like to call the mystical and spiritual. These underlying unconscious processes enable us to connect to the large group experience, and let us begin to understand what really happens 'underneath.'

The oceanic feeling and the mystical

Freud wrote to Romain Rolland in March 1923: '...your name has been associated with the most precious of beautiful illusions, that of love extended to all mankind. But a great part of my life has been spent (trying to) destroy illusions of my own and those of mankind' (E. Freud 1970, p.346). In his correspondence with Rolland, Freud was impressed with Rolland's ability to transcend the scientific and emotionally relate to others in brotherly love. This major difference between Freud and Rolland came to the fore after Freud sent Rolland a copy of *The Future of an Illusion* (1927). Rolland expressed disappointment that Freud had neglected to include subjective feelings which Rolland called 'a sensation of "eternity", a feeling as of something limitless, unbounded – as it were, "oceanic"' (Freud 1930, p.64). (See Jones 1974, p.594)

Freud the scientist noted: 'I cannot discover this "oceanic" feeling in myself. It is not easy to deal scientifically with feelings (1930, p.65)...it is very difficult for me to work with these almost intangible qualities' (1930, p.72). Since these amorphous feelings could not be defined objectively,

Freud did not investigate the intangible. He never stated that these feelings did not exist, they just weren't part of his *Weltanschauung*. He admired Rolland for being able to feel and express these emotions. In a 1929 letter, Freud writes to Rolland: 'How remote from me are the worlds in which you move! To me mysticism is just as closed a book as music' (Freud 1970, p.389). And in January 1930, Freud states that the mystical experience is 'highly valuable for an embryology of the soul when correctly interpreted, but worthless for orientation in the alien, external world' (Freud 1970, p.393). It sounds as if Freud might be fearful of entering the mystical 'orchard' because of its association with organized religion, which he rejected.

In 1936, Freud dedicated a paper to Rolland on his 70th birthday in which he related a recurring psychical situation which appeared to him confusing. Freud had a momentary feeling: '*"What I see here is not real."* Such a feeling is known as a "feeling of derealization"' (Freud 1936, p.244). As Freud notes, they are '"sensations"…attached to particular mental contents and bound up with decisions made about these contents' (*ibid.* p.244). Defensively operating, 'they aim at keeping something away from the ego…' (*ibid.* p.245). One can attempt to make a strong case for understanding derealization as a psychological mechanism that operates in a mystical sort of way. Freud alluded to this, but wasn't willing (or able?) to pursue it any further. No doubt, since Freud was very caught up emotionally with Rolland, he wanted to identify, on some level, with Rolland's interest in mysticism. Meissner feels that Freud was trying to convey to Rolland 'that what he calls "oceanic feelings" may well provide the basis and springboard of religion – insofar as they are a defense against depression and the memory of a buried wound' (Meissner 1984, p.48). Harrison felt that Freud's 1936 paper was a response to Rolland's implicit request that Freud attempt 'a psychoanalytic consideration of mysticism' (Harrison 1979, p.407). The closest Freud came to this was his brief notation in 1938 (published posthumously): 'Mysticism is the obscure self-perception of the realm outside the ego, of the id' (Freud 1941, p.300).

For all that we have so far stated, we have not yet put forth a 'working definition' of the 'oceanic feeling' or mysticism. Freud (1930) stated that the 'oceanic feeling' is bound-up with the concept of ego boundaries: '…the ego detaches itself from the external world' (p.68). It is precisely this regressive state of the ego that gives one the 'oceanic feeling.' This is the feeling 'of limitlessness and of a bond with the universe' (p.68). Milner called this 'a sea of undifferentiated being' (Milner 1969, p.29) and Werman the 'confluence of the inner and outer world' (Werman 1986, p.125). Others have likened this 'oceanic feeling' to the blissful state of the infant–mother relationship (Harrison 1979), and to the Buddhist meditation state which recalls 'vestiges of primary narcissism' (Epstein 1990, p.163). Milner was 'not entirely satisfied with the use of the word "mysticism" for psychoanalytic thinking' (Milner 1973, p.273, footnote 16) but could not find a better word. What seems clear is that the 'oceanic feeling' seems bound up with our understanding of consciousness. When one attends to something and is aware (Freud's attention cathexis), this is consciousness. Any change from that attention to another state is referred to as an alternative or altered state of consciousness (Werman 1986).

This brings us to the concept of mysticism. Ostow tried to anchor the 'floating' definition of mysticism with religion and wrote that 'religion seems to be the natural medium for the evolution of the mystical experience' (Ostow 1995, p.13). Bettelheim who was 'born into a middle-class, assimilated Jewish family' (Bettelheim 1984, p.3), did not write in 'religious' terms. Instead he spoke of a spiritual feeling that was pervasive in Freud's writings and conspicuously absent in Strachey's (mis)translation. When Bettelheim spoke of the necessity of emotional closeness on the part of the staff to the children they were treating, he wrote that what was needed was 'a spontaneous sympathy of our unconscious with that of others, a feeling response of our soul to theirs' (*ibid.* p.5). Underhill, in a classic definition of mysticism, wrote that: 'mysticism (is) the art of establishing one's conscious relation with the Absolute…' (Underhill 1912, p.97).

It seems obvious from the above citations that mysticism oftentimes was identified with religious practice. One can readily see how many shied away from any identification or association with religious feelings or practices. Spirituality and religion became theosophical systems to be avoided. Thus, anything that was related in any way to organized religious feelings or practices was shunned and rejected. This situation didn't allow spirituality or mysticism to develop in psychological contexts as divorced from any religious connotation.

Jung, who tried to place a strong emphasis on the occult and spirituality, wrote: '...the various forms of religion no longer appear to come from within, from the psyche; they seem more like items from the inventory of the outside world' (1928, p.466). This was an expression that something was missing in modern man; something called 'spiritual' or 'mystical.'

Bion tried to relate to this *feeling* quality by creating a distinction between knowing (K) and being (O). As he states: 'Reality has to be "been"' (Bion 1965, p.148). In 1970 he referred to O as the experience or thing-in-itself (Bion 1970, p.4). He continues:

> I shall use the sign O to denote that which is the ultimate reality represented by terms such as ultimate reality, absolute truth, the godhead, the infinite, the thing-in-itself. O does not fall in the domain of knowledge or learning save incidentally, it can 'become,' but it cannot be 'known.' It is darkness and formlessness but it enters the domain K when it has evolved to a point where it can be known, through knowledge gained by experience, and formulated in terms derived from sensuous experience...
> (*ibid.* p.26)

Bion, unlike Freud, was able to go beyond the purely scientific and allow himself to 'float' (something akin to free-floating attention) and be able to pick up mystical cues. Grotstein had personal communication with Bion and relates that Bion was keenly interested in Kabbalah (Grotstein 1996, p.122) and mysticism (see Eigen 1998, p.25). As Grotstein writes:

> I believe Bion left behind the saturated pre-conceptions of the psychoanalytic establishment and ventured inward in a soul-searching, mystic journey with what I have come to believe was a mission to transcend the positivistic certainty of its determinism and 'messianically' return it to its provenance in numinous parallax and doubt, where the ultimate mystic and relativistic 'science of man' truly resides. What emerged perhaps became the state of the art in psychoanalytic metatheory and metapsychology. (Grotstein 1996, p.115)

Mystical influences were 'in the air.'

In 1933, Freud stated an opinion that brought his public coolness towards the occult closer to his private interest and desire for further understanding:

> No doubt you would like me to hold fast to a moderate theism and show
> myself relentless in my rejection of everything occult. But I am incapable
> of currying favour and I must urge you to have kindlier thoughts on the
> objective possibility of thought-transference and at the same time of
> telepathy as well. (Freud 1933, p.54)

Freud explained his earlier fear of recognizing the validity of such
paranormal phenomena (this was similar to the views he had expressed in
1921, pp.177–181, although here they were expressed more strongly) in
the following manner:

> When they first came into my range of vision more than ten years ago, I
> too felt a dread of a threat against our scientific *Weltanschauung*, which, I
> feared, was bound to give place to spiritualism or mysticism if portions
> of occultism was proved true. To-day I think otherwise. (Freud 1933,
> p.54)

The need to protect the scientific discipline of psychoanalysis even at the
expense of avoiding potentially conflictual issues is the central theme. This
'admission' by Freud augurs well for our understanding of the underlying
unconscious elements operating in the large group.

Psychic susceptibility

An overview of psychotherapeutic principles and methods runs the gamut
from Freud's earliest drive theory conceptualizations to object relations
and intersubjective theoreticians. Over the past 100 years, clinicians have
been grappling with how and why emotional interactions occur. As
Stolorow, Brandshaft and Atwood (1987) describe it:

> Today, the study of intersubjectivity seems to be another medium for
> trying to understand interactive processes, as it focuses on the analytic
> work that takes place within the realm of '... *subjective reality* – that of the
> patient, that of the analyst, and the psychological field created by the
> interplay between the two. (p.4)

Bion tried to find the 'right word' to describe this transcendental, mystical
feeling that somehow gets conveyed between patient and therapist. 'I
propose to use the term "intuit" as a parallel in the psychoanalyst's domain
to the physician's use of "see," "touch," "smell," and "hear"' (Bion 1970,

p.7). This is similar to Bollas' comment about '…psychoanalysis…the reliving through language of that which is known but not yet thought (what I term the unthought known)…' (Bollas 1987, p.4). Something very mystical occurs within the therapeutic experience and especially in the large group experience.

As Eigen noted: 'There are mysticisms of emptiness and fullness, difference and union, transcendence and immanence' (Eigen 1998, p.13). Anyone who has had large group experiences knows the feeling of wanting to say the 'right thing' and not to say the 'wrong thing.' What seems to happen is that the large group, as Le Bon (1896) wrote, exerts a tremendous unconscious and conscious pull upon its members. Not all the time is the effect an anticipated, expected or 'moral' one. One can be influenced by the large group and propelled to think and act in ways that one would never have thought, imagined or wished for. '…by the mere fact that he forms part of an organised crowd, a man descends several rungs in the ladder of civilisation' (Le Bon 1896, p.32). Morality is used by Le Bon 'to mean constant respect for certain social conventions, and the permanent repression of selfish impulses…the moral standard of crowds is very low' (*ibid.* p.56). In effect, the large group or crowd, which is impulsive, fluid and constantly moving in and out of chaos, brings to the fore morality sentiments which may be lower or higher than those of the individuals composing them, and this further influences group members to act potentially out of role (Sandler 1976).

Interestingly, Trigant Burrow, a man 'ahead of his time,' started searching for the underlying reasons why people behave in the way they do. This innovative exploration, starting in the 1920s, cost Burrow his university appointment and had him excommunicated from the American Psychoanalytic Association. This was connected to Burrow's wanting to investigate what fueled societal behavior, and what he called the 'preconscious foundation of human experience' (1964, p.ix). Burrow was talking about a personality template that influenced the individual and society. As he wrote: '…this preconscious matrix of personality persists as a sort of background of consciousness, representing a biologically permanent mode that is inherent in human development… The preconscious type of personality is sensitive, inspirational, intuitive and creative' (*ibid.* p.47). If we are not cognizant of this preconscious element in the human personality, i.e. society, or in our terminology, the large group, it's like having an unanalyzed person 'on the loose.' There will be a tendency to act out, respond symbolically or metaphorically – not be rooted in the actual 'here-and-now.' Burrow called this 'a flight toward the mystical' (*ibid.* p.56). Le Bon termed this 'a religious shape assumed by all the convictions of crowds' (Le Bon 1986, p.72). It is important to note that the terms 'mystical' and 'religious' do not necessarily have to have a religious-as-religion connotation. Rather, we are dealing with concepts and ideas that relate to the underlying, unconscious emotional receptivity and awareness that enable us to pick up on unconscious cues, affects and behaviors. Interestingly, Grotstein noted: 'I posit that the unconscious is perhaps as close to the 'God Experience' as mankind can ever hope to achieve' (Grotstein 2000, p.xvii). Not religious experience *per se,* but a spiritual, mystical, unconscious perception.

Schermer wrote recently about his conceptualization of the group therapist as a mystic. Utilizing what he termed 'a Bionic object relations perspective,' Schermer stated that 'mystical awareness is pertinent to the conduct of therapy groups' (Schermer 2001, p.505). But this is really not new. Burrow had earlier remarked that 'this element of mysticism underlies and animates many phases of thought and activity commonly regarded as normal' (Burrow 1964, p.94). Burrow borrowed from ancient Semitic (Hebrew, Egyptian), Buddhist, Indian, Greek and Roman sources in order to show how ancient civilizations possessed and applied understanding of these 'primary or elemental "forces"' (Burrow 1964, p.88). Let us look a bit further into some of the ancient roots surrounding mysticism and spirituality.

Mysticism (from the Greek *mystikós*: 'revealed only to initiates into the mysteries') is an attempt to transcend ordinary understanding in order to seek and 'know' on an experiential and cognitive level the 'inner reality' of the divine majesty – the spiritual. This can be done on a religious or non-religious plane. The mystic endeavors to attain this state of union without getting lost in the divine abyss; without sinking (Idel 1985). In our terminology, mysticism is a type of 'floating' whereby the group members connect to a spiritual, mystical unconscious. There evolves an unconscious union in the here-and-now which connects *all* group members together on a subliminal level.

Jung wrote: 'Whereas the personal unconscious consists for the most part of *complexes,* the content of the collective unconscious is made up essentially of *archetypes* (Jung 1936, p.60). Jung described the archetype as 'a pre-existent form' (*ibid.* p.60). It's something that doesn't exist alone, by itself, but resonates and reverberates with those who are in the same social sphere, at a specific moment in time. In the large group, there is an underlying unconscious feeling of connection and belonging that resonates and echoes with existing collective, group (societal) commonalities.

In his treatise on the fundamentals of Buddhist thought, the Dalai Lama discusses the principle of interdependent origination, which he defines as 'all conditioned things and events in the universe come into being only as a result of the interaction of various causes and conditions' (Dalai Lama 1997, p.12). Even though this principle negates the possibility of a Creator or God, we can still find parallels in other religious and philosophical systems, where something happens because of something we do not control. In the Zen mind, 'when you try to understand everything, you will not understand anything. The best way is to understand yourself, and then you will understand everything... So we say that true understanding will come out of emptiness...' (Suzuki 1970, p.111). In the large group we oftentimes have a chaotic process that seems to force us to deviate from knowing what is going on. We need to understand that this chaos is an important part of our connecting on a pre-conscious/unconscious level to what is really happening in the group. The mystical or spiritual dimension has to be subliminally connected to; we cannot allow ourselves to be shifted away from unconsciously connecting to the underlying themes and feelings '...chaos helps us to see what is underneath all these thought patterns...' (Trungpa 2001, p.75). We need to allow ourselves to be unfettered in the large group so that we can connect to the underlying themes and affects. As the Buddha says 'To be attached to one thing (to a certain view) and to look down upon other things (views) as inferior – this the wise men call a fetter' (Rahula 1959, p.10). In order to be free emotionally so that we can connect to the underlying thematic idea or emotion in the large group, we need to avoid rigidity or, as the Buddhists call it, attachment. 'Attachment is an attitude that overestimates the qualities of an object or person and then clings to it... Attachment is an unrealistic view and thus causes us confusion' (Chodron 1990, p.29).

Eastern philosophical systems can relate much more easily to the large group. The lay-back, searching and experiential aspect of their philosophical system allows an unfettered, more flexible sway of subliminally attuning to the underlying themes and affects. The fact that the large group oftentimes seems so chaotic, is the challenge we face in accepting the importance of unconsciously drifting – what Freud had termed 'evenly suspended attention' (1912, p.111). This allows us to receive all that is being expressed: consciously, unconsciously, metaphysically, mystically and spiritually. If the large group members, and the conductor(s), connect to the mystical unconscious messages that are being expressed, the chaotic feeling will dissipate. This is seen very well in the following Zen story.

> Chuang-tze of the third century BC, has the story of *konton*, Chaos. His friends owed many of their achievements to Chaos and wished to repay him. They consulted together and came to a conclusion. They observed that Chaos had no sense organs by which to discriminate the outside world. One day they gave him the eyes, another day the nose, and in a week they accomplished the work of transforming him into a sensitive personality like themselves. While they were congratulating themselves on their success, Chaos died. (Fromm, Suzuki and De Martino 1960, p.6)

In the Jewish Kabbalistic system, there is a connection between our present or lower world and supernal upper worlds. This explains the underlying unconscious feelings in large groups. Man has cosmic influence – lower and upper worlds have a symmetrical correspondence. As the Talmud (Ta'anit 25b) states: 'No drop comes down from above without having two drops come from below' (cf. *Zohar III*: 247b). Kabbalah is a mystical search which uncovers the hidden and the revealed.

The 'oceanic feeling' and the mystical quality that is 'felt' parallels the movement from one world to the next in Kabbalistic thinking – especially movement within the last two worlds. However, Freud had great difficulty in accepting the fact that there was a mystical nature of the soul, as we stated earlier on in our paper. This was one of the reasons why Freud and Jung separated. Jung's early works contained within their titles the words 'so-called occult,' 'spiritualistic medium,' 'symbols of rebirth,' 'the collective unconscious,' 'the soul and death,' to name a few. Jung was willing to extend his observations to the parapsychological world, which allowed him access to the realms of the hidden, unconscious worlds.

Melanie Klein tried to further develop Freud's theories but she too was stuck with the one-sided influence of the internal world on the external thinking, feeling and actions of the individual. While she emphasized a psychic world of introjections and projections, the resultant was always to influence the outside object.

It wasn't until the object relations theorists of the late 1930s that we began to see an active – interactive relationship emanating from either or both sides. In the paradigm of infant–mother – there is the possibility of both influencing one another. From Heinz Hartmann to Mahler, the direction was to leave behind the skewed instinctual discharge theory. But it wasn't until the late 1970s and early 1980s, that Daniel Stern, Robert Emde and Stanley Greenspan advanced Mahler's theory and expanded it to include the importance of the infant's influence on the mother – not just that of the mother on the infant. Here we have a perfect parallel of dual influence from inferior to superior and back – from inner to outer and outer to inner. This dual influence theory in psychoanalysis comes closest to paralleling the dual influence theory of the Kabbalah, and of mystical and spiritual preconscious feeling.

In psychoanalysis we have different levels of consciousness. According to Freud (1900), one could live in two spheres simultaneously. On the conscious level, we live our lives in thought and action that we are aware of: the manifest content. But there is another level, the unconscious level or latent content. The unconscious level, likened metaphorically by Freud to that part of the iceberg that is beneath the surface of the water, has major influence in both thought and action over the conscious level, the above-the-water part of the iceberg. We are constantly influenced by the latent content, by the unconscious. In the large group we need to be able to sit back and take in the chaotic world around us in order to connect to our own unconscious thoughts and feelings as well as the collective unconscious of the other large group members. It is the role of the conductors to allow this unfolding process to occur.

References

Bettelheim, B. (1984) *Freud and Man's Soul*. New York: Vintage Books.

Bion, W. R. (1965) 'Transformations.' In *Seven Servants*. New York: Jason Aronson, 1977.

Bion, W. R. (1970) *Attention and Interpretation*. London: Tavistock Publications.

Bollas, C. (1987) *The Shadow of the Object.* New York: Columbia University Press.

Burrow, T. (1964) *Preconscious Foundations of Human Experience.* New York: Basic Books.

Chodron, T. (1990) *Open Heart, Clear Mind.* New York: Snow Lion.

Dalai Lama (1997) *The Four Noble Truths.* London: Thorsons.

Eigen, M. (1998) *The Psychoanalytic Mystic.* London: Free Association Books.

Epstein, M. (1990) 'Beyond the oceanic feeling: Psychoanalytic study of Buddhist meditation.' *International Review of Psycho-Analysis 17,* 159–164.

Freud, E. (1970) (ed) *Letters of Sigmund Freud.* London: Hogarth Press.

Freud, S. (1889) 'Review of August Forel's *Hypnotism.*' Standard Edition, Vol. 1. London: Hogarth Press, 1981.

Freud, S. (1900) *The Interpretation of Dreams.* Standard Edition, Vol. 5. London: Hogarth Press, 1981.

Freud, S. (1912) 'Recommendations to physicians practising psycho-analysis.' Standard Edition, Vol. 12. London: Hogarth Press, 1981.

Freud, S. (1921) 'Psycho-analysis and telepathy.' Standard Edition, Vol. 18. London: Hogarth Press, 1981.

Freud, S. (1927) 'The future of an illusion.' Standard Edition, Vol. 21. London: Hogarth Press, 1981.

Freud, S. (1930) 'Civilization and its discontents.' Standard Edition, Vol. 21. London: Hogarth Press, 1981.

Freud, S. (1933) 'New introductory lectures on psycho-analysis: Lecture 30, Dreams and occultism.' Standard Edition, Vol. 22. London: Hogarth Press, 1981.

Freud, S. (1936) 'A disturbance of memory on the Acropolis.' Standard Edition, Vol. 22. London: Hogarth Press, 1981.

Freud, S. (1941) 'Findings, ideas, problems.' Standard Edition, Vol. 23. London: Hogarth Press, 1981.

Fromm, E., Suzuki, D.T. and De Martino, R. (1960) *Zen Buddhism and Psychoanalysis.* London: Condor, 1993.

Grotstein, J. S. (1996) 'Bion's "Transformation in 'O,' 'the Thing-in-Itself,' and the 'Real': Toward the concept of the 'Transcendent Position'."' *Journal of Melanie Klein and Object Relations 14,* 109–141.

Grotstein, J. S. (2000) *Who is the Dreamer who Dreams the Dream?* Hillsdale, NJ: Analytic Press.

Harrison, I. B. (1979) 'On Freud's view of the infant–mother relationship and of the oceanic feeling – some subjective influences.' *Journal of the American Psychoanalytic Association 27,* 399–421.

Idel, M. (1985) 'Prophetic Kabbalah and the Land of Israel.' In R. I. Cohen (ed) *Vision and Conflict in the Holy Land.* New York: Yad Ben Tzvi.

Jones, E. (1974) *The Life and Work of Sigmund Freud.* Edited and abridged by L. Trilling and S. Marcus. Harmondsworth, Middlesex: Penguin.

Jung, C. G. (1928) 'The spiritual problem of modern man.' In J. Campbell (ed) *The Portable Jung.* New York: Penguin, 1976.

Jung, C. G. (1936) 'The concept of the collective unconscious.' In J. Campbell (ed) *The Portable Jung.* New York: Penguin, 1976.

Jung, C. G. (1951) 'On synchronicity.' In J. Campbell (ed) *The Portable Jung.* New York: Penguin, 1976.

Le Bon (1952) *The Crowd.* London: Ernest Benn. First published as *La Psychologie des Foules.* Paris, 1896.

May, R. (1969) *Love and Will.* New York: Dell, 1974.

Meissner, W. W. (1984) *Psychoanalysis and Religious Experience.* New Haven: Yale University Press.

Milner, M. (1969) *The Hands of the Living God.* London: Virago Press, 1988.

Milner, M. (1973) 'Some notes on psychoanalytic ideas about mysticism.' In *The Suppressed Madness of Sane Men.* London: Tavistock Publications, 1987.

Ostow, M. (1995) (ed) *Ultimate Intimacy: The Psychodynamics of Jewish Mysticism.* London: Karnac Books.

Otto, R. (1958) *The Idea of the Holy.* London: Oxford University Press.

Rahula, W. (1959) *What the Buddha Taught.* New York: Grove Press, 1974.

Sandler, J. (1976) 'Countertransference and Role-Responsiveness.' *International Review of Psycho-Analysis 3*, 43–47.

Schermer, V. L. (2001) 'The group psychotherapist as contemporary mystic: a Bionic object relations perspective.' *International Journal of Group Psychotherapy 51*, 505–523.

Stolorow, R. D., Brandshaft, B. and Atwood, G. E. (1987) *Psychoanalytic Treatment: An Intersubjective Approach.* Hillsdale, New Jersey: Analytic Press.

Suzuki, S. (1970) *Zen Mind, Beginner's Mind.* New York: Weatherhill, 1991.

Trungpa, C. (1975) *Glimpses of Abhidharma.* Boston: Shambhala, 2001.

Underhill, E. (1912) *Mysticism.* London: Methuen.

Werman, D. S. (1986) 'On the nature of the oceanic experience.' *Journal of the American Pschoanalytic Association 34*, 123–139.

CHAPTER 5

Chaos and Order in the Large Group

Gerhard Wilke

Emergence of a group analytic perspective on the large group

Group analysts tend to agree that in large groups we learn about primitive defence mechanisms, the fear of psychotic fragmentation, the fragility of communication and the socially divisive and destructive potential in the foundation matrix of each culture. The focus of attention in the literature has been on the decivilising and not on the civilising processes within the interactions between social actors in the large group setting (Elias 1976). Despite their differences, Foulkesian and Kleinian thinkers agree that the large group repeatedly fails to learn from experience and almost always regresses into a psychotic state of mind. This negative dialectic between large group, individual member and conductor is so unquestioned that it is the first thing that deserves rethinking.

Foulkes, in his refusal to integrate his work with that of Bion, shaped the understanding of small and large groups in three generations of group analytic practitioners. The founding father of group analysis was traumatised in the Third Reich and dealt with the pain of displacement through the mass and its leader by idealising a smaller version of the group. The pre-war generation of analysts was preoccupied with finding a set of defences against the decivilising monster of fascism. The fascist followers and their seducing, charismatic leaders drove the grandfather of group analysis out of his homeland. Foulkes wanted to create applied models of psychoanalysis which could act as a sociopsychological vaccine. In Kreeger's classic book on the large group all the contributors have a passion for invoking dialogue in the face of psychic fragmentation and mass-psychosis. They search for more mature social exchanges through the use of the large group (Kreeger 1975). The contributions in the book read as if this task mirrored the labour of Sisyphus. It is as if basic trust had been damaged for this second generation and as if the work in the large group was, in part, serving the function of healing this transgenerational wound (Balint 1968). The impression one gets, rereading the book, is that it is a delusion to think that the genie of human destructiveness can be kept in the bottle through work in small therapy groups alone, so that analysts have a duty to avoid a split between the idealised clinical and denigrated societal settings.

Foulkes' pro-group perspective has effectively influenced the development of a practice for conducting small therapy groups throughout Europe. His description of the group as a matrix of transpersonal relationships and not a dualistic opposition between the individual and collective gives the analyst permission to adapt the method to a range of settings and patient groups. Foulkes' non-dyadic vision of the group took him beyond Freud and Klein and enabled the group-analytic conductor to work simultaneously with the individual, the pair, the subgroup, the whole group and the context (Foulkes 1986). This is celebrated as a freedom from fear in the small group, as consequently its dynamic process does not have to be mastered, merely worked with.

The group-analytic conductor and therapy group are described as being always on the way to widening and deepening communication, though they don't know how to accomplish this task when they set out on their journey of interaction and communicative exchange. Group analysts have sat easy with a Winnicottian style of working with the group as a transitional object and the group process as a transitional space (Winnicott 1971). What group analysts have been very reluctant to do is transfer this open and optimistic attitude towards the healing powers of the group from the small into the large group setting. Almost against their better natures, group analysts have held on to the idea of the 'good' small group and the 'bad' large group. This is a noteworthy pattern which is in need of deconstructing.

In my experience of sitting in large groups as a participant and conductor over the last 15 years I have become convinced that group analysts who practice the art of the large group resort, on the whole, to a non-group-analytic, negative-group perspective in order to master the Freudian and Kleinian dyadic scene of a fused large group wrestling with a lone and heroic conductor. Group-analytic large group conductors knowingly or unknowingly tend to underpin their interpretations and interventions in a large group with Bion's basic assumptions theory or his ideas on thinking and linking (Bion 1962). Unconsciously, this stance brings two gains: by denigrating the large group in comparison with the small group, the latter remains the theoretically unchanging self-object for each group analyst; and by sharing the non-group-analytic assumption that the large group process is condemned to be just frustrating and destructive, group analysts pull back from attacking their founding father, who was profoundly ambivalent about this methodology.

Foulkes tells us very little in his work about the nature and the workings of the large group. He limits himself to saying that we can work with it in the same way as with the small group; and he reveals his fear of mass phenomena by striving to find the image of the group conductor so as to avoid any association with the leader – the embodiment of the seducer of the large group as mass. This dictum left the successor generation with the problem of looking elsewhere for a theory which could be used to make sense of what goes on in a large group. The unclear legacy led to the emergence of two related but radically different positions in the second generation of group analytic thinkers on the large group – both rooted in Bion, not in Foulkes.

Kreeger, for instance has, for a group analyst, an unnecessarily pessimistic view of the kind of social therapy that can be accomplished in the large group. He describes the conductor as a kind of survivor who appears to be as helpless in relation to the large group as the Kleinian mother is in the face of the death instinct inside the newborn baby. His thinking on the large group process draws imaginatively and creatively on Bion's work on basic assumptions and object relations ideas about pre-oedipal fears and inter-personal defences. Pat de Maré, on the other hand, made use of Bion's theory of thinking in his book *Koinonia*, and begins to overcome the split between the good and benign small group, with its tendency towards integration and relatedness, and the bad and malignant large group with its propensity for disintegration and fragmentation (de Maré *et al.* 1991). He argues that the large group frustrates the satisfaction of libidinal needs and thereby causes hate in and between the participants. Resentment builds up and then finds a channel for expression in subgroups, which contain the hate, and turn it into the desire to think and speak. Through dialogue between the subgroups hate is transformed into frustration, which is, according to Bion, the precondition for thinking and linking (Bion 1967). De Maré thinks that a large group can weave a holding matrix between differing subgroups and develop the capacity for human fellowship. It is this capacity that makes the large group an ideal setting for working through historical trauma and intergroup conflict.

The second generation of Foulkesian large group conductors were split between overly optimistic and pessimistic views of large group work. Kreeger and de Maré accepted their group analytic inheritance, consolidated it and developed a large group tradition beyond the father. They ended up in the roles of competing siblings and have handed the current generation a clear choice: to attach to de Maré's model of using large groups to help deepen and widen democracy and fellowship in society; to follow Kreeger in his quest to work more consciously with the pathology that is part of the unconscious interactions within society; or, to work simultaneously, in the moment as it were, with co-operation and rivalry, order and chaos. The previous generation worked with the unfulfilled dream of the founder to apply analytic thinking in society. We now have the chance to integrate the work of the grandparents, Bion and Foulkes, and the parents, de Maré and Kreeger. Morris Nitsun paved the way for this integrative work by his de-idealisation of the small group object (Nitsun 1996). I would turn his thesis of the small group being not just good and healing, but also bad and destructive, on its head. I want to free group analysts up for the thought that the large group is not just bad and psychosis-inducing, but potentially a good and nurturing object at times (Wilke 1999). We can open a thinking space for working with the propensity for chaos and order in any group, not just the small one.

The symbolic construction of social order and chaos

The iconoclastic way Foulkes looked at the components which structure a group allows group analysts to treat the group as a social and psychological space, not simply as a fused 'as if' individual. Group analysts challenge the artificial dichotomy between individual and group, and society and citizen, so prevalent in the work of classical philosophy and psychoanalysis. Foulkes and Elias gave us an insight into how the individual, the group and society are inseparably connected by means of translucent boundaries. Individual, pair, subgroup, whole group and context can only be understand as a process where the pattern of the interaction, not the separateness of each component, is the focus of understanding – just as the relationship between mother and baby, not their separate identities, is at the core of Winnicott's thinking (Winnicott 1990).

This way of seeing implies that the conductor cannot be confined to confronting the group with its social defences but must open up spaces for the emergence of a sense of interdependence and social connectedness. A large-group conductor who tries to remain a classical analyst, as he struggles to keep an aloof position, and treats the group as a projective myth pays a heavy theoretical and practical price. By reducing the social process of the group to a defensive fantasy against reality he reduces the group members to actors on a dyadic stage which is pluralistic and complex. So, the way a conductor classifies the interactions within the large group shapes the way that reality is perceived, worked with and interpreted.

The anthropologist Edmund Leach argued that a myth constitutes lived reality, not an ideological or psychological rationalisation of it (Leach 1969). Human beings are compulsive classifiers and meaning-makers, and each encounter in a sociopsychological space turns into a ritualised exchange which, through the interaction of the participants, ends in a re-statement of the cosmological order of the belonging group. This dramatisation of social order contains the potential for regression, affirmation and renewal, and draws on the collective cultural, social and psychological memory which those present embody. In that sense it matters absolutely whether the conductor has a dyadic (pre-Foulkesian) or pluralistic (Foulkesian) view of the group process.

In a tribal society aristocratic and religious authorities function to help accomplish the journey through a social space-and-time continuum. In a large group, the group analytic conductor can function as a transitional being in the same way by attempting to contain the space for the emergence of regressive and psychotic forces. If both ends of this tension spectrum are held in the conductor's mind, then reassuring re-enactments of familiar ways of talking together, as well as disturbing and novel patterns of relating, doing and being can emerge in most large groups.

If we transfer the group analytic view of the group conductor as dynamic administrator, translator and analyst to the large group setting, then we will be set free to explore psychological, sociological and historical issues in a regressive and reflexive space. The complexity of this role description means that the conductor must separate from the detached position and adopt, like an anthropologist, the role of a participant observer in a network of transference and counter-transference relationships, embedded in a historical and cultural context. The conductor in the large group has to enact the role of the analyst, the participant observer and the 'individual member'. Writers on the large group have neglected the significance of the psychosocial methods we all use in groups to create the social order we hold on to, in order to cope with the tension involved in retaining a sense of self whilst also accepting our interdependence. Significant numbers in a large group retain the ability to see the positive function of our seemingly pathological social and personal defences against the underlying anxiety of sharing the group with others. With the help of this significant subgroup, the conductor can connect work with the push for order and the pull towards chaos in the large group through the triangulation of psychoanalysis, group analysis and social anthropology.

Social anthropologists show how tribal groups need rituals, leaders and symbolic gift exchanges to structure the transition from one social and cultural state of being to another. A large group has similar needs during its development, and we can regard projection, splitting and projective identification as defences against anxieties, and attempts at communication which need to be accepted and contained. A large group member who is desperate enough to engage in self-destructive patterns of feeling and thinking relates to others in the position of a delinquent who expresses the hope of contact and holding (Winnicott 1968). Such a person seeks to prevent a repetition of the original trauma and looks for an object which can respond to his real inner self, without recourse to persecution and demands for submission.

In the same act of provocation and disconnection, the group member seeks assurance, recognition and social connectedness. The conductor needs to see the attack not just as envious but also as a gift, designed to facilitate the construction of a matrix of interdependence, in which members secure their positions by the obligation to return projective gifts. The act of exchanging projections itself carries the implied message that the group is felt to be containing and deserves basic trust. Group members who present as being at the edge are unconsciously used by the large group to reassure itself of its capacity for sanity. In response, the conductor is called upon to model a form of blind trust in the free associative process, and give the group the feeling that it can accomplish the transition from a state of disconnectedness to re-connectedness.

The conductor creates a space for an experience of environmental mothering that can have a civilising influence both on the group culture and on each individual member. By trusting in the vacillation of the group process between order and disorder, the analyst can help the group integrate destructive forms of exchange through dialogue and the acknowledgement of interdependence. If this toleration of the good and the bad in the relationship with the object can be repeatedly internalised, then the large group will, like society itself, hold and affirm the integrity and the sense of fragmentation in the same act of communication and exchange.

Large group practice

In society we live suspended in psychosocial webs of meaning which we weave ourselves through our daily interactions. These invisibly connected group-webs make up our culture. Group analysts try to create a translucent boundary between the individual, the group matrix and the societal foundation matrix, so as to nurture attempts at recovering the work-group function in the large group or keep hope alive in its constituent subgroups. The following case illustrates how the unconscious mind of the different subgroups within a large group begins to exchange undigested psychic material and dramatise cultural and historical patterns of relating, in a way that is both novel and affirming.

An architect whose parents are concentration camp survivors embraced the fate of being a 'memorial candle' (Wardi 1992). In this role he has not really been able to create his own true self but serves the memory of his lost relatives through reparative work which his own parents are unable to accomplish. He asked me to participate in a project designed to highlight the fact that the second largest Jewish community in Germany still did not have a synagogue 45 years after the end of the war. The community itself was reluctant to settle in a place associated with the mass murder of their own relatives. The local political élite had given the community a piece of land in the Sixties and promised large subsidies for the construction of a community centre and place of worship. This piece of prime real-estate held a secret. Under the ground lay the bunker for the Nazi élite, designed to let them carry on their work whilst the Allies bombed the city. A surveyor's report showed that the cost of removing the bunker would be greater than that of building a new synagogue. Nothing happened for almost 30 years. The community built a car park on the land, made money for its coffers, and attracted the publicity and exposure it feared by creating an eyesore in the middle of the historic town centre.

In the early Nineties three things changed: my client was driven yet again to build another synagogue; a new head of town planning wanted to re-open the case and look with fresh eyes at the project; the newly elected president of the community, herself a survivor, decided that the synagogue should be built on top of the bunker – thereby symbolically signifying the community's survival. Public awareness was raised through an unusual architectural project. The final-year students from two architecture schools in Germany and Israel were invited to visit the site, interview the locals and the Jewish community, consult with the planners and then submit designs for a new synagogue. When the consultation process had ended and the designs were in first draft form, the two student bodies met for a workshop. Integral to this training event was a large group that took place in the cafeteria of the university. The seating area for the students was built like a Roman amphitheatre in the shape of a triangle with three tiers of seating and an empty space in the middle.

The group comprised about 65 students and four professors. After a short introduction in which I stated that we were here to explore the emotional aspects of the encounter with the site, the task and each other, there was a short silence. As I wondered what the effect on the group would be of sitting in an oedipal triangle, the caretaker of the building stormed into the hall. He somehow sensed that I was the leader, although I was one among many sitting in the triangle. He started shouting at me: 'Do you have official permission for this illegal assembly? Wait until the Director gets to hear of this... Get out... I will call the Director now... Don't move... It is disgusting... I never know what is going on in this place!'

I did nothing and waited.

There was a very brief stand off between the caretaker and the group. Most of the group turned away and stared into the empty space in the centre of the seating area. Suddenly a German professor stood up and started to shout back: 'Of course we have permission, you stupid fool! Stop bothering us. Do your own work and leave us to do ours.'

The caretaker went away in a huff. The professor sat down, his whole body shaking. There was another short silence. The group looked stunned and mesmerised. Another staff member started speaking about the task in hand and wondered whether a synagogue was any different from building a mosque or a church in modern Germany. Another person said that he was just going to design an empty building which could also be a fire station, what the community did with it was their business. They, not he, had to give meaning to the space. He was willing merely to design it. The words 'fire station' were a trigger for another student to say that this project was different, that a synagogue in Germany could never be viewed as a neutral construction. Too many of them had been consumed by fire during *Kristallnacht* in 1938.

The group carried on working like this. It became clear that splits were opening up around whether the design for this synagogue should resemble a modernist, functional and rational construction or take on the shape of an emotional, historically rooted holocaust memorial. These two paradigms established themselves very firmly and were not shifted for a long time. Towards the end of the session a third perspective emerged. An in-between subgroup thought that both the modernist and memorial perspective needed to be reflected in the design of this building. The difference between these ways of seeing seemed to be shaped by the influence of childhood experience. The subgroup who wanted to build a memorial to the holocaust victims had parents who had talked about their wartime suffering; the subgroup who wanted to exclude the history of persecution from the design of the building came from families who had remained silent. The in-between group of students seemed freer to choose their response in the here and now. As they were not aware of any shameful or traumatised family past they had responded in an empathic way to the holocaust story during their secondary education.

Though it was comfortable to find this neat fit between the design and inner history of Germans and Jews via the family or the school, the really significant event took place at the boundary of the group. While we were working on the emotional dimensions of designing a synagogue, the caretaker assembled his team and started to move furniture around us in a bizarre and mindless way for the remainder of the session. In a synchronic sequence, they ended their re-arrangement in such a way that by the end of the group the furniture was back in its original position. Almost simultaneously with the end of the group, the noise surrounding and uniting us, stopped. I was left with just sufficient quiet time to thank everyone and summarise the major patterns which had emerged during the session. Everyone got up looking like Munch's scream and full of dis-ease about the power of the social unconscious, which had driven them to sit in a public forum surrounded by people who had regressed into what Bollas has called a fascist state of mind and re-dramatised the traumatic scene between the Nazis and their enemies – the Jews and intellectuals (Bollas 1987). By moving the furniture they attacked thinking and wanted to reduce all of us to a state of mindlessness in which the unthinkable could be re-enacted.

This case material gives us a glimpse of the way in which inner object relations determine re-enactment and reparation processes. The group process revealed how attempts to integrate the disconnected parts of the past in the individual and group mind is subject to destructive and recreative forces. The work group, sitting inside the boundary, worked on reparation and recreation; the basic assumption group, beyond the boundary, worked on envy and re-dramatisation. What seemed to be an unrelated meeting of a work group and its envious enemies became a shared experience in a common social universe. Boundary events surrounding a group process signify the attempt to connect what is internal and external: what can be kept in mind and what needs to be expelled from it. The dis-ease between the group of intellectuals forming the work group inside the boundary, and the group of alienated labourers embodying a very primitive group outside the boundary, re-dramatised the trauma between perpetrators, victims, resisters and bystanders. The synchronicity of the encounter showed that the group process always has the potential to widen and deepen the civilising and decivilising forces. I regard the group of architects and the surrounding group of caretakers as part of the same societal figuration, given the ground of a shared and traumatising history. The inner subgroup struggled with reparation and social order; the outer subgroup displayed a valence for disturbance, loss of social control and subservience to a pathological leader.

Delinquency can be a sign of hope and must not be mistaken for the psychotic act itself. This delinquent subgroup fused in a relentless, timeless and envious attack, but simultaneously expressed its desire to belong and be connected. The attacking subgroup ultimately wanted to be tolerated and was clinging to a holding environment which could tolerate the pain, loss and incomplete mourning contained in its own social unconscious. The conducted large group symbolised the official public dialogue about the inheritance of the Third Reich, with its focus on guilt and reparation. In contrast, the destructive outer group represented the hidden trauma of the failed dependency, the incomplete mourning and the valence for envy on the part of the victim contained in the psychological inheritance bestowed upon the children of the perpetrators (Hopper 1997).

Conclusion

The large group process confronts us with the fact that civilising and decivilising processes are as inseparable as regression and progression. It makes sense to integrate preventative and curative models in large group work. Paradoxically, globalisation has disembedded cultural boundaries sufficiently to allow us to work with our common humanity much more openly, and it has re-awakened the human propensity to secure a group identity by denigrating the neighbouring stranger (Giddens 1999). The large group not only frustrates the satisfaction of libidinal needs and causes hate, but also opens up spaces for containment and development between individuals and a variety of subgroups. In the large group hate is transformed into the capacity to be frustrated when some of its members begin to feel heard and reconnected. As the capacity to tolerate frustration increases, so does the ability to think reflectively. The push for thinking and linking becomes as strong as the pull towards fragmentation and disintegration within the evolving group matrix. The conductor's perspective of the large group process as primarily pathological or as a balance of destructive and creative forces will significantly shape the experience of the process for the members, as well as determining how the case is analysed and presented.

References

Balint, M. (1968) *The Basic Fault: Therapeutic Aspects of Regression.* London: Tavistock Publications.

Bion, W. R. (1962) *Learning from Experience.* London: Heinemann.

Bion, W. R., (1967) *Second Thoughts.* London: Heinemann.

Bollas, C. (1987) *The Shadow of the Object: Psychoanalysis of the Unthought Known.* London: Free Association Books.

de Maré, P., Piper, R. and Thompson, S. (1991) *Koinonia: From Hate, through Dialogue, to Culture in the Large Group.* London: Karnac Books.

Elias, N. (1974) *Die Gesellschaft der Individuen.* Frankfurt: Suhrkamp Wissenschaft.

Elias, N. (1976) *Über den Prozeß der Zivilisation, I and II.* Frankfurt: Suhrkamp Wissenschaft.

Foulkes, S. H. (1986) *Group Analytic Psychotherapy: Method and Principles.* London: Maresfield Library.

Foulkes, S. H. (1990) *Selected Papers: Psychoanalysis and Group Analysis.* London: Karnac Books.

Giddens, A. (1999) *Runaway World: How Globalisation is Reshaping our Lives.* London: Profile Books Ltd.

Hopper, E. (1997) 'Traumatic experience in the unconscious life of groups: A fourth basic assumption.' *Group Analysis 30, 4,* 439–470.

Kreeger, L. (ed) (1975) *The Large Group, Dynamics and Therapy.* London: Constable Publishers.

Leach, E. (1969) 'Genesis as myth.' In *Genesis and Myth and other Essays.* London: Jonathon Cape.

Nitsun, M. (1996) *The Anti-Group. Destructive Forces in the Group and their Creative Potential.* London: Routledge.

Wardi, D. (1992) *Memorial Candles: Children of the Holocaust.* London: Routledge.

Wilke, G. (1999) 'Grossgruppenleitung und Gruppenentwicklung.' Heidelberg: *Gruppenanalyse 2, 99,* 133–148.

Winnicott, D. W. (1968) 'Delinquency as a sign of hope.' *Prison Service Journal 7, 27,* 90–100.

Winnicott, D. W. (1971) *Playing and Reality.* London: Tavistock Publications.

Winnicott, D. W. (1990) *The Maturational Process and the Facilitating Environment: Studies in the Theory of Emotional Development.* London: Karnac Books.

CHAPTER 6

Experiences in Large Groups

Bion's Influence

Robert M. Lipgar

Introduction

The central chapters of Bion's seminal work in group psychology, *Experiences in Groups* (1959), report his study of small groups with out-patients and staff at the Tavistock Clinic directly after World War II. These chapters, in which he explores 'basic assumption' and 'work' mental activity, have received the most attention over the years and were first published in *Human Relations* Vols. I–IV, 1948–51. The first chapter, 'Intra-group tensions in therapy: their study as the task of the group,' is one written and published during the war in collaboration with John Rickman (Bion and Rickman 1943). This earlier work reports groundbreaking, psychosocial, in-patient treatment of psychiatric disorders sustained in battle (Harrison 2000; Bridger 2000 in Pines 1985) – arguably the first report of 'milieu therapy.' Together with a final chapter, 'Group dynamics – a re-view' (first published in 1952), this small volume, *Experiences in Groups*, remains Bion's most cited and best-selling publication. These reports and analyses have been foundational for a large body of work in group psychotherapy, organizational and community consulting, and the study of authority, leadership, power and influence in social systems (Bion Talamo, Borgogno and Merciai 1998; Bion Talamo, Borgogno and Merciai 2000; Colman and Bexton 1975; Colman and Geller 1985; Cytrynbaum and Noumair in press; Lipgar and Pines 2003a, 2003b; Pines

1985). From his early experiences in World War I (Sandler, in Lipgar and Pines 2003a) to his later writing about the 'container and the contained' (Bion 1970), Bion never left his interest in group psychology.

Bion's work with groups came to our attention early in 1950s at the University of Chicago Human Dynamics Laboratory (HDL) directed by Herbert A. Thelen. Bion's ideas blended well, for us, with those of John Dewey, Kurt Lewin and Freud, and supported our studies of leadership and group dynamics in an experiential laboratory setting. It was his attention to, and respect for, group-as-a-whole phenomena, particularly his attention to the emotional life of the group at a macro level, that both resonated with, and added to what we were doing (Thelen in Pines 2000; Stock and Thelen 1958).

For many of us, Bion was a towering intellect committed to making sense out of human 'groupishness.' He reinforced our own commitment to group psychology and social betterment. We were of the generation deeply affected by the horrors of both World War I and World War II. Many of my fellow graduate students, I believe, shared a passionate (naive?) belief that the world could be made better and that the social sciences, including psychoanalysis, provided instruments and methods with which we would bring this about. By taking psychoanalysis beyond the study of the individual, Bion personified the kind of leadership that strengthened our resolve and fed our hopes.

A 'Manteno experiment'[1]

In the early 1960s, I was offered a rare opportunity to apply and test what I had learned at the HDL and during my internships in clinical psychology. On the basis of my specialized background in group psychology and psychotherapy, I was invited to join an interdisciplinary team of mental health professionals organized by Joseph Kepecs, a Chicago psychoanalyst, to provide consultative support to Manteno, the largest of the state's hospitals for the mentally ill. For a little more than two-and-a-half years, I was able to consult weekly to the staff and patients on a ward, James I, which housed 140 women diagnosed as 'combative, chronic schizophrenics' (Lipgar 1968). This was for me a rich field laboratory, and I approached the challenge eagerly, with confidence and optimism. I was able to select James I because Dr Kepecs gave us almost complete autonomy, and the condition of the hospital gave the superintendent little opportunity to direct our efforts otherwise.

Built in 1928 to house approximately 2000 patients, Manteno was now overcrowded, with 8700 patients, and understaffed – an example of what Karl Menninger called 'human warehouses.' Hospital personnel were stretched beyond the limits of their training and resources. Only the super-intendent was a board-certified psychiatrist; other physicians on staff had had little psychiatric training; there were no psychologists trained at the doctoral level; social work and nursing staffs were similarly staffed with few well-qualified personnel. The activities therapy staff was relatively strong. While most patients came from ethnic and racial minority groups in Chicago, the front-line staff were almost all white and from rural villages near the hospital. Typical housing for patients was in large locked wards of 100 or more. Most of these wards were divided into two dormitories, one on each side of a large 'dayroom,' each dorm with beds for 50–75 patients.

James I was one of the neediest wards, in the most wretched condition, known to both patients and staff throughout the hospital as a dumping ground for the most difficult and regressed women patients. The two dor-mitories on James I held only beds, in two long rows along opposite walls; there were no side chairs, no bureau drawers, no other space for personal items. These bare dormitories were locked during the day, confining patients to the dayroom. When I began my work, the 'day shift' consisted of only two 'mental health workers' (this allocation of staff was soon increased to three) under the supervision of a registered nurse with super-visory responsibility for several such wards. Personnel from the other departments divided their time among at least six or more such wards and provided very little support to the aides or service to the patients. Given the condition of the patients and the ward, personnel from other disciplines were reluctant to set foot on the ward.

My work started with my knocking, quite literally, on the front door of the locked ward. The charge aide answered and I explained briefly who I was and why I was there. The dayroom was filled with rocking, sleeping, pacing patients. Many were shouting epithets and obscenities, arguing with themselves and with each other. Sitting down to discuss my role and plans with the staff present was out of the question. My wish for a better introduction and authorization seemed rather beside the point, quixotic. Instead, I set directly about my task. I arranged a large circle of chairs in the middle of the dayroom, announcing as I did so that I would be conducting a meeting for all patients and staff who wished to attend.

As I did this, there was, of course, among both patients and staff, a considerable increase in tension, curiosity, consternation, anxiety, and a buzzing, chaotic flurry of activity. The aides clearly felt my presence and behavior to be eccentric, egocentric and ill conceived. They were, however, grudgingly compliant, perhaps helpless. They seemed resigned to yet another inexplicable intrusion over which they had no control and which would surely be as short-lived as all the other attempts to improve the situation on the ward. Both aides voiced their fears to me as I continued to set the chairs for the meeting: my initiatives would disorganize the ward, cause patients to act out, and make controlling the situation more hazardous and difficult than it already was.

Amid a din of fear and curiosity, I sat down in the circle of chairs I had arranged in the center of the dayroom. Approximately 20 patients took seats. The circle seemed filled with frustration, anger, neediness, despair and pain. I began, nevertheless, to relate in public, relying entirely on words. My efforts were meant to demonstrate my ability to be attentive and responsive in the 'here-and-now' – to link, keep track and make sense of what was occurring among us. I sought to make the manifestly public events available for all to attend to and comprehend. I sought to use words to make our common experience as plausible, comprehensible, and shareable as possible. Under these unusual and primitive circumstances, I set about establishing a social discourse that would be feasible and relevant to the patients and staff.

As I had been warned, one patient during the first session fell on the floor in a pseudo-epileptic fit. Having assessed this behavior to be primarily functional rather than neurologic, I continued the meeting, leaving the patient on the floor to be tended to by the aides or other patients. I managed in some fashion to stumble through a meeting of approximately 45 minutes' duration.

I remember that after this first meeting, when it was time for me to leave the ward, the 'charge aide' led me to the door, and unlocked it for me. (I had no key, and for all these years chose not to have one.) She followed me outside onto the small front porch, burst into tears, and told me that what I was doing would be disastrous for her small staff and the patients. She implored me to stop. I expressed my understanding of her fears, and tried to be reassuring. I attempted to persuade her that what I had planned was feasible and would be worthwhile, and stated that I would continue at the same time each week to bring patients together for discussion in an open group setting. It was my intention to provide patients with a positive opportunity to interact verbally with each other, with staff and me. I expressed my hope to meet with staff before and after each large group meeting as their time and other duties permitted.

The extent of the ward's isolation, the dominance of primitive processes, as well as the pervasive sense of helplessness and deprivation, put the usual group goal of identifying common interests beyond reach. In a very real sense, what people had in common was the dismal and often dangerous milieu, the locked doors, the disarray and deprivation. Under these circumstances, I saw my task as making a space for coherent public discourse. Each week I invited patients to sit in the arranged circle of chairs and proceeded to conduct large group meetings. My intention was to instigate an orderly transformation of the ward's social system, an evolution rather than revolution. I meant to respect the power structure in existence, while moving to empower patients, alter their relations with each other, and alter relations between patients and aides.

For two-and-a-half years I kept to this plan. Gradually it became clear to both patients and staff that I was not to be defeated, damaged, or captured. I continued in each meeting to listen, link and translate to the best of my ability – to acknowledge what was happening and make it as relevant and comprehensible to as many in the circle as possible. Patients often made recitations of past traumas, grievances, personal disclosures, and attacked other patients. My response to such personal complaints and disclosures often was to show that the person was heard in such a way that others might also hear what each woman had to express to the group. Often there were demands directed to me, demands that I write relatives or the Governor. Often I would acknowledge emotions and their relation to behaviors, rather than simply 'reflect feelings.' I would rephrase to clarify the manifestly public 'here-and-now' events. This meant translating and clarifying patients' attempts to express themselves, selecting words and themes to provide some degree of coherence in the public discourse. In all, I conducted approximately 130 weekly meetings – same time, same place, same format, same role.

As these weekly patient–staff large-group meetings progressed, I was able to have more time for post-meetings with the aides and other personnel. We discussed what had just taken place in the group meeting and more of what I was trying to accomplish. I learned more from them about what it was like to work with these patients under these most difficult circumstances. Over the months, the staff time from other disciplines was expanded and staff attendance at the large group meetings as well as willingness to spend time on the ward and with patients increased. Our post-meetings became more inter-active, more candid and productive. Gradually, we were able to talk together about current problems of patient care, patient–patient and patient–staff relations, and ward management, as well as the large group sessions.

Gradually, a working relationship and trust developed between the aides, other staff, and myself. Relationships among the patients became less violent; and relationships between patients and staff became more collaborative. The meetings became more coherent and more relevant to daily problems of living and working together. For example, forks and knives, as well as sugar and salt, were now made available to patients in the dining hall. Patients were permitted to have a coffee-maker during the day in the dayroom and were able to take responsibility for maintaining it. Toilet paper was made available next to the toilets so that patients no longer had to ask for a roll of toilet paper each time they needed to use the bathroom. Incidents requiring patients to be placed in leather restraints or sent off the ward for 'hydrotherapy' (submersions in cold baths) were greatly reduced.

These developments confirmed my belief that treating the ward as a whole, as an interacting social system of staff and patients, would result in benefits for both. Focusing on individuals would have been counterproductive, intensifying primitive feelings of deprivation and rageful competition.

During this time, changes were also occurring in other parts of the hospital as well, and more staff were being made available to James I and other wards. However, these large groups meetings were critical, I believe, in enabling other personnel to invest their time and efforts in working with these patients on this ward, and in contributing to the evolution of the ward from a locked one to an open one.

Building on Bion and lessons learned

In choosing to 'treat' the group, I was working in Bion's tradition as a 'taker of groups' (Bion 1961). Grotstein (2003) has noted that Bion was a social psychiatrist before he was an analyst. Bion had a far-reaching vision of psychiatry's task and potential (Bion 1948). His own personal experiences (Bleandonu 1994) deepened his broad interests in issues central to civilization and group life. Bion had taken his education, his values, his intellect and himself out of the laboratory, out of the doctor's office and into the broader 'real' world of social and political dynamics.

Although I did not have a good cognitive grasp of Bion's theories until after participating in group relations conferences later in the 1960s, there were, nevertheless, critical aspects of his thinking that influenced my work at Manteno. Prominent among these I can list the following:

1. Bion's regard for groups as essential to the understanding of human psychology and as an appropriate domain for scientific study

2. his attention to, and analysis of group phenomena at a macro level

3. his insights into the emotional and fantasy life of groups (the 'basic assumptions') and their relationship to a group's adaptive work

4. his appreciation for 'binocular vision' which enabled the study of the interplay between individual psychology and group dynamics, covert and overt processes, desires as well as task

5. the inevitability of experiencing those terrors, as well as gratifications, particular to our 'groupishness' as 'group animals.'

Even without my consciously applying Bion's or Melanie Klein's theories of primitive and psychotic processes, the patients' hungers were palpable and the power of these to destroy thought and relationships was obvious. For instance, volunteers would come to the ward for special occasions such as Easter and Christmas to provide small gifts and refreshments. Seldom would the same women return the next season[2] – one small indicator of 'burnout.' Crossing the threshold into James I felt like entering a toxic zone. In response, I confined myself, intuitively perhaps, to a disciplined demonstration of a group consultant's role. I managed my role boundaries with deliberate consistency by minimizing contact with individual patients, avoiding as tactfully as possible the incessant requests for cigarettes, accepting no coffee or donuts myself, and offering nothing to staff or patients beyond task-related conversation – and that almost entirely in a group context. Although this stance and the power of large group meetings may not be deemed sufficient conditions for change, they were necessary ones.

In retrospect, it seems to me that the persistence and consistency with which I pursued my vision were critical to the positive outcomes. My youthful idealism, a particular respect for the education and training I had obtained, and a conviction that these indeed gave me the authority and competence to bring about change – all were contributing factors. Commitment to task, desire to make the most of this rare opportunity to test my training and confidence in my clinical approach, as well as the pre-dictability of my attendance and role behavior[3] – all were manifest and all, I believe, had a positive impact on both patients and staff.

Further, one should not overlook the impact of my initial encounter with the charge aide on the front porch of the ward. Without deliberating or having theory in mind, I held to task and set a boundary. Although her sentiments and tears had affected me and moved me to reconsider my plans, I 'held the line.' This was, I believe, critical to the establishment of a 'beachhead' for thought and communication in this sea of despair, fear, frustration, anger and psychotic confusion.

My 'Manteno experiment' was a treatment of the social context and social relations within which the other work of a hospital takes place. As such it can be viewed as an exercise in 'sociotherapy' very much as Edelson (who also had studied at the HDL as a graduate student) explicates it theo-retically (1970a) and explores it clinically (1970b). Although guided by therapeutic principles, my consulting on James I was not group therapy, psychotherapy, or organizational consulting. It was therapy *of* the group.

Leadership and task

Since the trials at Manteno, I have had at least three venues for further testing of the principles applied there. Over the years, I estimate that I have participated in several thousand large group meetings in a variety of private and public mental health institutions.

In my experience, large group meetings work best when leadership is able to bring to the meeting a clear understanding of the distinctive purpose of the gathering on each particular occasion (Lipgar 1999). The primary task (Rice 1965) should be conceptualized and presented directly in the simplest terms, and should be both feasible and relevant to those gathered at this particular time and place. Leadership should function in as consistent a way as possible with regard to advancing work on the primary task and managing boundaries of task, time, space, and role in as sensitive yet as firm a way as possible. As the primary task and the leadership functions become more apparent to more of those gathered for the meeting, then these large group meetings become more coherent, more useful, more supportive of common interests, and participation becomes less threatening.

In a hospital setting, the distinctive purpose of a large group patient–staff meeting is to provide opportunity for expressing and exploring the relationships among the constituents of the ward or unit as a living entity. There is no other time or place, no other occasion when relations between patients and staff (and their constituent subgroups) can be explored first-hand. Such shared first-hand observation, participation, and exploration of a social system is a source of knowledge, a well of understanding, quite different from secondhand reports or separate inter-actions with segments of the whole. A large group meeting, in this sense, is unique. Only large patient–staff meetings can provide this quality of first-hand experiential reality, informing both management and patients. It follows that these meetings can be most productive, when all members of the social system are present or clearly represented by delegates. In the case of hospital settings, this caveat translates in practical terms to include all patients who are able to participate even minimally, and all staff or designated representatives of each administratively defined staff subgroup. Only then can real understanding be advanced of how patients and staff are 'living and working' together. Managing the tensions among and between subgroups as they affect relationships and the ability to work together, can only be advanced in meaningful and useful ways when the flow of relevant data is maximized and shared.

Successful meetings require that those present experience themselves as needed or relevant, that their presence and participation is required for the work at hand. The primary task of large group meetings of patients and staff is to learn how the various members of various subgroups are relating to one another, not particularly as individuals but especially as constituents of subgroups. In this way insight into impediments, tensions and obstacles to working and living together can be advanced and awareness of common interests can be enhanced (Edelson and Berg 1999).

This particular work, which I believe to be essential to the maintenance of any sophisticated working social system – community group, institution, organization, program, school, or hospital – cannot occur in any venue other than large public meetings. Such psychosocial work requires not only the participation, the input of all those persons, roles, sectors, disciplines, and constituencies who compose the unit, but also effective leadership.

Good leadership essentially participates in ways that enable others to do likewise. Having said this, however, it must be added that participation, or enabling others to join the group, is as much a means to an end as an end itself, and is as much a function of group-as-a-whole processes as of one's own intentions. Group-as-a-whole or systematic manifestations of transference phenomena must be addressed and managed. Otherwise, the potential for competence (individually and as a group) will be compromised. Competence must emerge, be tested and confirmed in public in order for groups to function at a sophisticated level. This process does not occur without the appearance of, and the resolution of competition, and the clarification of those resources and competencies most relevant to the tasks at hand (not to those which may seem to have potency and salience to imaginary or irrelevant tasks).

Bion makes both these points in most compelling ways. He helps us understand the inevitability of having to live with and channel the desires or emotional strivings of what he called the 'Basic Assumptions' (Bion 1959 [1961]) within group life while at the same time developing and maintaining the capacities to think, learn, and adapt to the challenges which interactions and confrontations with reality impose upon us. In short, neither belonging nor love is enough; work, thinking, and learning are also required. 'Learning from experience' (Bion 1977) requires linking feelings and thoughts.

Group analysts, following Foulkes, have long recognized that leadership for the group therapist involves administrative and executive functions as well as facilitative, interpretative, and holding or containing functions (Ettin 2003; Wilke 2003). Leadership in the context of large groups, following Bion, I would add, requires experience with, and understanding of the complexity and paradoxes governing individuals' social contributions and influences in the particularly daunting circumstance of groups larger than 12 or 15 (Turquet 1985). Whether one is formally authorized as 'the leader,' or is simply 'a group member,' participant, or citizen, one cannot contribute meaningfully without considerable and well-honed inner resources.

This conception of leadership has many behavioral implications for when one speaks, why one speaks, what one says in a group, and to whom. For instance, one thinks twice before responding directly to the needs, solicitations, invitations, requests, proposals, and questions of an individual, and instead looks for ways to respond to the impact such requests or questions have created for you, the solicitor, and the group. One endeavors to participate creatively in the here and now as events unfold and interact, as they stir new feelings, new questions, reactions and initiatives, moment by moment. This is not to imply that one is merely a reactive instrument to be played upon, nor does it mean that in order to be independent and creative one is required to be remote, opaque, inaccessible, mysterious, or emotionally distant. (One does, however, often have to risk being perceived as such.) Leadership, as Bion describes it, is participatory as well as independent, and, by example, demonstrates that the group situation must be dealt with as something other than a collection of individuals.

My sense of large group leadership builds on Bion and Lewin, borrows from Whitaker and Lieberman (1964) and, more recently, from Agazarian (1997). More than interpersonal events, more than displays of individual needs, proclivities, traits, agendas or pathologies, and more than the explicit and public issues, group and organizational objectives, proposals, and agendas must be acknowledged and addressed. Especially in large groups, leadership must be capable of providing interpretive as well as administrative structure based on insightful responsiveness in the here and now to covert as well as manifest group processes. Constructive leadership is able to manage the multiple ways in which people divert themselves from joining together to accomplish work and collude to defeat the common good.

Bion's example of leadership is neither passive nor absent, and neither pessimistic nor optimistic concerning the drives basic to life, learning and survival. Rather, it seems to me (Lipgar 1993; Lipgar 2003), his model is actively engaged in the here-and-now ebb and flow of learning. Such psychological work requires engagement with feelings, private and public fantasies; the linking of thoughts and feelings, testing facts and fictions through learning encounters with reality, and making adaptive behavioral changes. Bion shares a broad, complex picture of our human 'groupishness.' It is left to us to discover and invent particular leadership actions relevant and effective under particular group circumstances. His insights and theoretical formulations take us to the water's edge and the swim in each instance is up to us.

Notes

1.   In referring to my consulting work at the Manteno Hospital administered by the State of Illinois Department of Mental Health as 'A Manteno Experiment,' I want to link my work at this hospital with Bion's innovative project during World War II, which has become widely known as the 'Northfield Experiment.' In doing so, I want to call attention to the intrinsic interdependence of theory and practice and emphasize the importance of reporting our experiences in groups so that we can build on each other's work. Advancement in knowledge and effective applications, especially with regard to large group psychology, requires all this.

2.   This pattern would change as the ward culture changed.

3.   For instance, I never missed a week and was always on time. Also, I would review the day's large group meeting and the pre- and post-meetings speaking into a tape recorder as I drove home the 55 miles from Manteno to Chicago.

References

Agazarian, Y. M. (1997) *Systems-Centered Therapy*. New York: The Guilford Press.

Bion, W. R. (1948) 'Psychiatry in a time of crisis.' *British Journal of Psychology XXI*, 2, 81.

Bion, W. R. (1959) *Experiences in Groups*. London: Tavistock Publications. Republished by Basic Books, 1961).

Bion, W. R. (1970) *Attention and Interpretation.* London: Tavistock Publications. (Also [1977] in *Seven Servants: Four Works by Wilfred R. Bion.* New York: Jason Aronson, Inc.).

Bion, W. R. (1980) *Bion in New York and Sao Paulo.* Perthshire: Clunie Press.

Bion, W. R. (1992) *Cogitations.* London: Karnac Books.

Bion, W. R. and Rickman, J. (1943) 'Intra-group tensions in therapy.' *Lancet 2,* 678–681.

Bion Talamo, P., Borgogno, F. and Merciai, S. A. (eds) (1998) *Bion's Legacy to Groups.* London: Karnac Books.

Bion Talamo, P., Borgogno, B. and Merciai, S.A. (eds) (2000) *W.R. Bion: Between Past and Future.* London: Karnac Books.

Bleandonu, G. (1994) *Wilfred Bion: His Life and Works 1897–1979.* London: Free Association Books. New York: Guilford Press.

Bridger, H. (2000) 'Northfield revisited.' In M. Pines *Bion and Group Psychotherapy.* London: Jessica Kingsley Publishers.

Colman, A.D. and Bexton, W.H. (eds) (1975) *Group Relations Reader 1.* Jupiter, FL: A.K. Rice Institute.

Coleman, A.D. and Geller, M.H. (1985) *Group Relations Reader 2.* Jupiter, FL: A.K. Rice Institute.

Cytrynbaum, S. and Noumair, D.A. (in press) *Group Relations Reader 3.* Jupiter, FL: A.K. Rice Institute.

Edelson, M. (1970a) *Sociotherapy and Psychotherapy.* Chicago: University of Chicago Press.

Edelson, M. (1970b) *The Practice of Sociotherapy.* Chicago: University of Chicago.

Edelson, M. and Berg, D. N. (1999) *Re-discovering Groups: A Psychoanalyst's Journey Beyond Individual Psychology.* London: Jessica Kingsley Publishers.

Ettin, M. E. (2003) 'Bion's legacy to median and large groups.' In R. M. Lipgar and M. Pines *Building on Bion: Branches, Contemporary Developments and Applications of Bion's Contributions to Theory and Practice.* London: Jessica Kingsley Publishers.

Grotstein, J.S. (2003) 'Introduction: Early Bion.' In R.M. Lipgar and M. Pines (eds) (2003) *Building on Bion: Roots. Origins and Context of Bion's Contributions to Theory and Practice.* London: Jessica Kingsley Publishers.

Harrison, T. (2000) *Bion, Rickman, Foulkes and the Northfield Experiments: Advancing on a Different Front.* London: Jessica Kingsley Publishers.

Lewin, K. (1951) *Field Theory in Social Science.* New York: Harper and Row.

Lipgar, R. M. (1968) 'Evolution from a locked to an open ward through therapeutically guided group meetings.' *Community Mental Health Journal 4,* 221–228.

Lipgar, R. M. (1993) 'Bion's work with groups: Construed and misconstrued.' In S. Cytrynbaum and S.A. Lee (eds) *Transformations in Global and Organizational Systems.* Jupiter, FL: A. K. Rice Institute.

Lipgar, R. M. (1999) 'Guide to patient–staff large group meeting: A sociotherapeutic approach.' *Group Dynamics: Theory, Research, and Practice 3, 1,* 51–60.

Lipgar, R.M. (2003) 'Re-discovering bion's experiences in groups: notes and commentary on theory and practice.' In R.M. Lipgar and M. Pines (eds) (2003) *Building on Bion: Roots. Origins and Context of Bion's Contributions to Theory and Practice.* London: Jessica Kingsley Publishers.

Lipgar, R. M. and Pines, M. (eds) (2003a) *Building on Bion: Roots. Origins and Context of Bion's Contributions to Theory and Practice.* London: Jessica Kingsley Publishers.

Lipgar, R. M. and Pines, M. (2003b) *Building on Bion: Branches. Contemporary Developments and Applications of Bion's Contribution to Theory and Practice.* London: Jessica Kingsley Publishers.

Pines, M. (ed) (1985) *Bion and Group Psychotherapy.* London: Routledge and Kegan Paul. Republished London: Jessica Kingsley Publishers, 2000.

Pines, M. (ed) (2000) *Bion and Group Psychotherapy.* London: Jessica Kingsley Publishers.

Rice, A. K. (1965) *Learning for Leadership.* London: Tavistock Publications.

Sandler, P. C. (2002a) 'Bion's war memoir: A psychoanalytic commentary.' In R. M. Lipgar and M. Pines (eds) *Building on Bion: Roots. Origins and Context of Bion's Contributions to Theory and Practice.* London: Jessica Kingsley Publishers.

Stock, D. and Thelen, H. A. (1958) *Emotional Dynamics and Group Culture.* Washington D.C.: National Training Laboratories, New York Press.

Thelen, H. A. (2000) 'Research with Bion's concepts.' In M. Pines (ed) *Bion and Group Psychotherapy.* London: Jessica Kingsley Publishers.

Turquet, P. M. (1985) 'Leadership: the individual and the group.' In A. D. Colman and M. H. Geller (eds) *Group Relations Reader 2.* Jupiter, FL: A. K. Rice Institute.

Whitaker, D. S. (1985) *Using Groups to Help People.* London: Routledge & Kegan Paul.

Whitaker, D. S. and Lieberman, M.A. (1964) *Psychotherapy through the Group Process.* New York: Atherton Press.

Wilke, G. (2003) 'The large group and its conductor.' In R. M. Lipgar and M. Pines (eds) *Building on Bion: Branches. Contemporary Developments and Applications of Bion's Contributions to Theory and Practice.* London: Jessica Kingsley Publishers.

CHAPTER 7

The Power of Projective Processes in Large Groups

Joseph H. Berke

My first experience of a large group occurred while working with Dr Maxwell Jones at Dingleton Hospital in Scotland in the summer of 1963. 'Max' as he was affectionately known, was trying to transform an old-fashioned hospital regime into a therapeutic community. Without warning, he suddenly suggested that I run a group of 50 ladies, many of whom had been residing in the chronic women's ward for decades. I tried to get them to talk about themselves, and to each other, without much success. I am sure that they were as frightened of me, a brash, bearded young American, as I was of them. But that was my job, to shake things up in whatever way possible.

The occasion also provided me with a concrete experience of projection. After hovering about during one of these meetings, a wasp stung me in the neck. The sting hurt like hell, but I tried to carry on as if nothing had happened. Did the wasp emanate from one of the women? Or, more likely, from the elderly ward doctor who so hated my intrusions into her domain? At the time it did not occur to me that the wasp could have been an 'envious ejaculation', or a projected expression of doctor's 'evil eye'. In fact this person used to hide behind the curtains in the ward in order to watch what was going on. If she found out that one of her charges had been talking to me, or had accepted a 'fag end' from a male patient, the woman patient would disappear. What had happened? I was mystified until I discovered that the individual in question had invariably been given a dose of ECT on the next day.

By 1965 I completed my medical training and returned to London to live and work with Dr R. D. Laing at his Kingsley Hall community. I have described this experience at length in the book I wrote with Mary Barnes, the woman I helped go through a psychotic regression, in *Mary Barnes: Two Accounts of a Journey Through Madness* (Barnes and Berke 1971). As I later realised, this community functioned like a large spoked wheel with Laing at the centre. All communications had to pass through him. All relationships were centred on him. He knew what everyone was thinking and doing, but most of the residents were dimly aware of what was happening on their periphery. This led to a lot of paranoia. The principle projective processes had to do with jealousy, who was close to him, and who had been shunted to the outer circle. Much of the psychotic interactions had to do with these highly charged, but vigorously denied, jealous emanations.

From all this I learned how projective processes dominate relationships, whether with and within individuals, small groups, or large groups like a therapeutic community.

By 'projective processes' I refer to projections as active psychological and interpersonal events. These are operations involving mental mechanisms like denial and evacuation, leading to a perceptual transformation both of the focus of this activity, the object, and of the person doing the projecting, the subject. Moreover, projective processes are not just mental events. They also include interpersonal transactions, something that the subject does to another person, the object, in order to arouse a further something in him or by her. By 'something', I refer to the contents of the transaction: feelings, thoughts, states of mind, primary process experiences, 'beta' elements; all the noxious stuff that people can and do evacuate into others. But it is very important to note that these projections can involve good or valuable experiences too.

The third component of a projective process concerns the reasons for these transactions. These include: getting rid of inner tensions, control of the other, envious attacks, scapegoating, as well as preventing separation, and nonverbal communication. As for the reasons for arousing good impulses, like love in others — these include control, avoidance of separation, and communication, but also primitive reparative efforts and protection.

Really I am discussing a projective/introjective system which my Kleinian colleagues and others have intensively explored under the term 'projective identification' and 'introjective identification'. In this chapter I wish to emphasise the system, or systemic aspect, of projective processes. It is necessary to look at where they come from and where they end up. I am speaking about the originator of the projections and the recipient or target of them, as well as the interplay between the projector and the recipient.

With this in mind I want to explore the power of projective process in a special projector and special recipient, the Arbours Crisis Centre. The Centre has been the major focus of my professional work. Here, as with Dingleton or Kingsley Hall, we can see the operation of a large group in the form of a specialised therapeutic community.

In the first part of this presentation I shall consider the Crisis Centre as a target of projections originating from outside the Centre. In other words, the originator is or was persons external to the Centre, and the Centre was the focus of intensely evacuated impulses.

In the second part I shall consider the Crisis Centre as both originator and recipient of the projections. In other words, I will be discussing what happens from the projections that originate from within the Crisis Centre and travel from one part of the Centre to another.

But before I begin let me provide a few details about the Centre. It is a facility of the Arbours Housing Association, a mental health charity which I and others founded in 1970. The Crisis Centre itself was established in 1973 and is now located in a large Edwardian house in Crouch End, North London. It provides intensive interpersonal and psychodynamic support to individuals, couples and families in severe emotional distress.

The Centre is a unique community because the staff whom we call the 'resident therapists' (or RTs) live at the house on a full-time basis. It is their home. People come not as patients, but as guests, and stay with them for days, weeks or months.

The term 'guest' conveys hospitality, and a 'treat', not a treatment. Many residents or guests have been in hospital before. Our aim is to help them to shed, or never take on, their learned role of mental patient, or institutionalised other. Moreover, we intend that they should achieve a position of respect and dignity, as well as relief from whatever pain brought them to the Centre in the first place. More information about our work can be found in two anthologies written by therapists and guests connected with the Centre. These are *Sanctuary: The Arbours Experience of Alternative Community Care* (Berke, Masoliver and Ryan 1995) and *Beyond Madness: PsychoSocial Interventions in Psychosis* (Berke, Fagan, Mak-Pearce and Pierides-M üller 2001).

My first example has to do with the power of projections or projective processes which arise from outside the Crisis Centre. Here external others are the originators and the Centre is the target or recipient of these events.

The Centre was the fruit of a year's discussions in 1972 between myself and therapists and residents of two initial Arbours communities. At that time the communities were young and there was a lot of uncertainty and inconsistency as to how to join one of our households. Sometimes it happened quickly, sometimes slowly and sometimes not at all. Often people were very caring for each other, but not infrequently they remained unconcerned. Moreover, there were no clear-cut lines of responsibility as to who did what for whom. I proposed to establish a household where people in acute distress could be accepted quickly and be offered very intense personal and psychotherapeutic support.

The small circle of people interested in the project first researched the literature on crisis intervention. Then we decided to push ahead and establish a new community where at least two residents would provide direct care (resident therapists, RTs). Other, experienced therapists would visit often and back them up (team leaders, TLs). But we had no money, nor a place where this could happen.

In the fall of 1972 one of the Arbours long-stay communities was in the home of Morty Schatzman and his wife Vivien Millett. They lived in a large house near Parliament Hill in Hampstead. Next to them there was a large church, a vicarage and unused church hall. During the course of a casual chat with his neighbour, the vicar, Morty mentioned the proposed crisis centre. The vicar immediately exclaimed, 'What a good idea! Why don't you use the church hall?'

Morty told me and I told others in the discussion group. We all agreed it was a grand idea and made imminent plans to move to the church hall. When we told the vicar, he was pleased, but suddenly sprung a condition. He recalled that there had once existed a neighbourhood association in the vicinity of the church and suggested that it would only be fair to get the neighbours' permission for the proposal. Thoroughly alarmed, because I knew how difficult it was to get any neighbourhood group to agree to a mental health project, I remonstrated that what was most important was to get the Centre off and running, before meeting with any such group. Then we would have something tangible to present. But all my arguments were to no avail. The vicar insisted we first activate the neighbourhood group, which had not met, as I subsequently learned, for ten years.

So notices were passed about, and on a wet and windy evening towards the end of November, we prepared to meet the neighbours. I tried to console my colleagues. How many would turn out on such a cold night? Five, ten at the most. In fact close to 80 irate men, women and children crammed the hall to vent their upset and anger at the prospect of 'mentals' moving to the area. One man in particular, a plumber who lived a block away, was apoplectic with rage. He screamed that he would not allow drug-crazed perverts, sex maniacs, violent and immoral lunatics, to roam freely in his street. His wife and children would be endangered. And if that weren't enough, house prices would plummet. Needless to say, these words carried the meeting. The project was turned down and all the Arbours people present fell ill with the flu.

It was obvious what had happened. The plumber and most of the neighbours who spoke up against the project had attributed their own denied sexual, violent, perverse and perverted wishes to the Arbours therapists and unnamed 'mentals' whom they imagined were about to invade their space. As for myself and my colleagues, one might say that we were made sick by their envious, hate-filled ejaculations. But it is one thing to know this. How can one prove it?

Some months later Morty was referred a young, pretty trainee accountant who lived nearby. She had been having a torrid affair with a married man who also lived nearby. But he had begun to frighten her with his possessiveness. She responded with panic attacks, crying spells and sleeplessness. Things had gone from bad to worse. Finally the man had taken to keeping watch all night in his car outside her flat. Most alarmingly, he claimed to carry a loaded shotgun, which he would use if any man dared to visit her. Who was her lover? None other than the plumber who had carried the meeting with his diatribe against sexuality, violence and immorality. Rarely can one see the evidence for a projective system so directly. This episode provides clear proof that the plumber had offloaded his denied perversities onto the Arbours project.

My second example has to do with the power of projections or projective processes which arise from within the Crisis Centre. Here one part of the Centre is the originator and another part of the Centre is the target or recipient of these projections.

'Akuna' ('A') is a 23-year-old young man of 'African' origin who was brought up in London by his mother, a woman who has been depressed all her life. She is a woman who dreads abandonment and has done everything in her power to keep 'A' close and dependent on her. In fact, various colleagues have referred to the mother's attachment to 'A' as a striking example of 'symbiotic enmeshment'.

When Akuna came to the Centre, he was tall and thin and silent. Perhaps because he had shown a lot of intellectual capacity, having read Shakespeare at school (he was particularly fond of *Hamlet*), there was a lot of uncertainty about what diagnostic category he might fall under, that is, what was he? Eventually the favourite category was 'elective mute', although 'simple or hebephrenic schizophrenic' were also considered. As 'A' grew older, he became more withdrawn and inactive, and was described by psychiatrists and social workers as 'passive and frozen.'

Akuna was an unusual person in that, while he appeared not to respond to anyone or anything other than his mother, large numbers of people took it upon themselves to provide for him, beginning with social services, and continuing with the therapists and guests at the Crisis Centre.

In fact, we broke all our own rules in accepting him as a resident. Our main criterion is that a person wishes to stay at the Centre. 'A' never indicated in any way that he wanted to come to the Crisis Centre. He never spoke, never gestured one way or the other. His carers both wanted to keep him, and knew he had to leave. It was never clear to me why we accepted him, although in retrospect I think we were engulfed by his need to be needed, and seduced by others feelings' for him. Akuna's team included Cath, his RT, Paul, a new but experienced team leader, and Neil, an Arbours trainee. Cath quickly became Akuna's primary contact and support. Their main exchange was his demanding and Cath's giving cigarettes. He could smoke a whole pack in one go. Aside from this, Cath said she felt as if she was on a 'wild-goose chase' of speculation, only to find at the end of the pursuit further confusion, and that an utterly, contra-dictory action had occurred. Cath remarked that it seemed like Akuna's main aim was to defy understanding.

To all this Cath responded by enmeshing herself as a mother substitute and sex object. Concurrently, Paul and Neil defended themselves by means of boredom and indifference on the one hand, or despair and rage on the other.

The Centre, in turn, seemed to be taken over by either paralysis or over-activity. Although 'A' missed most meetings and meals, did not join the cooking rota, smoked in non-smoking zones, wore clothes till they stank, and often appeared in semen-stained underpants, this all seemed to be taken for granted. Then some therapists and guests would get so concerned and angry that they began to intrude into his life in a myriad of ways, as his mother so often did when she visited the Centre, barged into his room, and dragged him off for an Afro haircut.

Akuna's exercise in non-being aroused a cascade of projections. Many of the ensuing emotions were very intense, both positive and negative. But there were considerable hints at their counter-transference components, such as the fact that 'A' continued his charming custom of putting raw eggs in the microwave and bombarding them with rays them until they exploded.

Similarly, the situation at the Centre continue to simmer until it exploded one day when another resident suddenly called Akuna 'a black baboon'.

'Abdul' was someone who had come to the Centre with the reputation of a monster: very loud and aggressive. During the first part of his stay most of the residents, including the RTs, were very frightened of him. Gradually he had modulated his vocal repertoire of demands and insults and had been grudgingly accepted by the group. But there was one aspect of Akuna's behaviour that Abdul found impossible to take, and that was 'A's' continual low-level giggles and inexplicable outbursts of laughter. Abdul thought they were particularly directed at him, and felt put down and humiliated by these noises. He hated 'A' for them.

One day Abdul joined one of the rare house meetings that 'A' deigned to attend. Whereupon Akuna dominated the meeting by prancing about, making silly giggles, and seemingly laughing at internal voices.

'Black baboon! Black baboon!' Horror of horrors, Abdul had articulated what some people had been thinking, but were reluctant to say. For this everyone pounced on Abdul. How dare he call 'A' a black baboon?

Didn't he realise this was racism? All the anger and aggro turned on Abdul. 'A' continued his silly grin.

The next day Abdul returned to the Centre in the evening after a trying visit with his family. He switched on the TV. He was wanting to bury himself in a maze of visual and auditory projections emanations. But then another guest, Zoe, came in. She wanted to watch another programme, or as I would see it, a different set of projections. In front of the TV, they fought for the controls. There were heated exchanges. The handset was thrown about. Zoe stormed up to her room with the house newspaper. (This is a cardinal sin. The paper is always supposed to be kept downstairs in the lounge or kitchen/conservatory.) Abdul ran after her, demanding that she return the paper. Zoe refused, but Abdul barged into her room, took the paper and whopped her on the head. A big commotion ensued, but Zoe, all 84 pounds and thin, was determined not to be intimated by Abdul (238 pounds and stocky).

Eventually the whole house got involved. Some guests felt that the ruckus was no big deal. Abdul should apologise. End of story. But Cath, who had been aroused from her sleep by what was going on, in conjunction with other guests and students, argued that on top of calling 'A' a baboon, Abdul had become abusive, dangerous and was a risk to others. He should be asked to leave.

Eventually the issue was put to me. I should be the judge, jury and executioner. The situation reminded me of a previous incident with Hamid, a guest who had surreptitiously eaten food laid out for a reception after a lecture. I described these events in my paper, 'Psychotic interventions', which was published in *Beyond Madness* (Berke *et al.* 2002, pp. 188–201).

Again I was chosen to be the executioner of a decision the RTs had made. But I refused. I made it clear that I didn't think that such an extreme measure was needed. More reflection was required. In the end Abdul was asked to leave for a few days while I was on holiday. He returned when I returned and said sorry, much subdued and appropriately depressed.

In retrospect it became obvious that whatever Abdul had done, he became the focus of and scapegoat for the anger and aggression of Cath, Akuna, Zoe, and many others in the house. Embodying 'A's' projections as the over-solicitous mother, Cath especially was determined to protect 'A' from others' aggression, which she saw as a threat to her own 'guest/son/lover'. Perhaps more important, she sought to protect 'A' from her own hostility, which she often projected onto Abdul. Why? Because Cath was in a constant state of frustration, as were others, about 'A's' giggly non being, in spite of their best efforts to get him to do things or not do things which upset them.

Akuna's insistence on loud music exemplified this. No, he didn't speak. But his ghettoblaster often spoke for him. It was a continual source of irritation which led to a rare occasion when 'A' was willing to speak up for himself. Once Lizzie, the nurse therapist at that time, who was staying over while the RTs had a night out, confiscated his stereo lead after repeatedly failing to get him to turn the volume on his set down. He replied in a loud, menacing, angry voice: 'It's my lead, give me my lead back, I'll fucking kill you. I'll cut you up, you cunt, you came in here and just took the lead, it's all on camera!'

At that moment 'A' catapulted out of his trance-like state and became a different person: angry, violent, threatening, but embodied, direct and dangerous. But it was not politically correct to see this, even if it stared you in the face.

Abdul completed his stay successfully and moved to another community. However, 'A's' undercurrents remained all-pervasive. They boiled over towards the end of his stay, for he was responsible for a series of fires in his room and in the kitchen. As a result, he was asked to leave. Much to everyone's regret, he was taken to hospital where he remained for some time. This was his way of cutting and running. In so doing he may have protected himself, *but he made a monkey out of us*: for allowing him to be an exemption, for breaking the house rules and for not challenging him much more.

Anyway, 'A' is out of hospital now. Cath ran into him a few weeks ago outside a supermarket in North London. He greeted her warmly and told her all he had been doing. At that moment he was on the way to his sports club.

As for Zoe, little Zoe…in spite of her size, as she came to life, so did her combativeness, anger, and aggression. She tried to hide this by starving herself and keeping to her room. But her feisty mannerisms belied her innocence.

I have just given two examples of how powerful projective systems have taken charge of a large group, the Arbours Centre. In the first instance they emanated from outside entities, neighbours, and were directed at therapists and residents. In the second example I showed how the projections took charge, like a 'malign and poisonous spirit', and how they jeopardize the life of the group.

In conclusion I would ask if is it possible for projective processes not to take charge in a large group like a therapeutic community? Stanley Schneider and Rena Bina address this very point in their chapter in *Beyond Madness*, 'The hierarchal authority pyramid in a therapeutic milieu' (Berke *et al.* 2002, pp. 255–268). First they point out that projections don't always have to be 'ejaculations or irradiations' of evil. They can also be idealisations such as accompany the medical model of the therapeutic dyad. Here the patient lies in the firm hands of the all-knowing, all-giving, all-controlling doctor or institution.

In fact many attempts have been made to circumvent the structural rigidities and anti-therapeutic implications of such a dyad. These go back as far as 1792 with the opening of the Retreat in York. There patients were encouraged to take power and control over their own disorders (Kennard 1983, pp.18–22).

More recently I can cite the pioneering group work of Wilfred Bion and S. H. Foulkes and the practical applications of Tom Main and Maxwell Jones. At Dingleton Hospital in Melrose, Scotland (where I spent a summer) and at the Henderson Hospital in Sutton, Surrey, and Cassel Hospital in Richmond, Jones and Main established therapeutic milieus where, to quote Stanley Schneider:

> Patients, guests, residents, group members: '...now become active agents in the treatment process. Staff members make great efforts to flatten the traditional authority pyramid. There is an effort to develop a community cohesion by frequent community meetings, and the deployment of patient government. In addition there is more open communication between staff and patients and constant re-evaluation of role and patterns of functioning. (Schneider 1978, p.257)

Essentially this means that the therapists make the effort to share power, rather than aggrandise it. Moreover, they don't have to take charge or control of the projective processes. They are much more concerned with empowerment. As we have seen, when events take a benign or creative course in a large group, empowerment signals that:

- the therapists are receptive to projections, instead of trying to squash them

- they are willing to suffer when projections hurt, rather than defend themselves from nasty narcissistic wounds, or counter-attack

- they try to negotiate boundaries, rather than impose them

- whenever they are knocked off course by the power of this or that projection, they are willing to expand their interpersonal field in order to regain their thinking process, rather than revert to omnipotent interventions.

Finally, we must realise that death impulses can be accepted, but especially be tempered by libidinal desires and reparative efforts.

I have tried to show how these positive steps ameliorate the hurt, distress and desperation for all members of the group. I think this capacity to overcome the power of harmful projections and potentiate authentic relationships is what therapeutic work with a large group is and should be all about. Maybe this doesn't happen all the time, but it does happen enough of the time, so that as Schneider and Bina (2002) point out, treatment can be a 'treat, and not an excuse for sustaining projective systems, nor perpetuating harm'.

References

Barnes, M. and Berke, J. H. (1971) *Mary Barnes: Two Accounts of a Journey Through Madness.* Third revised edition, 2002. New York: The Other Press.

Berke, J. H., Masoliver, C. and Ryan, T. (1995) *Sanctuary: The Arbours Experience of Alternative Community Care.* London: The Process Press.

Berke, J. H., Fagan, M., Mak-Pearce, G. and Pierides-Mü ller,S. (2002) *Beyond Madness: PsychoSocial Interventions in Psychosis.* London: Jessica Kingsley Publishers.

Kennard, D. (1983) *An Introduction to Therapeutic Communities.* London: Routledge and Kegan Paul.

Schneider, S. (1978) 'A model for an alternative educational treatment program for adolescents.' *Israel Annals of Psychiatry 16*, quoted in Berke *et al.* (2002).

Schneider, S. and Bina, R. (2002) 'The hierarchal authority pyramid in a therapeutic milieu.' In Berke *et al. Beyond Madness: PsychoSocial Interventions in Psychosis.* London: Jessica Kingsley Publishers.

Part II

The Large Group

Application to Society

CHAPTER 8

Socially Sanctioned Violence

The Large Group as Society[1]

Otto F. Kernberg

I. The psychodynamics of group psychology

When small groups of 7 to 15 members are formed to carry out a task, a functional organization for task performance sustains the group's adherence to reality, permits the desire for mutual affiliation to prevail in the coordination of work, and facilitates the emergence of task-oriented leadership. The authority of that leadership derives from its institutional authorization as well as from the group's acknowledgement of the technical, conceptual, and human qualities of the leader. The group operates on the basis of these factors in a rational mode, adapted to reality. When such a 'work group,' however, is rendered ineffective by the lack of a realistic task or by overwhelming demands for performance or threats to its security, two sets of primitive reactions rapidly emerge. They were originally named by Bion (1961) the 'dependent basic assumption group' and the 'fight–flight basic assumption group;' but they might equally well be called, respectively, a narcissistic regression and a paranoid regression. These two reactions can be observed systematically by giving to the group the task of observing its own behavior without any other work commitment that relates it to its environment.

A narcissistic regression of the group (corresponding to Bion's 'dependent group') stimulates the emergence of a narcissistic, self-conratulatory, self-assured leader who thrives on the admiration of others

125

and assumes the role of an 'all-giving' parental authority, on whom everybody else can depend for sustenance and security. In the throes of its regression, the group's members become passive and dependent upon that leader, and assume that it is their right to be fed and taken care of. They begin to feel insecure and confused, unable to take an active stance toward their assigned task, instead competing with each other in a greedy, envious way, for the attention of the leader. This constellation of leader–follower behavior describes the 'dependent basic assumption group.'

A group involved in a paranoid regression conforms to Bion's descriptions of the 'fight–flight basic assumption group.' It becomes hyper-alert and tense, as if there were some danger against which it would have to establish an aggressive defense. The group selects a leader with a strong paranoid potential, a hypersensitive, suspicious, aggressive and dominant person, ready to experience and define some slight or danger against which he and the group following him need to protect themselves and fight back. The members of the group, in turn, tend to divide between an 'in-group,' rallying around the group leader, and an 'out-group' who are suspect and need to be fought off. The mutual recriminations and fights between the in-group and the out-group give a frankly hostile and paranoid quality to the entire group, and may lead either to splitting into paranoid splinter groups, or to the discovery of an external enemy against whom the entire group can consolidate around the leader. The fight then evolves between that paranoid group and the external world.

The narcissistic regression of the dependent group is characterized by the prevalence of primitive idealization, projected omnipotence, and acting out of a regressive parasitic dependency; by contrast, the paranoid regression of the fight–flight group is dominated by projective identification, splitting, and acting out of rationalized aggression. If the leaders of the work group fail to conform to the respective expectations of the narcissistic or the paranoid regressive group, the group will find alternative leaders that correspond to its expectations, and with an unerring certainty such groups tend to select the most narcissistic or the most paranoid individual of the group for their corresponding emotional needs.

Unstructured small groups such as those assigned no task other than to observe their own behavior, may oscillate relatively quickly between the paranoid and the narcissistic form of regression; or they may experience the development of still a third alternative, Bion's (1961) 'pairing basic assumption group.' In this third type of regression the entire group develops a focused interest in the relationship of a particular couple whose fantasied relationship gives the group a sense of meaning and purpose. The pairing basic assumption group creates a 'messianic' hope for the future of the group, promoting cohesiveness, mutual gratification of the members, and protection against the dangerous ('pregenital') narcissistic and paranoid developments of the dependent and the fight–flight groups. The messianic hope for a better future conveyed by the pairing group wards off the sense of helplessness, of overdependency on an idealized leader, and of easy frustrability of the dependent group, and protects the paranoid group from its potential destruction by the mutual aggression of all involved: it may be considered a flight into a primitive oedipal structuring of the regressive group.

Pierre Turquet's (1975) and Kenneth Rice's (1965, 1969) observations regarding large group processes replicate these phenomena in an astounding way. Large groups of 30 to 150 members, if they meet regularly in a stable place for an established time, can hear, observe and communicate with each other so as to carry out a task such as a construction, the acquisition of learning, clarification and decision-making regarding tasks that the group or components of it have to perform in relation to external reality. Such work orientation and its corresponding work-oriented structure bring about a perfectly 'normal,' rational and reality-oriented functioning. When the rational task that brings such a large group together is lacking, or fails, or if the group is unstructured by design, it tends to generate intense anxiety, and rapidly regresses to a generally shared sense of danger and chaos.

Systematic observations of such large groups when they are unstructured or at points of failure of the task that related them to their environment demonstrate consistently a sense of fear, irritation, apprehension and impotence in most of the members of the group. Some individuals may make efforts to consolidate subgroups that might provide some protection against the large group psychology, but these efforts usually fail. The lack of stable individualized relationships in the large group prevents effective mutual control, and promotes unsuccessful reliance upon the mechanisms of projective identification, omnipotent control, denial of aggression and gratifying passivity to protect the participants against the common anxiety which may rise very high very quickly, and at times can reach the level of panic. The outbreak of random individual aggression in the midst of the general fearfulness intensifies the chaos and the shared sense of danger. Some members may succeed in isolating themselves from the group's mood, but at the cost of increasing their sense of impotence or paralysis. Efforts on the part of level-headed individuals to control this situation by means of a rational analysis of the vicissitudes of the shared group experience usually are condemned to failure. The reason is the strange and fascinating shared emergence in the large group of intense resentment against individuals who seem to maintain their autonomy, integrity, clear thinking, and intelligent analysis of the situation. Unmistakable evidence of inordinate envy and even hatred towards such individuals rapidly evolves. The unstructured large group does not tolerate rationality, regardless of the maturity and knowledge of the group members.

There are two major roads to organizing this regressive group and relieving its panicky atmosphere, corresponding respectively to the narcissistic and paranoid developments in the unstructured small group (Kernberg 1998). In a narcissistic reorganization, the group intuitively selects a leader with strong narcissistic features – that is, a person who is self-assured, enjoys being the center of attention, and spews reassuring banalities and clichés that have a tranquilizing effect. The group accepts the leader's proffered 'wisdom' with a subtle ironic disqualification of it. A shared passive dependency on a mild grandfatherly or grandmotherly patron prevents the emergence of mutual suspicion and of destructive envy and resentment of members possessing authentic autonomy and depth. The narcissistic large group, under these conditions, tends to acquire the characteristics of what Canetti (1960) has described as the 'feast crowd,' a shared enjoyment of the gratifying expectation of being safe and taken care of. The content of the group interaction now takes on features of marked conventionalism and superficiality of cognitive elaboration.

If, to the contrary, the group regresses to a paranoid mode of functioning, it may select a leader with unmistakably paranoid features, who rallies the group in preparation for a fight against the enemies he defines. He transforms the disorganized large group into a 'mob.' The group is now united in idealizing the paranoid leader, who helps them to project all aggression onto an out-group, and transforms the intragroup aggression into loyalty to the group, derived from the shared identification of all members with the leader. The group thus acquires the embryonic structure of what, on a larger scale with a more permanent organization and the development of an ad hoc paranoid ideology, might become a political mass movement.

Whether the unorganized large group will shift in a paranoid or a narcissistic direction depends on a number of influences: the composition of the group, the nature of the sociocultural environment within which the large group operates, the extent to which all the members are under realistic, external pressures or constraints affecting their economic, social, or political well-being. Influential as well will be the characteristics of the leadership that emerges and whether the pre-existing ideology of the group reflects a static, self-assured, conventional political environment with a low level of conflict, or one in which social unrest or rapid social change are accompanied by the formation of a strong ideology with powerful paranoid elements.

It is of interest that, once a crowd is transformed into a paranoid mass or a spectator mass, it immediately tends to select the kind of leadership that corresponds to its psychology: only a 'merchant of illusions' (Chasseguet-Smirgel 1975) who provides reassuring banalities will gratify the feast crowd, and only a paranoid and possibly demagogic warrior who appeals to the fear, anger, and thirst for aggressive action of the multitude will be listened to by the paranoid mass.

This outline brings us to the psychoanalytic theory of mass psychology first spelled out in Freud's classic book *Group Psychology and the Analysis of the Ego* (1921). Freud described the mutual identifications of all the members of the mass movement with each other in their joined identification with the leader, onto whom they collectively project their superego, and whom they become willing to follow wherever he directs them. The projection onto the leader of the mass members' ego ideal frees them to express their instinctual urges, particularly those of an aggressive kind, and the mass becomes willing to attack, destroy, and murder at the leader's behest. The mutual identification of all the members of the mass provides them with a sense of belonging and strength, and the projection of their responsibility onto the leader gives them a sense of exhilaration and exciting freedom from moral constraints.

In the light of the psychoanalytic explorations of the psychology of large and small groups, important additional implications of Freud's analysis emerge. These explorations reveal the regular emergence of

aggression in group situations of all kinds when such groups are unstructured, and particularly when their task structure fails. The dread of the consequences of such aggression mobilizes defenses of a narcissistic or
paranoid kind. Although Freud stressed the importance of the libidinal
linkages among the members of the mass, and the libidinal implications of
the idealization and potentially blind following of the leader, the
importance of the underlying aggression was evident to him although he
had not yet formulated the theory of the death drive at that time. In fact, it
is striking how intensely aggression is activated in small groups, in large
groups, and in mass movements (however short-lived or enduring they
may be), enabling individuals to behave in violent ways that would be
unthinkable for them under ordinary life circumstances structured by
ordinary status-role relationships. In other words, the normal processes of
socialization in the family; the elaboration, sublimation, repression, and
reaction formations dealing with primitive aggression; the normal
tolerance of ambivalence with a corresponding dominance of love over
hatred; the normal acknowledgement of aggression with efforts toward its
rational and conscious control, all seem to get lost almost instantaneously
under certain conditions of group functioning. In the process of group
regression, all those normal functions and defensive operations are
replaced by the broad gamut of primitive defensive operations typical of
the paranoid-schizoid mechanisms originally described by Melanie Klein
as predating the stage of total object relations, or object constancy in ego
psychology terms.

I have proposed in an earlier work (1994) that the situation in the
unstructured large group prevents the enactment of ordinary status-role
relationships, so that the relations to parental objects and siblings,
neighbors, employers, and friends, slowly developed throughout life,
become inoperant. At the same time, a multiplicity of simultaneous
relations evolves among the members of the large group that cannot be
managed by enactment of ordinary defensive operations, particularly
because of the ineffectiveness of primitive defenses, such as projective
identification, omnipotent control, denial and splitting operations in
unstructured large group situations. To this is added the disappearance of
ordinary confirmation of the perception of self by significant others; and
all of this uncannily reproduces the psychological conditions that predate
identity integration and object constancy, when a multiplicity of

non-integrated representations of partial aspects of others coexists with a lack of an integrated concept of self. Therefore the characterologically anchored behavior patterns that normally reflect and confirm ego identity are not operant in the large group situation. The consequent experience of helplessness reinforces the emergence of primitive aggression and fears and promotes regression to the structural conditions of very early – paranoid-schizoid – development.

From a different perspective, the rapidity of onset, the intensity, the surprisingly universal nature of group regression under unstructured conditions, point to a persistent, unmetabolized core of primitive aggression, primitive object relations, and primitive defensive operations as an important, perhaps even essential part of the psychological make-up of the individual, and to a surprising frailty of the mature defensive operations, centering around repression and characteristic of normal identity and ego integration, that function in ordinary life situations. This uncontrolled, powerful, regressive potential towards primitive defensive operations centering around splitting to deal with primitive aggression may be most important evidence for the basic motivational system that Freud designated as the death drive, the counterpart to libido.

Another aspect of Freud's contribution to mass psychology that acquires a new meaning in the light of experiences with unstructured small and large groups is the projection of the ego ideal onto the leader. For the sake of semantic clarity, I am using the term 'superego' to refer to the integration of conscious and unconscious internalized demands and prohibitions, value judgements and ethical principles. They include, as part of that structure, the 'ego ideal,' namely, an integrated set of ideals, demands for and aspirations toward ethical behavior.

Freud (1921) described the projection of the 'ego ideal' (his term for what I have just described as the superego) onto the leader. The projection Freud described obviously is facilitated if the leader enunciates his system of morality as corresponding to his perception of his leadership role. But the massive projection of superego features, in fact, occurs spontaneously and consistently even without the crystallizing presence of an individualized leader. Here, the contribution of Serge Moscovici in his seminal book *The Age of the Crowds* (1981) expands Freud's analysis to the consideration of the influence of mass communication on individual regression. Freud had defined mass psychology as including both the behavior of masses, and the attitudes of individuals when they experience themselves as forming part of a mass.

Moscovici pointed out how modern communication creates temporary masses on the basis of large numbers of individuals experiencing themselves as part of a mass while receiving communication from mass media that reaches them simultaneously, with all the other individuals with whom they are thus connected. Proceeding from the medieval gathering of all the village by a drummer who would announce in a loud voice the latest developments of importance to all of them (thus instantaneously transforming the crowd of villagers into a large group), to the revolutionary effects of the printing press that permitted simultaneous communication to the masses by printed edicts and proclamations, western society then advanced to newspapers as the most efficient modern simultaneous communication of information to the masses. We do not read newspapers as we read books. Unwittingly, the reader of the newspaper perceives the communication as if he were part of a large group of readers, while the selection of a book has a quality of individual choice, and even implies an act of separation from what is commonly absorbed and reacted to in daily life. The functions of the radio as the communicator and instant activator of mass reactions was consistently exploited by the Soviet Union and Nazi Germany as a powerful and highly effective instrument for creating a mass susceptible to indoctrination with the dominant state ideology.

The central role of television in contemporary political life reflects a culmination of communication that is both powerfully immediate and clearly perceived as being directed to the entire population. Moscovici proposes that mass media create mass psychology, and that mass psychology, in turn, stimulates the elaboration of mass culture, and brings about its immediate acceptance. Mass culture may include both objects that have economic and commercial interest, and ideas the propagation of which is facilitated by mass psychology. We do not have, as yet, a comprehensive analysis of the corresponding functions of the Internet. However, insofar as the Internet includes a bewildering simultaneity of contradictory and confusing appeals to ideological and cultural orientation and biases, it may serve more of a function for consolidating the membership of regressive groups rather than organizing public opinion into the direction of one prevailing ideology. In recent political campaigns, at least, television has continued to play a central role in influencing mass behavior.

Insofar as mass media provide a powerful gratification of affiliative needs, recreation, a socially sanctioned gratifying fantasy life and a means of experiencing one's self linked with and accepted by the group, mass psychology fosters the narcissistic group regression described in the large group experience and the dependent small group.

Mass media, however, may equally exploit and intensify the paranoid regression of the paranoid large group and the fight–flight small group, by developing information that conforms to a sharp division between good and bad, between loyal friends and dangerous enemies. Mass media achieve this regression by presenting a world picture in which the individuals addressed are described and confirmed as part of a good, valuable, progressive, superior, rightfully dominant group, in contrast to a threatening outsider group portrayed as aggressive, malignant, sadistic, revengeful, and above all, dangerous and threatening. Here the mass psychology originally described by Freud comes into full development, even in the absence of a specific, defined paranoid leader.

In fact, the development of a particular ideology, that is, an integrated cognitive system that explains to a mass its origin and sense, its purpose and future, may contribute to the severe paranoid regression of an entire community, or an entire nation. Mass psychology, in short, resides in a profound potential of all individuals, easily activated by mass communication. Mass psychology, in this regard, is a most powerful amplifier, both of paranoid ideologies and of the leadership provided by the narcissistic merchants of illusions or by the paranoid revolutionary.

II. Regressive pull of ideologies

Ideology, as I stated earlier, refers to an integrated system of beliefs that provides a social group with an explanation and rationale for the nature of its existence and origin, a sense of common purpose, an ideal condition to which it aspires, and potential or assumed means for achieving that condition (Althusser and Althusser 1976; Green 1969). Ideologies, in short, reflect the value systems of a social group; they include national, social, racial, religious, and political belief systems. Because of its reference to a preexisting or transcendent deity, religion occupies a particular place within ideologies, ranging across a broad spectrum, from primitive assumptions of ad hoc deities only related to a particular social group, to what Canetti (1960) calls mature religions, with a universal deity and moral value system that transcends any particular social group.

What interests us here is the possibility of detecting the narcissistic and paranoid dimensions as potential extremes of all ideologies, with an intermediate realm characterized by a focus on individual rights and obligations, and, particularly, on the value of the individual within that particular ideological system. This intermediate realm of ideologies has a definitely humanistic core, with respect for the privacy and autonomy of the individual and of the sex life of the couple. It is thus a bastion against the perilous loss of identity that both promotes and results from the regression of the large group. But the proposal that our 'normal,' civilized stance is poised perilously on a continuum between the two potential threats of the narcissistic and the paranoid dimensions is a key assumption of this paper.

For example, exploring the dominant political Marxist ideology of the Soviet Union and Communist China (Kolakowski 1978a, 1978b), we find its paranoid extreme in the doctrine of total warfare against the remnants of bourgeois culture as part of the cultural revolution sponsored by Mao Tse Tung in China, and the terror regime of the Stalinist times in the Soviet Union. The ideologies of the Pol Pot regime in Cambodia and the Shining Path in Peru are other examples. In contrast, the dominant cultural Marxist ideology in the Soviet Union during the Brezhnev years manifested the typical characteristics of the narcissistic, in contrast to the paranoid, polarity. Official Marxism, at that point, constituted a type of state religion universally accepted and repetitively proclaimed, but without any implication that it had any particular relevance to the nature of daily life, or any shared ideological impetus toward change. It was the commonly accepted doctrine, the formal adherence to which conferred social legitimacy and secure expectations for advancement in work and profession upon individual citizens. At the intermediate area of Marxist ideology we might place the humanist Marxism of Western Europe, with its emphasis on social equality and responsibility, a progressively egalitarian distribution of wealth, and respect for the authentic autonomy of the individual (Anderson 1976; Haberman 1987; Marcuse 1964).

From the viewpoint of our analysis of social violence it is, of course, the paranoid extreme of ideologies that is particularly relevant. In fact, paranoid ideologies are a powerful facilitator of social violence by directly neutralizing individual moral constraints against personal perpetration of suffering, torture, and murder. What is characteristic of paranoid ideologies is that the world is divided between the good and ideal carriers of the ideology, and the bad, dangerous, threatening enemies of the ideology, who must be destroyed in order to prevent them from destroying the true believers. Here the world is clearly split along the lines of the good and the bad, and the good are called upon to destroy the bad. Typically, paranoid ideologies stress mass action, seeking to arouse a group spirit that promotes the sacrifice of individual autonomy, reasoning, interests and rights in the service of the community. Equally typical, as Freud (1921) pointed out, is that such paranoid ideologies significantly restrict the autonomy of the sexual couple, curb the freedom of love relations from social regulation, and recruit the establishment of intimate pairs to the service of the community. Fundamentalist ideologies, that is, religious systems of ideas that take the form of the paranoid polarity of ideologies, may express all these characteristics in essential ways. The division of the world into the faithful and infidel, the need to fight the latter, the promise of an utopian future once the world is freed of all the 'bad,' the strict submission of the chosen to a sexually restrictive morality, and strict boundaries separating 'bad' social groups, are typical of fundamentalist ideologies. The leader, who may represent the deity, also demands and receives total, uncritical submission.

Individuals born into a totalitarian system and educated by it from early childhood have very little choice to escape from total identification with that system unless hidden resistances against it still operate in the intimacy of the family or a restricted social circle. Totalitarian educational systems permit a systematic indoctrination of children and youth into the dominant ideology, including the adoration of the omnipotent and omniscient leader. Those exceptional individuals who are able to stand up to such a system and reject it out of their personal growth and maturity deserve particular attention and admiration, but historically these have been small minorities.

The dimensions of narcissistic and paranoid regression thus emerge as major axes around which regressive social pathology crystallizes, and they link the psychopathology of the leader with the nature of regression in small and large unstructured groups, and with the regressive quality of paranoid mass movements and ideology formation. In fact, in studying the nature of ideologies and the 'entrance' of individuals into them from a psychological viewpoint we re-encounter the same two dimensions: ideologies 'click' with the psychology of their standard-bearers.

There is a complex relationship among the nature of the leadership, the dominant ideological system, and the efficiency of the bureaucratic organization of society at large. A humanitarian ideology may 'dampen' the regressive effects of mass psychology and of an authoritarian, paranoid leadership; and an efficient bureaucracy may prevent or reduce the regressive effects of mass psychology and unstructured group processes, by establishing or maintaining stable social task systems.

However, the same features – ideology and bureaucracy – also may worsen the effects of pathological leadership. A leader with malignant narcissism may increase the level of terror and submissiveness around him by means of the official adoption of a paranoid ideology. And an efficient bureaucracy may augment dramatically the speed and power of a totalitarian ideology and leadership. The efficient German bureaucracy combined with the paranoid features of Nazi ideology to enhance the power of Hitler's malignant narcissism. The rapidity with which the ordinary rules of law and basic human decency could be eliminated in daily social life in Nazi Germany illustrates the combined effect of leadership, ideology, bureaucracy, and the state control of the armed forces, economy, and media.

Vamik Volkan (1988, 1999) has provided us with fundamental contributions to the understanding of the interrelationships among historical traumata, identity formation, and intergroup conflict. What interests us here is how, from very early on, the linguistic and cultural characteristics of a particular social subgroup to which the individual belongs become integrated with self representations to consolidate ego identity. I referred earlier to the 'groupishness' of the small child entering the educable period of the school years, and the adaptation to the group as a first effort of the child to distance himself from threatening oedipal conflicts. The identification with a culture and a language, however, occurs, of course, from the moment of the very acquisition of language; and the identification with oedipal figures includes identification with their relationships with the surrounding culture and religion as well.

A major political upheaval, a lost war, an historically longlasting, ongoing rivalry with another social group, are included with early learning of culturally shared myths about the origin and history of one's family and intimate social group. 'Other' groups become objects of early splitting mechanisms, narcissistic and paranoid regressions and defenses against them (Volkan 1999). A sense of personal value becomes attached to belonging to a certain language, culture, or religion as part of normal narcissism. The powerful effect of the social commonality of language, rituals, art and myths is a reflection of the integration of self-representaions into a cohesive self, and of partial object representations into total object representations as part of the consolidation of ego identity: the similarity of others assures the integration of their images as well as that of the multiple self-representations that reflect those interactions with 'similar' others. At the same time, the demands and prohibitions that are part of the cultural heritage or of the particular religious beliefs of the family are integrated into early superego structures, together with the more idiosyncratic parental value systems, and with the culturally shared aspirations, biases, and frustrations that link the individual and his family to a particular social group (Volkan 1999).

As Volkan (1988) has pointed out, such shared historical heritage, particularly when it involves significant social traumata, becomes part of the individual's narcissistic equilibrium. Social trauma coalesces with personal trauma and narcissistic frustrations, and these may reinforce each other. The violent redress of a social injustice becomes the violent redress of a narcissistic trauma, while narcissistic traumata may become integrated into and rationalized in the form of the redress of a social trauma.

Violent behavior of one social subgroup against another may become a preferred channel for the expression of individual psychopathology. Acceptance into a violent subgroup is often contingent upon the individual's willingness to commit acts of violence. When historical traumata facilitate the physical separation between social subgroups (as in the 'racial cleansing' that separated Christian Serbs from Moslem Albanians), or highlight such differentiating characteristics of subgroups as language or skin color, and when a paranoid ideology promotes dehumanization of one group by the other, a leadership characterized by malignant narcissism or paranoia can readily create the circumstances that trigger social violence. Once massive propaganda has succeeded in separating and dehumanizing a subgroup, the physical extermination of such a subgroup may be widely tolerated and supported, as was the case of the Jews in Nazi Germany (Dawidowicz 1975; Goldhagen 1996; Klemperer 1995a, 1995b).

From individual psychopathology we have learned that the only way to escape from this traumatic vicious circle is an internal process of recognition of the identification with self and other, with victim and aggressor, and a process of mourning that, through overcoming the split between these representations, leads to the resolution of that identification, to efforts to bring about sublimatory resolution of the damage caused by the trauma, and, potentially, even a reconciliation with an erstwhile enemy. Mitscherlich (1963), Segal (1997), and Volkan (1999) have pointed to the pathology of the lack of mourning processes resolving a historic past traumatic experience, and the danger of the repetition of the trauma on a social level when such socially anchored mourning does not occur. Here lies the role of a humanistic ideology as a precondition for the resolution of social trauma, and as an alternative to the exacerbation of social and historical traumata by new social crises.

In conclusion, the unconscious potential for primitive aggression available in different degrees in every individual may be activated rapidly in regressive group processes. Group-activated aggression, in turn, may be amplified by the combination of the collective internalization of historical traumata, an acute or chronic social crisis that disrupts ordinary social structures, the paranoid polarity of a dominant ideology, and an effective bureaucracy that can be absorbed easily into the power of a sadistic tyrant. What warrants to be explored, in this context, is the psychology of terrorism, the transformation of a fundamentalist ideology into a terrorist subculture.

III. Fundamentalist ideologies and terrorism

The terrorist attack on the United States on September 11 2001 has naturally focused attention and concern upon the nature, causes, and implications of this dramatic expression of social violence. Because the event is so recent and its immediate psychological, political, ideological and military consequences so serious, it is difficult to examine its psychological characteristics, as contrasted with other forms of social violence, from a 'technically neutral' psychoanalytic viewpoint. Sociological and historical analyses of terrorist movements, clinical studies of actual and potential suicidal bombers, and the ongoing consequences of terrorist attacks elsewhere, serve as elements for exploring the relationships of terrorism with the general area of socially sanctioned violence (Armstrong 2001; Bergen 2001; Galanter 1989; Guzman 2000; Haynal 1983; Hoge and Rose 2001; Juergensmeyer 2000; Kakar 1996; Kepel 2000; Laqueur 1999; Post 2001; Reinares 1998; Volkan 2001a, 2001b).

Terrorism as a social phenomenon must be differentiated from fundamentalist ideologies, although the latter constitute the most common basis of terrorist motivation and action. It also must be differentiated from the severe regressive group processes described earlier as developing into socially sanctioned and organized manifestations of brutal, sadistic behavior against a persecuted minority, and justified in terms of the ideology of the dominant group.

Fundamentalist ideologies divide the world into ideal and evil realms; their own ideology belongs to the ideal realm and its proponents are thus guaranteed goodness, survival and redemption, happiness, harmony, and moral triumph. The ideas, beliefs and behavior of the realm of evil are immoral, dangerous, destructive, and threatening to everything that the good stand for. The triumph of the good and the destruction of evil will bring about universal peace and harmony, and the end to all conflicts and grievances. Typically, such an ideology projects all aggression onto the evil social group, while justifying aggression against the infidel as a necessary defense and retribution if not a moral imperative. The fundamentalist ideology requires strict adherence to its basic theories and assertions; mutual confidence and trust of the idealized social group of believers is based on the assurance of such total ideological adherence. Characteristically, within the belief system of a fundamentalist ideology, the individual is less important than the community, and submission to the values of the community overrides any conflicting needs or desires of the individual. Fundamentalist ideologies frequently have a puritanical character, are suspicious of individual sexual behavior and the private life of the couple, and tend to regulate and restrict sexuality in the process. They usually also require submission to an absolute leader who incorporates all the values of the ideology, and is imbued with total knowledge and absolute certainty as to how to interpret the fundamentalist ideology to his followers. In the case of religious fundamentalism, the leader assumes the authority of the deity.

As Freud originally stated, the mutual identification of all the followers in terms of their idealization of the leader, and the projection onto him of their ego ideal and superego functions, frees them from moral responsibility for actions demanded by the leader, and fosters the relentless, brutal attack on the infidels. Volkan (2001a, 2001b) has stressed that religious fundamentalism, in addition to these characteristics, typically implies the wish to return to an original and idealized past, involves a pessimistic outlook regarding the present, and the confidence that the specialness of their faith derives from a divine text that justifies the specialness of the group, while the absolute leader is the only one authorized to interpret the text. Fundamentalist groups are often dominated by a feeling of victimization, a belief in magical signs, and a combination of a sense of danger from evil forces with a sense of omnipotence in their belonging to the elected group. Religious fundamentalism, Volkan states, stresses the sharp boundaries that separate the believers from dangerous or at least negative outside groups or forces, a differentiation often expressed literally or symbolically by dress codes or modes of presentation in public.

Because of the religious commitment to an absolute belief system and trust in the deity, the manifestations of mass psychology described by Freud acquire the greatest intensity. As Kakar (1996) points out, total commitment to the deity is condensed with an emotional, basic religious experience derived from the earliest longings for fusion with an idealized protective parental figure. That experience confers a sense of emotional integrity, calmness and security which is enhanced by participating in a benign and supportive matrix of social goodness. As Kakar suggests, a systematic and massive indoctrination with a fundamentalist religious ideology in the context of isolation from the family of origin and total submersion within a group setting may facilitate a shift from a personal religious feeling into the socially resonating sense of oneness with a community that shares absolute ideological convictions.

Terrorism is a type of socially directed violence committed against the surrounding social group by individuals and groups who live in relative loneliness, secrecy, and defiance, united by a fundamentalist ideology. Their fervor is reinforced by a personal disposition to primitive hatred, ruthlessness, sadism and cruelty, totally rationalized in terms of the corresponding fundamentalist ideology. Their hatred is expressed in the commitment to destroy the infidel, the enemy power, group or forces that stand between the fundamentalist ideology and the eventual utopia, the reign of human brotherhood, or the Kingdom of Heaven. The splitting of the world into an idealized and a persecutory region is accompanied by a commitment to the goal of destroying the enemies of the utopia. Typically, individual terrorists have undergone a strict and consistent training that intensifies both their hatred toward the representatives of evil, and a commitment to total indifference or the suppression of any concern for the victims of the terrorist act. This permits killing of women and children, of innocent bystanders, with a sense of excitement in fulfilling the ideology's moral demands.

The literature on the personality features of individual terrorists frequently describes a history of severe trauma, a sense of inferiority or abandonment in infancy and childhood, compensated later on by an aggressive self-affirmation and the transformation of a sense of victimization into an ideologically rationalized passion for sadistic revenge as the redress of earlier grievances (Haynal 1983; Post 2001; Volkan 2001a, 2001b). While describing the surface calmness and pseudo-rationality of the terrorist, Volkan has explored how, behind the imperviousness to ordinary logic, one typically finds an ideology that permits no questioning and, tested regarding its internal logic, reveals both an underlying confusion as well as the total inability to negotiate that confusion rationally.

The cultural ambiance of regressive mass psychology that constitutes the social and cultural background of the future members of terrorist groups does not have a uniform quality. Such mass psychology may derive from a historically given religious fundamentalism that is accentuated under the effects of a contemporary traumatic situation or reactivated in response to massive social trauma, a set of circumstances that may promote followership by a relatively broad variety of frustrated, impoverished, disappointed, and isolated individuals; but immersion in such a mass psychology may also lead to the emergence, from a highly individualized background of ideological indoctrination, of an individual with strong paranoid, narcissistic, and/or antisocial features. Often the leadership of fundamentalist and terrorist groups is taken by individuals presenting the syndrome of malignant narcissism, individuals stemming from an elitist class within which they felt rejected or traumatized, subsequently identifying themselves with the oppressed and humiliated as a justification for their revengeful attack on the environment from which they proceed (H. Neira, personal communication). They gather their followers from the members of the disadvantaged or traumatized social group that is experiencing an acute or chronic regression into mass psychology.

We find, in short, the typical combination of circumstances that facilitates the outbreak of sanctioned social violence in any case, but can be transformed, under the influence of specially predisposed individuals, into an exhilarating sense of mission and total commitment to the destruction of the enemy. That mission confers a sense of control, omnipotence and triumphant sadism, entirely split off from the idealized ideology that provides the terrorists with a community with their own group. This radical split contributes to an overall dynamic stability throughout the period of patient preparation and execution of the terrorist acts.

The commitment to terrorist action implies a particular orientation toward both the terrorist in-group and the external reality that complicates the situation of ordinary fundamentalist ideologists. Toward the 'in-group,' the terrorist presents absolute submission to the leader and to the leader's delegates, and acceptance of whatever limitations of private life are decreed by the leader, as well as preparedness to watch for the maintenance of the purity of the in-group. This includes the selection for immediate elimination of any traitor or comrade whose commitment to the group and its ideology seems to weaken. Absolute obedience, cruelty, and fearlessness are the guiding principles of this moral system, and the brotherhood of the conspirators provides the compensating sense of warmth and humanity. In relation to the 'out-group', the enemy world, the terrorist is committed to its destruction as his main or only objective in life, by whatever cruel and dehumanized means, disregarding the nature of the victims, obeying orders slavishly, and being totally focused on the mission.

The primary objective of terrorism is the production of terror, that is, a paralyzing, disorganizing sense of dread that spreads among the enemy, destabilizing and eventually delegitimizing the enemy's social structure, way of living and leadership. The long-range objective of terror is the destruction of the enemy, although it may involve tactical flexibility as a preliminary step. Terrorist groups may enter into negotiations with the enemy, but by definition those negotiations must be dishonest, because the ultimate objective is not conciliation of differences or reconciliation, but destruction of the enemy. Any compromise would imply a weakening of the boundary between the ideal and the persecutory world, and threaten the purity of the terrorist's utopia by contamination, and therefore, in the process of conciliation, the very survival of the fundamentalist ideology.

By projective identification, the terrorist's dread is his own ruthless destruction by the enemy, so that death becomes an essential aspect of the terrorist's mental world. Death inflicted upon the enemy signals triumph, while the death of the terrorist before the mission is accomplished is seen as a catastrophic failure. Death in the successful accomplishment of the mission itself expresses the deepest commitment to the mission. Self-sacrifice in the course of inflicting a maximum of terror and destruction on the enemy is an additional source of moral triumph and, in the case of religious fundamentalism, a guarantee for happy survival in the Kingdom of Heaven. Islamic suicide bombers often refuse indignantly the implication that they are suicidal: death in the fulfillment of the terrorist act is only a moment of transition to entrance into heaven, to martyrdom and immortality (Post 2001).

Laqueur (1999) points out that, while self-sacrifice has been a characteristic of terrorist movements throughout many centuries – like, for example, the Islamic sect of the 'Assassins' of the eleventh century – different historical periods and social circumstances of terrorism have modeled the relationship of terrorists to punishment and death. So, for example, nineteenth-century anarchic terrorists directed their aggressive actions only against perceived leaders of the social or political establishment, tried to avoid hurting innocent bystanders, women or children, in the process, and expected to be punished with long prison sentences. Self-sacrifice also might be induced by a commitment to nationalist fundamentalism, such as the ideological commitments of the Japanese kamikaze pilots during the Second World War. The profoundly masochistic implications of self-sacrifice may emerge in pure form in ideologically motivated self-immolation as a social protest. In this latter case, the split between the ideological ideal and the dissociated aggression is achieved by an exclusively self-directed aggression as an assumed expression of altruistic love.

Obviously, the outline presented above is a necessary simplification of more complex, individual variations of entrance into the terrorist system and the idiosyncratic motivations of the individual terrorist. From the rather simple-minded follower who obtains a sense of personal signifi-cance in belonging to a terrorist group, to the narcissistically isolated, omnipotent fanatic, to the individual with antisocial tendencies who expects financial gains for himself or his family without significant concern for himself, to the severely traumatized, paranoid individual searching for personal revenge, there is a broad spectrum of individuals who engage in terrorist acts, similar to the diversity of the spectrum of the leaders who induce such individuals to the terrorist commitment and remain distant from the terrorist act itself.

The struggle against terrorist movements is a particular challenge for a democratic society that, while protecting its citizens from the socially dis-organizing consequences of terror, needs to avoid seduction, by the very terrorist challenge, into its transformation into an authoritarian state. A frequent misconception in this area is the confusion between authority and authoritarianism. Authority is the rational, socially sanctioned, function-ally necessary exercise of power in the pursuit of realistic and socially acknowledged goals (Kernberg 1998). Authoritarianism is an exercise of power that exceeds that functionally required by the task, and leads to dis-tortions of organizational and political structures that destroy, eventually, the task-oriented functionality of social and political systems. A task-oriented analysis of the functional requirements of authority com-mensurate with the necessary power to carry out the task, corresponds to the legally defined nature of authority commensurate with a democratic state's obligation to protect civil rights. The degree of authority required to protect an open society from its potential enemies varies from country to country, from social situation to social situation; the definition of functional authority required to deal with a social emergency needs to be clarified and negotiated in each concrete instance.

Most authors seem to agree that the causes of terrorism are multiple, and cannot be reduced to any single one such as poverty, population pressures, religious conflicts, massive migrations, ethnic pressures, nation-alist aspirations, uncontrolled growth of mega cities, etc. (Hoge and Rose 2001; Huntington 1996; Kakar 1996; Kepel 2000; Laqueur 1999). With some frequency, religious and nationalistic aims may combine, as in the Islamic terrorist groups in the Middle East and Central Asia, the IRA in Ireland, and terrorist groups in Kashmir. However, in the search for causes of terrorism, and hence for prevention and treatment, it has to be kept in mind that typically, the professed statement of the 'cause' that justifies a terrorist group's actions is itself part of the terrorists' strategy, and follows political objectives rather than corresponding to authentic causes. As Hugo Neira (personal communication), referring to the Shining Path movement in Peru, put it: 'terrorists often wrap themselves in the flag of grievances for the oppressed, whom they themselves attack ruthlessly.'

Laqueur (1999) in agreement with other authors, points out that terrorists tend to escalate terrorist actions until they obtain a significant reaction from the enemy. Lack of response to terrorist provocation usually increases terrorist action, to a point where terrorist action becomes so outrageous that the society threatened by it reacts strongly, and usually manages to defeat terrorism. Efforts to compromise with terrorist organi- zations usually fail: at the bottom, compromise and conciliation are anathema to the terrorists because they threaten the very basis of their ideological commitment. For all these reasons, the only effective way to deal with terrorism is to control and defeat it, while studying the long-range causes that fostered its development. Both processes must go on simultaneously, and that requires complex combinations of social, economic, political, diplomatic, and military means.

Terrorist movements thrive in open societies that they can exploit relatively undisturbed for setting up their operations. The fight against terrorism, therefore, necessarily means some restriction of civil liberties, with the danger that an excessive restriction of civil liberties may play into the terrorists' hands. There is a delicate balance between sufficient control of the social structure to stop terrorist activities, and the protection of civil liberties against an excessive exercise of control; to establish such a balance is a general principle, with which all states affected by terrorist onslaughts have to struggle. This struggle is exacerbated by the particularly dangerous nature of contemporary terrorism with its access to biological, chemical, or nuclear weapons. Protection against these dangers implies expensive, long-term, global measures of prevention and control, disconnecting terrorists from their sources of financial and political support, be it state-sponsored terrorism, religious fundamentalist supported terrorism, nationalist terrorism, or politically inspired terrorism. The gradual, effective cutting off of the support that terrorist movements such as the IRA in Northern Ireland, the ETA in the Basque country, and the RAF in Germany had obtained from corresponding nationalist, religious, or political groups was successfully achieved by the concerted efforts of the political, social, and cultural community of those countries, together with police and military action to control terrorism. Once terrorists lose their support from silent sympathizers, they have difficulty surviving, and this reinforces the effectiveness of cutting them off from sources of international funding and logistic support.

Where terrorism is an open or secretively used instrument of a state, political action, economic pressure, and/or military intervention by outsiders may be required to control such a state's behavior. British political intervention in Ireland regarding the IRA, West German economic pressure on East Germany regarding the RAF, and the military intervention of the United States in Afghanistan to destroy the effectiveness of Al Q'aeda illustrate the measures that have been used recently in the attempt to control terrorist organizations.

Where long-standing independent educational systems linked with fundamentalist religious organizations are given a free hand by the state, they are able to exacerbate religious, racist, nationalist or other social prejudices. They thus become the breeding-ground for future terrorist recruitment and state-sponsored terrorist activity. Such educational systems must be brought under the control of responsible governments as part of the effort to protect open societies and prevent fundamentalist groups from regressing into terrorist activity. Islamic fundamentalist schools such as the Palestinian educational system controlled by Hamas are the backbone of a social structure that fosters the psychology of suicide bombers and terrorist groups in general.

As mentioned before, the terrorist commitment cannot be influenced, and the terrorist movement must be controlled and defeated. But the masses of passive sympathizers who constitute the social and political world within which terrorism develops can and must be influenced in order to isolate the terrorist group.

Here understanding of the immediate consequences of group regression and mass psychology is helpful. Historically determined biases and hatred may be transmitted transgenerationally, but do not necessarily interfere in the peaceful coexistence of different social groups under ordinary social and political circumstances. In the same way as, under the influence of acute socially traumatic circumstances or crises, immediate regression to violent mass psychology may emerge, such violence may be decreased equally rapidly by the reduction of such regressive phenomena in the context of social reorganization, political action, conciliatory efforts with political and social forces related to but not identical with the terrorist group (Huntington 1996; Volkan 1988). For example, Christians Serbs and Bosnian Muslims have been able to live together peacefully over many decades, with outbreaks of intercommunal violence closely related to concrete political developments, war, and, particularly, the falling apart of the Soviet system at this particular historical juncture. The rapid disappearance of the remnants of Nazi ideology and mass psychology at the point of Nazi Germany's defeat and Hitler's death illustrates the same phenomenon: the fundamentalist ideology died with the leader.

This brings us to the role of the media in triggering mass psychology and in influencing its change and demise. For reasons mentioned above, mass media are able to generate a rapid psychological regression to large group psychology in viewers or listeners who absorb media information while experiencing themselves as the simultaneous receptors of information broadcast to a large mass. Violence stirred up by mass media at the service of fundamentalist ideologies may be influenced rapidly by mass media 'daring' to challenge that ideology. By the same token, mass media, in their commercially driven thirst for sensationalist news, unwittingly reinforce the impact of terrorist action, and, in fact, become the tools of terrorist strategies. This development demonstrates the social responsibility of the media in the war against terrorism, a responsibility that is the counterpoint of a naïve defense of total freedom and irresponsibility to publish what may sell. This lesson has been absorbed by the European and Latin American press of countries subjected to long-term terrorist threats and anti-terrorist efforts. In short, the manipulation of mass psychology by the media may be used to reduce terrorism as well as to amplify it.

It would certainly be naïve to imagine that the principles outlined in this presentation are adequate and sufficient for all situations of socially sanctioned violence. They reflect general approaches, from a psychoanalytic viewpoint, that should be integrated with other approaches derived from social-psychological, political, historical, and socioeconomic 'know-how.' Insofar as psychological factors influence conflicts and violence both at individual, group, and national levels, and provide understanding for the structural analysis of ideological systems as well as leadership, it is to be hoped that they will become part of our social armamentarium for reducing, if not eliminating, the terrible problem of violence in our human reality.

Note

1.   This chapter will appear in a more expanded version, as two manuscripts, in the *International Journal of Psycho-Analysis.*

References

Althusser, E. and Althusser, L. (1976) *Positions.* Paris: Editions Sociales.

Anderson, P. (1976) *Consideration on Western Marxism.* London: NLB.

Armstrong, K. (2001) *The Battle for God.* New York: Ballantine Books.

Bergen, P. L. (2001) *Holy War, Inc.* New York: Free Press.

Bion, W. R. (1961) *Experiences in Groups.* New York: Basic Books.

Canetti, E. (1960) *Masse and Macht.* Frankfurt am Main: Fischer Taschenbuch Verlag.

Chasseguet-Smirgel, J. (1975) *L'Idéal du Moi.* Paris: Claude Tchou.

Dawidowicz, L. S. (1975) *The War Against the Jews 1933–1945.* New York: Bantam Books.

Freud, S. (1921) 'Group psychology and the analysis of the ego.' *Standard Edition 18*, 65–143.

Galanter, M. (1989) *Cults: Faith, Healing, and Coercion.* New York: Oxford University Press.

Goldhagen, D. (1996) *Hitler's Willing Executioners.* New York: Alfred A. Knopf.

Green, A. (1969) *Sexualité et idéologie chez Marx et Freud.* Paris: Etudes Freudiennes, 1–2, 187–217.

Green, A. (1993) *Le Travail du Négatif.* Paris: Les Editions de Minuit.

Guzman, N. (2000) *Romo: Confesiones de un torturador.* Santiago: Planeta.

Haberman, J. (1987) *The Philosophical Discourse of Modernity.* Cambridge, MA: MIT Press.

Haynal, A. (1983) *Fanaticism: A Historical and Psychoanalytical Study.* New York: Schocken Books.

Hoge, J. F. Jr and Rose, G. (eds) (2001) *How Did This Happen?* New York: Public Affairs.

Huntington, S. P. (1996) *The Clash of Civilizations and the Remaking of World Order.* New York: Touchstone.

Juergensmeyer, M. (2000) *Terror in the Mind of God.* Berkeley: University of California Press.

Kakar, S. (1996) *The Colors of Violence: Cultural Identities, Religion and Conflict.* Chicago: University of Chicago Press.

Kepel, G. (2000) *La Yihad. Expansión y declive del islamismo.* Barcelona: Gallimard.

Kernberg, O. F. (1994) 'Aggression, trauma, hatred in the treatment of borderline patients.' *Psychiatric Clinics of North America 17, 4,* 701–714. (ed. I. Share) Philadelphia: W. B. Saunders.

Kernberg, O. F. (1998) *Ideology, Conflict, and Leadership in Groups and Organizations.* New Haven and London: Yale University Press.

Kernberg, O. F. (2000) 'Socially sanctioned violence: A psychoanalytic view.' German translation: 'Sanktionierte gesellschaftliche Gewalt: eine psychoanalytische Sichtweise.' *Persönlichkeitsstörungen: Theorie und Therapie 4*, 1–64, 4–25.

Klemperer, V. (1995a) *Ich will Zeugnis ablegen bis zum letzten: Tageb ücher 1933–1941*. Berlin: Aufbau-Verlag.

Klemperer, V. (1995b) *Ich will Zeugnis ablegen bis zum letzten: Tagebü cher 1942–1945*. Berlin: Aufbau-Verlag.

Kolakowski, L. (1978a) 'The founders.' In *Main Currents of Marxism 1*. New York: Oxford University Press.

Kolakowski, L. (1978b) 'The breakdown.' In *Main Currents of Marxism 3*. Oxford: Oxford University Press.

Laqueur, W. (1999) *The New Terrorism*. New York: Oxford University Press.

Laqueur, W. (2001) 'Left, right and beyond: The changing face of terror.' In *How Did This Happen? Terrorism and the New World* (eds J. F. Hage, Jr and G. Rose). New York: Public Affairs.

Marcuse, H. (1964) *One-Dimensional Man: Studies in the Ideology of Advanced Industrial Society*. Boston: Beacon Press.

Mitscherlich, A. (1963) *Auf dem Weg zur vaterlosen Gesellschaft: Ideen Zur Sozial-Psychologie*. Munich: R. Piper.

Moscovici, S. (1981) *L'age des foules*. Paris: Librairie Arthème Fayard.

Neira, H. (2001) Personal Communication.

Post, G. (2001) 'The mind of the terrorist.' Presentation to the Association for Psychoanalytic Medicine, New York, 30 October 2001.

Reinares, F. (1998) *Terrorismo y Antiterrorismo*. Beunos Aires: Paidós.

Rice, A. K. (1965) *Learning for Leadership*. London: Tavistock Publications.

Rice, A. K. (1969) 'Individual, group, and intergroup processes.' *Human Relations 22*, 565–584.

Segal, H. (1997) 'Silence is the real crime' and 'From Hiroshima to the Gulf War and after: Socio-political expressions of ambivalence.' In *Psychoanalysis, Literature, and War: Papers 1972–1995* (ed. J. Steiner). London: Routledge.

Turquet, P. (1975) 'Threats to identity in the large group.' In *The Large Group: Dynamics and Therapy* (ed. L. Kreeger). London: Constable.

Volkan, V. D. (1988) *The Need to Have Enemies and Allies: From Clinical Practice to International Relationships*. Northvale, New Jersey.

Volkan, V. D. (1999) *Das Versagen der Diplomatie*. Psychosozial-Verlag, Giessen.

Volkan, V. D. (2001a) *From Waco to the Bomian Valley: Violence and the Psychology of Religious Fundamentalism* (unpublished manuscript).

Volkan, V. D. (2001b) *September 11, 2001: From the Bomian Valley to the Twin Towers and Pentagon* (unpublished manuscript).

CHAPTER 9

The Large Group and Political Process

Josef Shaked

Each analytic experience encompasses not only the working through of one's own life history, but also a confrontation with cultural norms and social conflicts, i.e. with political processes in a broad sense. This applies especially to large groups that are composed of participants coming from different social classes and diverse countries and cultures. In such groups, which in the last decades have increasingly been integrated into training programmes and group analytic workshops, social and political issues occupy a significant part of the group experience. My own experience with large groups, I must admit, is limited to such gatherings attended mainly by professionals. Colleagues working with patients in psychiatric institutes have made, however, similar observations (cf. Ardjomandi, Dally and Kü hn 1995).

The large group is also especially suitable for the study of mass psychology. We experience in it vividly how uncertain and unstable we are and how suggestible and susceptible we may become to simplistic political slogans. If we reflect on these phenomena, we may become less likely to be seduced. Experience teaches us, however, that individuals repeatedly succumb to the regressive influence of the large group (and to the impact of mass media and public opinion).

My experiences with large groups

Some examples may be used to exemplify this thesis:

1. In the group analytic training in Austria, twice yearly I conduct a daily* large group for eight days. The bulk of our participants come from Germany, Austria and Switzerland. Furthermore, we have participants from Eastern Europe. When we initiated our workshops in the middle of the 1970s, Europe was still divided by the Iron Curtain, and the different ways of life and thinking of the participants from the two divided parts of Europe were reflected in our group processes. In the last two decades, Europe has undergone marked transformations, and the political changes in the various societies are felt in our groups.

    In the 1970s and early 1980s, our large groups were dominated by the generational conflict between the German participants. The younger group members accused their parents for being entangled in the crimes committed by the Nazi regime, while the older participants, who had served in the German army, tried to justify themselves. National differences became apparent in dealing with collective history: the Swiss, but also the majority of the Austrians, who initially had kept apart, in the course of time gradually altered their attitude and also got involved in the critical scrutiny of the past. The participants from Eastern Europe usually avoided political issues. The confrontation in the large group with experiences in communist countries was only possible after the fall of the Iron Curtain.

    In the 1990s we had a new generation of participants from the western countries, which was less interested in social and political issues. (A notable exception was the terrorist attack in New York, which generated immense anxieties in the large group.) By and large, however, the members of the large groups devoted most of their time to dealing with their individual anxieties and difficulties of relating to each other. This retreat into the private sphere was not utterly detached from the political changes that have taken place in the last decades. The globalisation of the world economy and the efforts undertaken to achieve a greater unity in Europe have entailed fears of economic insecurity and loss of identity. The present-day participants are more anxiously concerned with securing their professional existence. This is reflected also in the more hesitant and less playful way of making contacts within the large groups.

2. The European symposium for group analysis in Heidelberg 1993, the first gathering after the end of the Cold War, turned out to be a remarkable transcultural meeting. English was agreed upon as the common language in the large group, but the communication was difficult, as some participants had difficulties expressing themselves in this language. Especially some Germans had a problem feeling like strangers in their own country. This led subsequently to a confrontation between Germans and Jews, since quite a few of the English participants were German refugees or their descendants. Another problem lay in the large number of 400–500 participants, which was a considerable handicap for the communication in the group. These difficulties fostered paranoid tendencies in the group. In the course of the week, however, the willingness of the participants to listen and to understand each other increased, and it became evident that the difficulty of hearing in the large hall was largely a psychological rather than a physical problem. The ability to overcome the language barriers could likewise be improved in the course of the sessions.

A peculiarity of this large group was also its transcultural composition. Participants from East and West, to a lesser degree also those from North and South, clashed with each other and caused a sort of a cultural shock. The social and political upheavals in Europe during recent years, especially the war in Yugoslavia that was then going on, found their expression in the group. The feeling of helplessness in the face of this war in the immediate proximity and the awareness one's own powerless entanglement were clearly perceptible in the large group. Serbian, Croatian, Muslim and Slovenian participants recounted their personal experiences during the war. Besides the horror of this war, the Holocaust was the subject that loomed large in the group. One had to acknowledge once again that the relation between Germans and Jews is still not 'normal', notwithstanding the passage of time. Some participants were irritated by this discussion and tried – similar to tendencies in society as a whole – to let the past go, in order to be able to proceed with business as usual. They remained, however, in the minority. This incisive historic event has proved resistant against all attempts of repression. The Holocaust served the group also as a metaphor for all collective crimes and threats to mankind. This was documented by sometimes moving personal accounts of humiliation and torture, to which East Europeans and Asians also contributed (cf. Shaked 1994).

3. A large group in the Ukraine, as part of a training programme organized by German and Austrian group analysts, clearly demonstrated two major taboos: it was hardly possible for the participants to tackle their Soviet past, and they avoided talking about intimate matters concerning their families or other relationships. All kinds of cultural and ethnological explanations for these differences of mentality between Eastern and Central Europe remained unsatisfactory. Right at the beginning of the first session of the large group, the route was set for the rest of the week. After I had asked the group to report their thoughts and feelings as unfiltered as possible, I found out to my amazement that the participants apparently understood the invitation to freely associate like a new teaching from the West, which should replace the old Communist ideology. The consequence was a stream of 'correct' – and consequently superficial – associations that were motivated by the ardent wish to follow the 'basic analytic rule' under all circumstances. Simultaneously massive fears emerged that unimpeded free speech could lead to a perilous moral decay. This apprehension culminated in a flaming diatribe by an elderly participant against the media, which propagated filthy sex. My ironical intervention, that the participants who did not follow the analytic rule of free association should be banished to Siberia, was not funny at all, and was followed by an embarrassed silence. Apparently, psychoanalytic 'truth', understood as dogma, was meant to replace the lost certainty of the Communist teaching. Behind the all too eager compliance with the basic analytic rule, massive apprehensions of not conforming to the standards of behaviour expected of the members of the group were discernible.

Another problem with the Ukrainian reality offered opportunity for an experiment: the large group took place in the dining-room of a resort hotel. Kitchen employees occasionally looked curiously in, and since the doors could not be locked, and some spa visitors came inadvertently into the group. The organizers wanted to post guards at the doors in order to shield the large group against the intruders, whereupon I proposed not to turn away the visitors. My recommendation proved to have bolstered the identity of the group by discovering that it was developing its own culture that distinguished it from the outside word. On their part, the foreign guests were taken aback by this strange event, which they could not classify.

Two years later, the participants were able to talk much more freely about their collective past. They evidently needed a latency period until they were able to talk about their painful experiences. However, the taboo of discussing intimate matters persisted. In the course of time, this problem could also be clarified in an amazingly simple manner. It turned out to be the consequence of the dismal living conditions in Eastern Europe, where often several families had to share a single apartment. In order to be able to get along together, they had to set up rigid shame boundaries. Such experiences have induced me to be cautious with all too hasty judgments about foreign cultures. This last example illustrates the realisation of the simple insight, often neglected in analytic settings, that the way people deal with problems of proximity and intimacy has to do not only with their psychological disposition and the peculiarities of their culture, but also with the material conditions under which they live. Further work with the Ukrainian groups showed that the shyness with regard to the intimacy in the group could also be gradually reduced.

At this point the special problem of working with interpreters can be touched upon. Translations are often elaborations and distortions of the contributions of the participants, in the course of which some nuances and delicacies of language get lost. Sometimes the interpreter gets emotionally involved with the group and is in need of subsequent psychological support in order to regain his composure. Such was the case with a large group session in Ukraine, where a participant asked the group members for their opinions about a highly emotional issue. Some participants, finding this request outrageous, jumped up and articulated their displeasure by shouting and gesticulating, among them my interpreter, who had completely forgotten his function in the group.

4. Over a longer period I have been conducting a yearly large group in Israel. The topics of the group focused primarily on the Israeli–Arab conflict and the tensions within Israeli society. During those years the large group echoed the changes in mood within large segments of Israeli society towards the conflict with the Palestinians, from self-righteous nationalism to a pensive and self-critical attitude, and again recently a defiant hardening of attitude. Notable was the fact that, with the exception of one female social worker who attended the group years ago, Israeli Arabs never participated in the large group. The group was composed of liberally

minded Israeli Jews, who treated the Arab colleague with caution. She spoke quite freely about her difficulties with her father, but refused to talk about politics. This demonstrates the deep gulf dividing Jews and Arabs in Israel not only since the Intifada. At the same time it indicates the potential of the large group to deal with political conflicts by uncovering painful personal and collective experiences and learning to empathise with one's enemies, provided that it comes to an encounter with the others and with unknown aspects of oneself.

Within Israeli society, the disparity between Jews of European and those of Afro-Asian origin, between immigrants from different cultures, as well as between religious and secular Jews played a prominent role in the group. The few religious Jews who attended the group complained of being considered by the others as narrow minded and conservative. A woman settler, who had attended the group years ago, was overtly rejected by the other members of the group and never showed up again. In this particular case I failed to confront the large group with the hidden aggressive aspects within everyone of us, rather than projecting them on a scapegoat. I am convinced that the group could have dealt fruitfully with this problem, had I coped better with my counter-transference, and provided that the group had more time to unfold itself.

On the whole, the large groups in Israel are characterised by the great intensity with which political issues are discussed. As a result of the special exposed geopolitical situation of Israel, the omnipresent experience of the Holocaust and the Jewish sensibility to potential dangers, the distinction between 'the public and the private realm' (Hannah Arendt 1958) tends to get obliterated, intermingling collective and private calamities.

5. A large group with around 100 participants in Budapest offered an insight into the problems of a society in transition. From the beginning there was some unrest and unease noticeable in the group. At the outset persons who made a sort of confession about their problems and sexual wrongdoings repeatedly occupied the inner row. This conduct was reminiscent of the Communist practice of public self-incrimination. It turned out, however, that several members of a Catholic community took part in this training programme. Later, the inner circle was replaced by a group engaged in intimate conversation, causing a large amount of irritation among the members of the large group. Finally the large group disintegrated into

small groups, whereupon the group in the inner circle began dancing around the hall, encouraging other hesitant participants to join them. Perplexed and confused, debilitated and debased, incapable of sorting out this happening, I felt like a confused anthropologist in an unknown culture. In order to salvage the rest of my authority, I seated myself at the beginning of the next session in the inner row, where I was left alone. As the group began reflecting on the course of the previous session, it came to light that the inner group consisted of graduates of a training programme, who wanted to 'assist' me by demonstrating their therapeutic skills. Since that curriculum laid emphasis on role-playing and psychodrama, the graduates endeavoured to activate the group and set it in motion. Not content with this superficial explanation, I interpreted this happening as an echo of the social instability and as the search for new norms and rules in the post-Communist era. The group became thoughtful and reflected subsequently on cultural change in the new Hungarian society. My intervention, which was clearly motivated by my hurt pride, enabled me to regain my lost analytic honour.

6. As the last example of a transcultural happening I would like to mention the large group that was held in the summer of 1999 during the World Congress for Psychotherapy in Vienna. The participants came from different cultures and continents, and were adherents of various psychotherapy methods. Since there was no common language and communication took place with the help of microphones, considerable bewilderment prevailed among the participants, which could be reduced to some extent by the translations into German or English that some compatriots provided for some contributions in foreign languages. These difficulties caused a chaotic situation in the group and confused the participants. After some time, they got used to it and even derived some pleasure from it. For example, an Italian participant recounted his difficulties with what he considered the exaggerated orderliness of the Austrians, while an Indian colleague declared she felt in the group as if she were at home, where numerous cultures lived side by side without generally binding rules.

Some reflections on the 'political' in large groups

On the whole, one can say that in large groups the complex interaction of social, historic, economic, cultural and national components is experienced emotionally on the one hand, as a threat to identity, but on the other hand it offers an opportunity for a broader understanding of ourselves. Our examples have documented that in multicultural large groups the confrontation with members of foreign nations and cultures, and as a consequence also the 'political' perspective, inevitably plays a prominent role and puts a strain on the ability of the participants to cope with conflicts and come to a consensus. This confrontation takes place first on a level which may be described as rather structured, differentiated and reflexive. It is true that the participants know or sense that their communication is subject to constant emotional and more or less unconscious distortions as well as contingent influences. Nevertheless they operate with a prerequisite that is inalienable also for other situations of verbal communication: namely that, should communication make sense at all, then contact with something alien to us – be it a foreign language, a foreign culture, a foreign history – must also be possible through reflection and rationality. Our examples mentioned above may be regarded in this sense as illustrations for the possibility of rational discourse in very large groups.

From the psychoanalytic viewpoint, the confrontation with the stranger and the unknown offers another chance: namely, to acquire an understanding of the 'stranger in us', that is, of the unconscious, deeply engraved elements of our soul, our 'group mind'. This is a second level, which may be apostrophised as archaic, a level representing undifferentiated, regressive and chaotic elements, which, anyway at first sight, seems immune to sociocultural and national peculiarities. The initial stage of a large group and the confrontation of the participants with the authority of the group, as well as with the group conductor, may exemplify this thesis.

A general feeling of dependence, helplessness, emptiness and insecurity marks the initial situation in the large group. In contrast to small groups, the anonymity of the large group impedes personal relationships, individual remarks are in danger of being condemned and mocked by public opinion; conversely, the individual is tempted to place himself in the centre, in order to get the applause of the multitude. The instability and unpredictability of such a situation generates in the participants archaic behaviour patterns with primitive object relations and defence

mechanisms. As our experiences show, the large group is especially susceptible to narcissistic, grandiose fantasies that offer protection against threats
and injuries. Even though the omnipotence fantasies may often be
expressed in ironically mitigated form, nonetheless the group clings to
them. They offer also protection against separation as well as the menacing
disintegration of the group, and produce the illusion of timelessness.

The need for narcissistic and pre-oedipal regression is emphasized by a
number of authors. The propensity for idealisation is considered especially
characteristic for the group, particularly the striving to create an illusory
world in which all are 'equal'. As Anzieu (1984) stresses, above all the
denial of differences between the sexes and of castration anxiety reinforces
this illusion. The group procreates itself with the help of grandiose
fantasies, thus feeling omnipotent and self-sufficient, it styles itself as the
ideal maternal breast. Chasseguet-Smirgel's (1984) broadening of Freud's
concept of mass psychology (1921) appears noteworthy. In contrast to
Freud's idea that the ego ideal represents the longing for the male leader,
she asserts a deeper, more archaic longing of the members of the groups
and masses, the yearning for the Great Mother (cf. Neumann 1972),
through whom primary narcissistic illusions should be fulfilled in an hal-
lucinatory manner.

Kernberg (1989) accentuates the tendency of the large group to
promote conformity. He claims that the conventional mass culture in
western societies promotes relatively mild forms of regression compared to
totalitarian societies. Large groups are inclined towards the formation of
illusions in order to fight anxieties and threats. An essential illusion is the
belief that the group is uniform and homogeneous, thus offering
protection and security for the individual who is a constituent part of it.
Identification with the state, the party or a church offers such narcissistic
gratifications as successors of the childhood family. According to
Kernberg the large group threatens the individual identity, compensates
for it, however, through an increase in the feeling of power. In contrast, a
deeper regression impairs the perception of reality; the super-ego is poorly
integrated and shows primitive forms of super-ego precursors. Simultaneously, primitive sexual and aggressive instinctual tendencies are
manifested.

Pierre Turquet (1975) makes out the main feature of the large group in
identity diffusion, originating in the fear of one's own loss of control and
the fear of the aggression of the other participants. Members of the large

group who are able to assert their individuality are envied and attacked, differentiations are denied and individuation is prevented. Thinking in platitudes is favoured, which creates the illusion of equality and serves as a defence against the feared rivalry and aggression.

The struggle with authority referred to above is an important step in the development of the large group, which marks the transition from trust in the caring and sheltering mother towards confrontation with the father, or, in other words, from the pre-oedipal to the oedipal level. The dependence on the group conductor not infrequently leads to his veneration, and nurtures hopes that order will be created out the chaos by virtue of his omnipotence, and that the bewilderment of the passions will be tamed. When the conductor fails to gratify this longing for security, aggressions are mobilised against him or are projected into external enemies or scapegoats.

The problem of authority

The confrontation with the group conductor as embodiment of social norms and public morals is a predominant feature of group experience. Other than the small group, which follows the family pattern of rebellion against the oedipal father, the large group represents the clan or society, in which the rebellion against authority stands for the generational conflict. The group conductor turns into the tyrannical ruler who indirectly symbolises the mythical primal father in Freud's *Totem and Taboo* (1913). Patricide and subsequent remorse stood, according to Freud's famous theory, at the onset of human cultural development. This development recurs in the oedipal conflict of the child through the setting up of the super-ego and the consequent taboos of murder and incest. In the large group, this process recurs with the rebellion against the group conductor, symbolising his elimination, and the subsequent remorse and submission to social norms.

This advance in the group process does not, however, come about smoothly, since the basic ambivalence towards the group authority contains enormous conflict potential, and makes the necessary subjugation under the reality principle appear fragile. Since the reality of the group is often experienced as unpleasurable and fearful, situations arise in which the participants behave like an unstable mass in situations of political crisis and follow those group members who offer simple solutions for complex problems of the group, like the persecution of scapegoats, who are blamed for the difficulties of the group. The group is especially prone to following seductive leaders, if the conductor's reserved and reticent behaviour frustrates it. Long periods of silence may indicate the presence of unsolvable conflicts in the group. In such situations, proposals are occasionally made by defiant members to escape the unbearable situation by leaving the room or by having a good time. In such cases the group finds itself involved in a loyalty conflict between the group conductor with his taxing demands of facing the group's problems, and the seducer, promising a pleasurable alternative to the group's discomfort. Such fake or alternative leaders lure the group away from an arduous solution of its difficulties towards a regression to primitive stages of instinctual gratification, with which the archaic forces win over reason.

To sum up, in analytic large groups the simultaneity of political, that is, of historically and socioculturally very divergent action patterns, as well as of archaic, uniform psychological kinds of behaviour is especially striking. On the one hand, transcultural large group gatherings may be labelled as miniature societies, in which heterogeneous forms of origin, socialization and philosophy are reflected, and which are also perceived with this diversity more or less consciously by the participants. On the other hand, it seems as if certain unconscious forms of coping with conflicts recur with strict regularity, or repeatedly follow the same basic psychological patterns. Beside the authors mentioned, Freud above all made momentous contributions, particularly in *Totem and Taboo* (1913) and in *Group Psychology and the Analysis of the Ego* (1921), which we can only touch upon here.

Freud's tendency to classify the psychic residues of humanity's prehistoric period as hereditary, is, however, not unproblematic, since it favours the notion of the unconscious as part of our biological heritage, i.e. it does not take into account that the unconscious itself is subject to social and historic influences. Mario Erdheim (1982) speaks in this sense of the 'social production of unconsciousness'. If, however, we are to perceive the unconscious as an historic category, then the differentiation that we have undertaken – for methodical reasons – between the culturally determined political and the psychological as determined by our natural disposition, becomes problematic. In fact, all experience teaches a fundamental dialectic between conscious as well as preconscious political and unconscious psychological processes. This correlation could be confirmed by the example of the initially mentioned social change in the western countries. The tendency towards globalisation and the endeavours in the direction of unifying Europe, in the wake of which economic uncertainty and threats to identity emerged, left their mark also in our large groups. They had the consequence that the rebellious, 'oedipal' confrontations within the group and with the group conductor that were nearly ubiquitous during the 1970s and early 1980s gradually lost their provocative character. The narcissistic retreat into the individual and private sphere did not supersede entirely the 'archaic' confrontation with the group authority, but the enactment of this confrontation followed ways that were drawn socially and economically.

In this sense, transcultural large groups are an excellent medium for the psychoanalytical illumination of communication patterns which are political in a wide sense of the term, and simultaneously for applying psychoanalytic concepts in a contemporary socio-political frame of reference, or – to put it differently – for linking the interactions and the intertwining of the political and the intrapsychic in an exquisitely experimental field.

References

Anzieu, D. (1984) *The Group and the Unconscious.* London: Routledge and Kegan Paul.

Ardjomandi, M. E., Dally, A. and Kü hnY. (1995) 'Und plötzlich war die Mauer weg... – Die "Wiedervereinigte Großgruppe" in der psychotherapeutischen Klinik.' *Gruppenanalyse 1*, 97–113.

Arendt, H. (1958) *The Human Condition.* University of Chicago Press.

Chasseguet-Smirgel, J. (1984) *The Ego Ideal.* New York: Norton.

Erdheim, M. (1982) *Die gesellschaftliche Produktion von Unbewußtheit.* Frankfurt: Suhrkamp.

Freud, S. (1913) *Totem and Taboo.* Standard Edition XIII.

Freud, S. (1921) *Group Psychology and the Analysis of the Ego.* Standard Edition XVIII.

Kernberg, O. F. (1989) 'The temptations of conventionality.' *International Review of Psycho-Analysis 16*, 191–205.

Neumann, E. (1972) *The Great Mother.* Princeton University Press.

Shaked, J. (1994) 'Die analytische Großgruppe – ein Experiment in Massenpsychologie.' In W. Knauss and U. Keller (eds) *9th European Symposium in Group Analysis: 'Boundaries and Barriers.'* Heidelberg: Mattes Verlag.

Turquet, P. (1975) 'Threats to identity in the large group.' In L. Kreeger (ed) *The Large Group: Dynamics and Therapy.* London: Constable.

CHAPTER 10

The Large Group
and the Organization

Joseph Triest

The following anecdote is brought by Watzlawick *et al.* (1979) in *Change*: during the French Revolution, a young army officer was ordered to evacuate – by any means and at any cost – an agitated crowd from the central square. 'If the mobsters refuse to leave, do not hesitate to shoot them,' came the order. The officer, quite shocked, went to the square and found there a large box he could stand on: 'Distinguished ladies and gents,' he shouted, 'I was given orders to evacuate this square from mobsters. I beseech you, distinguished ladies and gents, to leave this place at once so that I could disperse the mob without injuring any of you.' A few moments later, the square was empty.

One might argue that it is one of the mob's traits that it never knows that it is a mob; but it may also be argued that something in the officer's respectful address really did turn the mob, for a moment at least, into 'distinguished ladies and gents.' 'Mobness' will be discussed here as a dynamic state, a type of chaotic and impulsive group mentality, and not as a socio-economic status. I wish to argue that the dialectic tension between the officer – a representative of the establishment – and the mob is an accurate representation of the linkage between the 'large group' and the organization.

The large group dynamics – the drive/structure point of view

The foundations for the discussion of any interrelationship between the 'large group' and the organization were laid in Freud's classical article 'Group psychology and the analysis of the ego' (1921), which deals with the transformation the individual psychology goes through when individuals gather and form a group. Freud did not initially intend to focus in this article on group processes, but rather, on the exploration of the unconscious; the group turned out to be a surprisingly fertile and useful framework in the service of proving the existence of the unconscious. In the chapter dealing with the behavior of the group, Freud mainly relies on French psychologist and sociologist Le Bon (1895), whose observations led Freud to the following conclusions: under the aegis of the anonymity provided by the group, the individual quickly sheds the outfit of culture in which he is imprisoned in discontent, releases his brakes, rises against his super-ego and lets loose his instinctual (sexual or aggressive) wishes. Since Le Bon's plastic descriptions are among the most vivid existing documentations of a large group behavior, they are well worth quoting directly.

> The most striking peculiarity presented by a psychological group is the following. Whoever be the individuals that compose it, however like or unlike be their mode of life, their occupations, their character or their intelligence, the fact that they have been transformed into a group puts them in possession of a sort of collective mind which makes them feel, think, and act in a manner quite different from that in which each individual of them would feel, think and act were he in a state of isolation. (Le Bon 1895, pp.72–73)[1]

Le Bon describes the change that occurs in an individual when he becomes part of the group:

> the disappearance of the conscious personality, the predominance of the unconscious personality, the turning by means of suggestion and contagion of feelings and ideas in an identical direction, the tendency to immediately transform the suggested ideas into acts; these, we see, are the principal characteristics of the individual forming part of a group. He is no longer himself, but has become an automaton who has ceased to be guided by his will. (p.76)

By the mere fact that he forms part of an organized group, a man descends several rungs in the ladder of civilization. Isolated, he may be a cultivated individual; in a crowd, he is a barbarian — that is, a creature acting by instinct. He possesses the spontaneity, the violence, the ferocity and also the enthusiasm and heroism of primitive beings. (p.77)

A group is impulsive, changeable and irritable. It is led almost exclusively by the unconscious.[2] The impulses which a group obeys may according to circumstances be generous or cruel, heroic or cowardly, but they are always so imperious that no personal interest, not even that of self-preservation, can make itself felt. Nothing about it is premeditated [...] It cannot tolerate any delay between its desire and the fulfillment of what it desires. It has the sense of omnipotence; the motion of impossibility disappears for the individual in a group. (p.77)

A group is extraordinarily credulous and open to influence, it has no critical faculty, and the improbable does not exist for it. It thinks in images, which call one another up by association (just as they arise in individuals in states of free imagination), and whose agreement with reality is never checked by any reasonable agency. The feelings of a group are always very simple and very exaggerated. So that a group knows neither doubt nor uncertainty. (p.78)

It goes directly to extremes; if a suspicion is expressed, it is instantly changed into an incontrovertible certainty; a trace of antipathy is turned into furious hatred. (p.78)

Inclined as it itself is to all extremes, a group can only be excited by an excessive stimulus [...] Since a group is in no doubt as to what constitutes truth or error, and is conscious, moreover, of its own great strength, it is as intolerant as it is obedient to authority. It respects force and can only be slightly influenced by kindness, which it regards merely as a form of weakness. What it demands of its heroes is strength, or even violence. It wants to be ruled and oppressed and to fear its masters. (pp.78–79)

The phenomenon we shall focus upon in this discussion is the large group's ability to generate, as cohesion is formed, what we might best describe as an 'atomic fusion' which disrupts the individual's intrapsychic balance and causes a twofold regression; a 'vertical–topographic' regression, caused by a breach of structural boundaries and expressed by a flooding of the 'conscious' (and pre-conscious) by the unconscious, and a 'horizontal regression,' on the separation–individuation axis, which 'melts down' the boundaries between self-representations and object-representations, leading to the loss of individuality in a group, the dropping of interpersonal barriers and a unity of affect and behavior. Being engulfed by the crowd allows individuals to escape social alienation or ostracism, which is in itself good enough reason, apparently, for them to let their drives loose. But they still have to overcome the super-ego's threats; which they do thanks to the fact that feeling 'part' of a group affords them the (often brief) illusion of power and 'ownership' on the society whose interdictions they have had to internalize; the individual would not miss such a golden opportunity to hush up that society's internalized representative, namely, his/her *inner* societal supervisor.

The large group and the leader's role

The neutralization of the super-ego's authority is mainly attributed to the quasi-hypnotic influence of the group leader. Through his/her 'charisma' the leader evokes in his/her subjects such identification that every subject's private and unique 'ego ideal' is converted to or replaced by a unitary 'group ego ideal' in the leader's own image. But the group itself plays an active role in this conversion, as groups have an *a priori* willingness to admire, and indeed adore, the leader, to exalt him/her and depreciate themselves before him/her. One reason is that group situations arouse in the individual an archaic memory originating from the dawn of the history of mankind: the gathering of the primitive horde facing the primordial father, whose repressed memory is still dreadful and awe-inspiring. Any grouping process generates a phenomenon of universal transference, which revives in the hearts of the group members the primordial father's castrating tyranny, as well as the memory of the primordial sin of patricide, immortalized and inscribed in the form of a taboo.

The relation between the large group and its leaders is therefore described as a balance of terror. Every leader automatically takes the primordial father's empty seat. The group projects onto him the power of the multitude and thus deifies him; after turning its leader into a god the group wishes to lie in his shadow and receive his protection. But at the same time the group is filled with dread and hatred for the leader, and feels frustration over its submission to a tyrant whom it has created for itself through the sheer power of imagination. Now the group gathers again in order to eliminate the leader (concretely or symbolically), but since the people's leader is also the people's symbolic representative, assassination does not only physically eliminate the leader but also eliminates the links between the group members. It is an act of murdering the existing social order, which is replaced by anarchy. The oedipal conflict, seen this way, inherently includes constant tension between chaos and order, organization (even if it is nothing but a primitive horde with its leader) and disorganization (crowd, mob).

Regression is explained, from this perspective, in terms of the drive model, as a consequence of two quite different elements of experience: on the one hand, the 'pleasure principle' (Freud 1911), which is associated with the liberation of sexual and aggressive drives, alongside an 'oceanic' feeling (Freud 1930) related to the fusion with the large group and identification with the venerated father; and, on the other hand, castration anxiety deriving from fear of the aggressive conflict with the omnipotent leader's tyranny, from which the members of the group – or organization – flee to regressive and pre-oedipal phases.

The organized group

But is regression a universal phenomenon? Is it characteristic of any group whatsoever? Freud, quoting McDougall (1920), thinks not. This, he says, is a description fitting only an unorganized crowd; but a group whose members identify with the group's goals and acknowledge its boundaries, a group that maintains historic and temporal continuity, defines inner roles, hierarchies, conventions and communication procedures, and inscribes laws, norms and traditions, *no longer exists – nor can it be considered as – a 'mob' or a 'crowd,' but in fact becomes an organization*. In this case, regression is held down and 'mobness' does not find any raw or crude expression.

True as it may sound, and contrary to what seems to be implied by McDougall's argument against Le Bon, I do not think that an organization is just another type of group, nor, alternatively, that it cancels out the dynamic of a 'large group' and thus ends its regressive tendencies. Rather, an organization traps the 'group spirit,' like a genie in a bottle, and by so doing in fact preserves an eternal tension, such as that which exists between the waves and the shoreline: the former ever attempt to erode the latter, and as it has no proper maintenance or support, they are bound to succeed sooner or later. The large group will always threaten the setting imposed upon it by the organization, although it is naturally dependent upon that setting for its existence. Only thus can the impulsiveness and instinctuality underlying any group be tapped into and become a mental power source generating life-energy for social and cultural processes.

The object relations point of view

The inherent tension between Le Bon's regressive group and McDougall's organization has found its way into Bion's theorization (1961); for what is a 'work group' if not an 'organized group' that recognizes and acknowledges reality and its own boundaries (as expressed in Bion's definition of the 'primary task'), a group capable of rational thinking and able to coordinate mental efforts for the sake of problem resolution and decision-making processes? And what is a 'basic assumptions group' if not a miniature regressive 'crowd' who fears reality and takes its strength from the world of fantasy, where wishes can come true and anxiety-evoking problems can be resolved by omnipotent means and solutions?

Formulated by Bion in terms of the object relations model, the regression of the group receives new meaning: Bion follows the group from a Kleinian perspective, far into the pre-oedipal realms (Klein 1935, 1945) and into the earliest and most primary phases of the mother–infant relationship. At this level of organization the notion of object–subject separation is dissolved, so as to form the illusion that the group does not consist of autonomous individuals but is an entity of its own 'in the mind' (Armstrong 1991), a sort of whole that is larger than the sum of its elements. The mechanisms of splitting and projection then allow one to see the group as a part object, detached – persecutory or benign – but in any event one whose existence is ostensibly independent of the people who in fact form the group. It can therefore be used as a 'toilet-breast,' that is, one that individuals suckle and feed from, fuse with, or onto which project all that the self refuses to own; this process is what eventually forms the group mentality. In this spirit, a group of 'paranoid-schizoid' phase (Klein 1935) 'little Red Riding Hoods' could fear and despise the 'bad wolf,' while being completely oblivious to the 'bad wolf' within each of them; differently put, despise the 'organization' even though all of its members are 'quite charming.'

The object relations model sees regression in the group as necessary and inevitable, deriving from the individual's innate and survival-related need to relate to others. Stephen Saravay (1975) suggests the following idea: every new relation is assimilated into an *a priori* matrix of internalized object relations perceived as relevant to the new relation. A primary matrix is formed via the internalization of archaic object relations, endowing it with the status of prototype matrix (or, one might say, 'prototype *patrix*') which is progressively enriched and added to as the individual acquires new knowledge and creates new relations (excluding states of traumatic fixation). When the individual wishes to relate to such a multifaceted and identity-ambiguous entity as a group, he finds himself in need of a pattern that would allow him to overcome abandonment and annihilation anxiety by forming a strong and immediate emotional and instinctual link, even at the expense of object differentiation. A matrix of primary mother–infant relations is naturally suggested as the most appropriate for the task in hand. The group is thus unconsciously identified with the mother's body, and its members develop a regressive dependence upon it, by virtue of which the group is perceived as either a 'good' feeding and nourishing breast, or a 'bad' abandoning and persecutory one. But in fact the latter option is more plausible. Turquet (1975), in a thought-provoking definition, suggests that a large group can be defined as a grouping of people which can never be fully contained in a single person's field of vision (that is to say, at any given moment there will always be people behind me whom I cannot see). This is, no doubt, a sure recipe for paranoia; no wonder, then, that group members make every possible mental effort, and cling onto any possible solution, to save themselves from disappearing (cf. Le Bon's 'disappearance of conscious personality' (1895, p.76)). Any of the following strategies: looking for an authority figure for dependency; fighting just for the sake of fighting; fleeing just for the sake of fleeing; 'pairing' in order to create a couple who will give birth to a new 'Messiah' and thus provide magic salvation for the group (Bion 1961); regressing to a narcissistic state of 'me-ness' (Lawrence *et al.* 1996); fusing with the whole (one-ness) as a defense against loneliness and abandonment (Turquet 1974); or 'schizoid' entrenchment in the status of a singleton (Turquet 1975) avoiding attachment or relation – is better than facing the great dread of annihilation and total disappearance of identity and self-knowledge.

Regression, then, according to Bion and Saravay, is inevitable and always occurs as a result of attachment efforts aiming to provide some protection from an anxiety-arousing reality that chases the group into the realm of fantasy, a schizo-paranoid world. But there (as with the gods of Hanna Green's psychotic refuge in *I Never Promised you a Rose Garden* (1964), who gradually turn into figures even more persecutory than the real objects in her world) the group faces the anxiety of annihilation and the total loss of identity, and clings like a drowning person to the primal mother's body, or that which represents her, namely, the parameters of the *setting*. This is naturally experienced as going from bad to worse, since the setting simultaneously represents not only a reality that protects against regression, but also the causes of the anxiety which led to the regression in the first place.

Self experience in the large group

Finally, a self psychology perspective (Kohut 1974, 1977) provides us with additional insight into the causes for regression in groups. In order to form an identity, the group must satisfy the developmental need of each of its members – the need to be reflected in it (in the object) as in a benign mirror. Any deprivation in this area will prevent the individual from developing the experience of a coherent, cohesive and integrative self. In other words, the group is supposed to serve as self-object, by providing its members with mirroring and idealization. The larger the group, the more vague and ambiguous the mirroring or reflection it returns to its members will be. Indeed, a 'large group' is a 'faceless mother' (Turquet 1975), and it is hard to imagine a more bizarre and awe-inspiring mirror for the baby's own reflection in his mother's eyes (Winnicott 1971). So this is where the empathic failure of any group or organization lies, since a group or organization cannot provide for its members that unique and exclusive place they need, which would facilitate regression to chaotic states.

Interrelationship between the organization and the large group

The organization, as a structure, therefore arouses ambivalence by its very nature: on the one hand it is 'called' by the 'large group' to provide it with a 'safety railing' against regression via the parameters of the setting it offers; but on the other hand, its laws, which are by nature impersonal, its task that requires reality testing, its teams which are based on differentiation and separation, its hierarchies – all entail some sort of narcissistic injury, and might be experienced as a limitation of freedom, as alienation, exclusion, persecution and engulfment.

Splitting mechanisms are then activated against the organization, and the setting is constantly attacked directly and indirectly (there is nothing people like more than hating the organization to which they belong). Such split situations make the individual choose between one of two possible and well-known extremes: either to identify with the organization as an alienated, mechanistic and non-human object, and so become a 'small part in a big machine' who only follows orders and instructions, even if such actions involve immoral, unthinkable and unacceptable cruelties and atrocities; or to rebel, to destroy the organization or to be persecuted by it, like Kafka's Joseph K. or Charlie Chaplin in *City Lights*.

Let us now consider three brief examples illustrating the underground 'volcanic' activity of the dynamic of a large group in the organization. The first example illustrates the attack on the organization's *primary task*; the second example illustrates the attack on the *system's boundaries*; and the third example relates to the way the organization uses the persons it has chosen to run the organization, that is, its *authority figures*.

1. Attack on the organization's objectives and 'primary task'

The weakness of McDougall's argument is illustrated by the historic example of the Third Reich. By any standard, the Third Reich was not a 'crowd' but indeed an 'organization' par excellence, and a highly efficient one. But its trajectory and its ideology were totally psychotic, and all of Le Bon's parameters can be used to describe it. How should we understand this? We might say that in this case, the psychotic processes characteristic of the 'large group' took over the definitions of the organization's goals, its 'primary task.' But attributing the concept of madness to Hitler's reign does not account for the entire phenomenon. For instance, it does not account for the German people's willingness to accept this sort of leadership, unless because it was expressive in some ways of its hidden and unconscious wishes. The fact that an organization manages to maintain all of the vital parameters required to turn a crowd into an organization does not ensure, therefore, a sublimatory channeling of the large group's drive-derivative behavior.

2. Attack on the organization's boundaries: a culture of lateness

Lateness is one of the most common patterns by which the 'large group' attacks the organization's structure and authority. Lateness has a 'domino effect' – every person who is late influences another person, who will also be late. But it has another advantage, as in this pattern the first domino block, 'patient alpha,' the cause of all causes, always remains anonymous; lateness could therefore really be described in terms of 'terrorism,' a subversive but well camouflaged attack on organizational order. A complex network of unconscious, condensed and encrypted communication is created around lateness. The organization's members develop various apologetic ceremonies, much in the spirit of Eric Berne's *Games People Play* (1964), the objective of which is, in this case, to 'launder' guilt. Even if the person who is late provides a totally credible and indeed true explanation for his lateness (they usually don't), and even if the lateness was really caused by this or that *force majeure*, the rite of confession and apology is still in force and will nevertheless be used for its designed purpose – to replace a true guilt with a false one. But what is that true guilt? In our perspective, the true guilt is related to the large group's unconscious hatred of the organization on which it depends, and whose authority it is forced to accept. This is why – regardless of whether the latecomer is forgiven and assured that he is still loved, despite having been 'bad,' or is punished by the archaic authority – an instinctual discharge has been achieved. But more than anything else, lateness is a sort of declaration of freedom, a promise of 'stolen moments' of privacy, which the individual manages to expropriate from the organization and from his or her own role in it.

3. Attack on authority – and the use of leaders and nominations

One of the central and more emotionally charged issues in organizations is that of the processes by which position holders are chosen. Although the best option would be to nominate the candidate who is most qualified for the job, what really happens in many organizations is that such decisions are often influenced by unconscious and irrelevant considerations, which are presented as 'rational' but in fact are nothing but rationalizations.

The following example relates to the election of Israel's prime minister on the 5th May 1999 elections. After all, democracy and its various agencies are a clear attempt to organize a crowd, so that it can function as a decision-making body while ensuring for its individual members freedom of thought and freedom of speech.

The said elections took place in one of the most difficult periods in the history of the State of Israel, when the Israeli public was torn and fragmented on the question of Israel's right to occupy the territories it conquered during the Six Day War, and at a time when suicide and other terrorist bomb attacks threatened personal safety so much that no normal life was possible. The prime ministerial candidate, Ariel Sharon, came from the opposition, and had strongly attacked all of Israel's previous prime ministers, regardless of their political views and whether they came from the same right-wing political party as himself (representing a harsh and more aggressive political stance on the Israeli–Palestinian conflict), or from the left (representing a calmer, more peaceful political platform). The slogan used for Sharon's campaign was 'Sharon will bring peace and security';[3] but on no public occasion was it ever clarified or explained how the prime minister intended to reach his objectives. This, however, was no mere coincidence; the election campaign managed by the candidate's consultants was in fact based on hiding him as much as possible from the public eye (e.g. in interviews in the media) and on blurring as much as possible his political and diplomatic platform. This strategy turned out to be well founded and based on a good understanding of the Israeli mass spirit, since the Israeli public acted as if it really did not care to be confused by knowing the facts. The wish 'not to know' was used to allow Sharon's voters to 'create him each in their own image.' Proponents of peace could imagine him as a peacemaker, whereas right-wing voters could imagine him as a war hero. Both sides did seem quite united, however, in their wish to leave to their leader the impossible task of coping on his own with reality and providing magical salvation for the impossible dire straits the two sides have created for themselves.

The way the organization uses (Winnicott 1969) its leaders is distinctly different from the way the 'large group' uses its leaders. In a 'work group' situation, group members understand that the leader's responsibility does not exempt them from taking personal responsibility. But this is not the case with a 'crowd dynamic.' The crowd or mob is not interested in reality. Its leader is idealized as long as he can provide magical salvation. He is 'assassinated' (abandoned, devalued, shot in the central square) once they feel he has let them down. The organizational mechanisms of Israeli democracy failed to prevent Ariel Sharon's election as prime minister of his voters' fantasy world.

Summary

In conclusion, there is a constant dialectic tension between the organization, which offers 'order,' and the 'large group,' which is a boiling caldron of chaos. The organization provides holding and containment, and serves as a defense against chaos. It gives group members an 'anchor' to hold on to and stop regression, prevents the blurring out of boundaries, blocks the desire for fusion and requires that each and every member assumes personal responsibility and acknowledges 'ownership' over all parts of the self – including those parts which are repressed and hated; but at the same time it also restricts the individual's freedom of wish fulfillment and pleasure. Constant maintenance of the 'organization' is therefore required to counter attempts on the part of the 'large group' to disrupt its systems and to take over its mechanisms.

Notes

1.   The page numbers of Le Bon's work, translated into English, are those cited in Freud's article.

2.   'Unconscious' is used here correctly by Le Bon in the descriptive sense, where it does not mean only the 'repressed' (Freud 1921 p.77, fn 2).

3. One must note that in the Israeli idiolect, 'peace and security' are taken as almost diametrically opposed concepts; proponents of 'peace' support the idea of evacuating the settlements and retreating from the occupied territories, whereas 'security' is identified with the need to hold on to the occupied territories and to deepen the military occupation even more.

References

Armstrong, D. (1991) *The 'Institution in the Mind': Reflection on the relation of Psychoanalysis to Work Institutions.* London: Grubb Institute.

Berne. E. (1964) *Games People Play.* New York: Grove Press.

Bion, W. (1961) *Experiences in Groups.* London: Tavistock Publications.

Freud, S. (1911) 'Formulations on the two principles of mental functioning.' *Standard Edition 12,* 218–226.

Freud, S. (1921) 'Group psychology and the analysis of the ego.' *Standard Edition 18,* 65–143.

Freud, S. (1930) 'Civilization and its discontents.' *Standard Edition 21,* 59–145.

Green. H. (1964) *I Never Promised You a Rose Garden.* Holt, Rinehart and Winston Inc. To Harcourt Brace, Orlando, Florida.

Klein, M. (1935) 'A Contribution to the psychogenesis of manic-depressive states.' *International Journal of Psycho-Analysis 16,* 145–174.

Klein, M. (1945) 'The Oedipus complex in the light of early anxieties.' *International Journal of Psycho-Analysis 26,* 11–33.

Kohut, H. (1974) *The Analysis of the Self.* New York: International University Press.

Kohut, H. (1977) *The Restoration of the Self.* New York: International University Press.

Lawrence, W. G., Bain, A. and Gould, L. (1996) 'The fifth basic assumption.' *Free Associations 6/1, 37,* 28–55.

Le Bon, G. (1895) *Psychologie des Foules.* Paris. [Translation: *The Crowd: A Study of the Popular Mind.* London 1920].

McDougall, W. (1920) *The Group Mind.* London: Cambridge University Press.

Saravay, S. M. (1975) 'Group psychology and the structural theory: A revised psychoanalytic model of group psychology.' *Journal of American Psychoanalytic Association 23,* 69–89.

Turquet, P. (1974) 'Leadership: the individual and the group.' In G. S. Gibbard, J. J. Hartman, and R. D. Mann (eds) *Analysis of Groups.* San Francisco: Jossey-Bass.

Turquet, P. (1975) 'Threats to identity in the large group.' In L. Kreeger (ed) *The Large Group.* London: Karnac Books.

Watzlawick, P., Weakland, J. H. and Fisch, R. (1979) *Change.* Palo Alto: Mental Research Institute.

Winnicott, D. W. (1969) 'The use of an object.' *International Journal of Psycho-Analysis 50,* 711.

Winnicott, D. W. (1971) *Playing and Reality.* London: Tavistock Publications.

CHAPTER 11

The In-patient Large Group Meeting

Rolf Schmidts

All groups have their own distinctive history since they are rooted, in all their shapes and forms, in a meaningful period of time which can be exactly determined and which is often narrated in a founding myth (Schmidts und Sandermann 2001).

For a therapeutic science such as psychotherapy, an image of man, methodically inevitable and content-determined, must assume 'the indivisibility of human beings and their relationships in the sense of a synergistic, dialectical principle' (Burbiel 1997, p.148). In his paper 'Theoretical aspects of milieu therapy,' Ammon (1959) establishes the transition from self-regulation, in the sense of Hartmann's psychology of self, to group interactions in formal milieu therapy treatment. He formulates much later: 'Group relations integrate people, their individuality separates them from the group' (Ammon 1982, p.11). At about the same time, he conceptualizes the 'social energy, i.e. the psychic energy that is generated in interpersonal contacts and functions as the mediator between individuals and the group' (Ammon 1982, p.15; Schmidts 1999).

The relation between groups and individuals

Malcolm Pines writes similarly in his paper 'There is something more — some ways in which group analysis heals: moments of meeting': 'The feeling of empathy allows one to share fear, sorrow and joy with others and yet to experience oneself as separate from others' (Pines 2001, p.163–164). This 'model of a jointly designed regulation pattern' corresponds to an 'open system theory which permits changes and actualizations with others and between others.' He emphasizes the importance of communication processes as a basic force for bringing about change in group analysis, and leaves the previous model of an object-relations theory behind according to Foulkes' paper 'Concerning criticism of inner-object theory' (1975).

In their paper 'Large groups from a sociological point of view,' Earl Hopper and Anne Weyman (1977) also consider the 'dichotomy between society and individuals' (p.155) and between human beings to be an abstraction. In contrast to this critical statement, they nevertheless refer to a 'primary and deliberate inner decision' (p.155) that must ensure cohesion, similar to the 'invisible hand' (Adam Smith) that, from the outside only, puts an end to Hobbes' selfish war waged by everyone against everyone else.

Implicitly, Christian Schwarz's (1994) criticism also attacks this point. He reproaches Pierre Turquet with having developed 'a phenomenology of threatened identities in large groups with relentless Kleinian single-mindedness' (Turquet 1977): 'What we experience here…is the descent into hell of the mass individual who is denied acting out the basic assumption of dependence' (Schwarz 1994, p.249). For this reason, the 'mass individual' can only defend itself against the large group by reacting as a 'singleton' (Turquet 1977). Not even the possibility of creative regression in the service of the ego remains open to him, as it was worked out by E. Kris (1952). It follows that only splitting mechanisms such as projective identification, paranoia and schizoid reactions, as well as depressions, can guarantee his/her autonomy.

A different perspective can only be found if one considers a person to be not only unique, but also, for that very reason, an integral whole in herself. In her explanation of Ammon's personality model, Burbiel (1997) explains that 'in his teaching, wholeness is something determined not only by its parts,' but ultimately by their 'structural coherence.' The term 'multi-dimensionality' of human beings (Ammon 1986), as applied not only to individuals, but also to groups combines and separates the various ego or 'human functions' of the members of a group.

Regression in the service of the group

The term 'regression' has never been conclusively defined in psychoanalytic literature, and so increasingly, specifically forms of regression in groups can be observed and call for new concepts. Hence, Ohlmeier (1975) spoke of regression in the service of groups, and went on to suggest that the function of individuals as speakers for the unified whole should be understood in the sense of a primary reciprocity of people in a group. Rafael Springmann, in his 'Psychotherapy in large groups' (Springmann 1977), reports that the therapeutic atmosphere clearly improved 'in a general assembly of patients and staff members with reciprocal feedback' (p.205), which facilitated the open treatment of patients to a large extent.

We also consider regressive phenomena in large groups to be more of a progressive development, typical for large groups, that starts out from an archaic level of functioning in the sense of the basic assumptions group. By means of group-dynamic work on the emotional networking of individuals, this development leads to a coherence of the entire group, making it strong in the sense of 'containment' (Bion 1971) and capable of dealing with conflict in the sense of being willing to change. Pines (2001) emphasizes that, beyond semantic and procedural thinking, there was an 'implicit relational knowledge' that was equivalent to wholeness or could be expressed in the sentence: 'There is something more than interpretation' (p.164).

In 1969 the German Group Psychotherapeutic Society was founded by Ammon, and its first international symposium on 'Psychoanalytic Group Psychotherapy' took place near Naples. The symposium tried to follow S. H. Foulkes, who recommended 'reviewing psychoanalytic theory in the light of group-psychotherapy' – an extension of psychology centered on the individual, in the direction of social-psychological approaches. Intellectually, politically and scientifically, the problem of groups, the meaning of aggression, the experience of the stunning power of masses, and the mental structure of new forms of group experience were in the air worldwide. The first postwar generation found and published their common topics. The so-called student movement of 1968 supplied the material for profound and momentous debates. In 'Some autobiographical notes,' Foulkes (1968) reported on the past history of these topics and emphasized how fundamental the experiences in the Northfield military training centre were for developing group psychotherapy and the concept of 'the hospital as a therapeutic community' (Main 1946). Janssen (1987 p.41) summarizes the developments at that time: 'Bion and Foulkes went new ways in group analysis, while Main tried to change the hospital as a therapeutic institution.'

In the article mentioned above, Foulkes also tells us about the visit of the Commission of the Menninger Foundation under the leadership of Karl Menninger in 1946. Ammon reports on the setting up of a psychoanalytic, group-psychotherapeutic program at the Menninger Clinic in 1960. The one-and-a-half-year preparation had been carried out by H. S. Perlmutter, a student of Kurt Lewin, and created a vivid 'awareness of the clinical necessity of the plan' (p.132). Tapping into his experience at the Menninger Foundation, Ammon made great efforts to integrate psychiatry and group dynamics once he was back in Europe, and in 1969 he founded the Institute for Dynamic Psychiatry and Group Dynamics in Berlin. He opened the Day Clinic for Intensive Group Psychotherapy near Passau in 1970/71 and the Clinic for In-patient Psychotherapy and Psychosomatics in Munich in 1975, the latter together with a team of collaborators in which the author played a substantial role. Finally, in 1979, the Dynamic Psychiatric Clinic Menterschwaige – Clinic for In-patient Psychotherapy, Psychoanalysis and Psychosomatics was established in Munich.

Large groups in the therapeutic community of the clinic

Large group sessions were already introduced twice a week for two hours when the first Munich clinic started. They took into account not only the manifestations of illness, but also patients' needs to have their daily living together made more advantageous. Above all, the relationships with therapists and the team of orderlies and nurses, unbalanced as they were because of strong transference manifestations, had to be considered. The idea was to have as many patients as possible attend these large group sessions, as well as the staff on duty at the time, under the central guidance of the head physician or the assistant medical director.

Our practical experience of many years confirms that it is possible to do successful psychotherapeutic work in a large group with about 60 patients and 10 co-workers taking part, especially in considerable emotional and reflexive depth, and with patients who, according to age, education, social status, cultural affiliation and symptoms of illness, are very heterogeneous.

According to Paul Janssen (1987), a clinic involved in psychoanalytic therapy is a social organization that, as a therapeutic community, shows a horizontal democratic structure in the interest of its emancipatory task. To counteract a tendency to ossify which is inherent in any hierarchically structured institution, and to avoid defensive attitudes resulting from change and leading to unimaginativeness and unethical indifference, Janssen recommends reducing social reserve by delegating responsibility step-by-step while observing cohesion and giving security needs as much attention as necessary to achieve a therapeutic atmosphere that makes change possible under such conditions.

According to Lohmer (2000), it is crucial that any organization is able to justify its existence. This is made more difficult because of the ambiguity discernible in the fluctuations between adapting to social expectations and supporting change – therapeutically wanted and socially relevant. To survive in society, an organization must be an open system that communicates with its environment in a regulated manner. According to A. K. Rice (1973), it can only do that if it has a clearly circumscribed 'primary task' and shows clear boundaries within itself as well as in relation to the environment. That is very important, because the leadership is positioned on the boundaries and controls the communication processes across them. That is why the director is the 'central figure' of a group *in statu nascendi* (Redl 1971b). In our opinion, he is obliged to balance the above-mentioned ambivalence. Hence, there is a close connection between defining the director's task and defining the primary task of an organization. In the outside world, the director has to justify the regulations that are necessary between the institution and its environment (e.g. contracts with health insurance companies). He has to ensure the integrity of the organization as well as the continuity of therapeutic goal-setting – tasks whose fulfillment is constantly threatened by internal and external resistance.

J. S. Whiteley (1978), who, according to Janssen, sees the therapeutic community as an ongoing large group, has also described this danger in his paper 'The awkward position of the leader in therapeutic communities and large groups.' His valuable concept of 'focal leadership' seems to offer a solution, in that it lists various aspects of responsible management. Accordingly, what is necessary is:

1. to create an atmosphere of openness

2. to convey an indispensable feeling of security

3. to be willing to perceive the group-dynamic conditions of conflicts and to reintegrate them

4. to grant protective functions in therapeutically meaningful situations where expectations in this regard appear, mainly for reasons of transference, and to accept, at least temporarily, a patient's wish to be dependent

5. to re-establish the connection to reality in a comrehensible way for the parties concerned – in spite of all pathological temptations coming from patients or staff.

The role of the director

As regards large groups, the director is, first of all, the representative of his institution and its embeddedness in society, which he personifies with the reserve appropriate to all institutions with a more or less developed aura of sovereignty. Second, as director, he will adopt a father's protective and a mother's sheltering manner, not only with regard to patients. Third, he will sometimes have to be authoritarian on the basis of his action competence and the resulting commitment to act in accordance with his specialist experience. In such cases, he will take into account the overall assessment that his team and patients give him. Fourth, he is the central figure, especially in view of the large group's psychoanalytic and group-dynamic goals. In this sense, he is a sympathetic observer who encourages spontaneity and attempts to create an atmosphere like Winnicott's 'facilitating environment' and, to that extent, grants freedom of thought.

He observes his role by establishing contact with the most timorous patient who is also the 'speaker of the group,' called the 'boundary person' by Ammon. He helps him find a place in the group or tries to reintegrate him in the case of his dynamically intensified role as a scapegoat. In this way, he provides the 'conditions for developing group boundaries, and only then does the group turn into that interpersonal inner space in which individual group members can design themselves by making creative and constructive contributions to group efforts' (Ammon 1976, p.60).

The director will then speak, depending on the level the group moves at in a given situation, and in a manner appropriate to that situation. He will talk to individuals in the group or to the group as a whole, or start a dialogue between various group members, thus interacting with the group at a great number of different intervention levels.

The place where large groups gather is the largest room in our clinic. It serves other purposes as well – milieu-therapeutic and non-therapeutic. Some architectural peculiarities make it possible to use the room for different events, e.g. theatre and music performances, dance therapy sessions, exhibition openings and celebrations.

According to a tendency existing in psychotherapeutic institutions to this very day, a 'real space' with entirely normal hospital conditions is separated from a 'psychotherapeutic space' in which transference manifestations are allowed (Schmidts 1996). Hence, one could assume that milieu therapy is more likely to represent aspects of reality. Milieu groups, with their focus on a common project, make therapeutic use of actions including constructive abilities and skills in the more nonverbal area of a uniform setting, with the aim of widening their experience and themselves and gaining more self-esteem, whereas large groups depend on communicating messages and contacts mainly through language. Their therapeutic goals are to integrate feeling and thinking and, conversely, thinking and feeling (de Maré 1977) by means of an intensive exchange process and, according to the semantic function of language, to negotiate distinctions and to distinguish relations. They do not want to blur distinctions, but rather to confirm them in their respective right to exist, i.e. in a kind of contact of distinctions, preserving their special qualities and re-delegating individual responsibility for contacts and relationships.

The face-to-face seating plan of large groups, usually in a circle, is prepared by arranging the chairs shortly before the session begins. The group leaders often sit together at the end of the dividing line between the milieu room and the room for large groups, opposite the entrance to the room. One enters it from a staircase that leads to the station rooms. Most of the time, the stairs and the landing are occupied by young people and by paranoid, suspicious, psychotically ill individuals who are easily offended and ready for escape.

Some patients have already gathered at the appointed time. They are scattered all over the circle. A process of making contact with each other in various small groups is taking place, whereas some individuals isolate themselves and, going their solitary ways, sit down on other chairs, appearing to contradict the spontaneous subgroups' wish to have contact. Nevertheless, a first, provisional shape of the group is recognizable.

As a rule, the circle now conveys a volatile atmosphere, often based on a specific attitude. The atmosphere at the beginning, which can be an intense experience, is mostly a feeling of incompleteness like an expanse full of holes, a disharmonious lack of symmetry, an anxious jostling, a suffocating denseness, sometimes the group's urgent wish to escape, or controlled rage and defiance, but also a mood of friendly relaxation. In this manner, large groups constitute themselves as a meaningful public space.

At the beginning, group leaders are highly involved, worrying about the existence and continuity of the large group, and together with the patients, whose numbers are increasing and who still seem to be rather carefree, they rack their brains over how to explain the absence of some group members. In this way, they develop a mental picture of the entire large group which is, in fact, and in contrast to this virtuality, already capable of doing concrete work.

One begins to sense how important those individuals who leave the group in the dark about their whereabouts are for the others. One knows that the 'boundary person' (who meanwhile has turned into the 'counter-leader'), has made the group-building function of an external enemy superfluous, and that his loud expressions of displeasure, supported by the paranoid staircase subgroup and directed against the late beginning of the session (as well as the group leaders, who show absolutely no interest in their patients), will not lead to a termination of his treatment. At this stage, one or the other of the patients begins to take on clearly distinctive roles. These are usually roles that typically correspond to the role dynamics described by Raoul Schindler (1957; 1960), but also more specific roles emphasizing kinds of relationship more clearly, e.g. the role of someone who is worried about a particular individual and wants to help her, or offers his own example as a piece of advice. By thus showing off their social integration in the group, these people gain more self-esteem, as do the others.

At this point, new patients are introduced to the large group. Birthday wishes, educational achievements or success in dealing with authorities can now be properly looked at and appreciated. Discharges are possible now, since some individuals have become increasingly clear about themselves, not only during psychotherapy, but also during the current group process, so that, in the best cases, they have concrete ideas about themselves, their future and the contacts they have maintained or would like to establish. In this way they have learned, in the encounter with others, to separate and detach themselves. In connection with that, the level of the whole group has also changed from the 'basic assumption' level (to cite Bion) to that of a 'working group' which can devote itself to task-solving, or at least make efforts in that direction, with only slight transferences occurring.

Large groups are structures which, according to de Maré (1977), hold up a double mirror to society and, in our case, to the whole organization of the clinic by making visible not only the social behavior of individuals, but also, simultaneously, the behavior of the larger community.

Thus, the large group is at the stage of a goal-oriented work group that is concerned both with therapeutic goals in the narrow sense and with real changes. This is the result of an intense process of communication about emotional contact needs, about split-off desires and fears, phantasies, utopias and dreams, but also the result of objective information regarding concrete changes that were important in the communication process of the meeting. In this manner, a structure emerges encompassing space, meaning, time and topics in a continuum of group processes and identity development in the here-and-now of the group, and leading to broader awareness. De Maré (1977) comments: 'Awareness itself originates in a cognitive process that takes place by associating with others' (p.142).

Subgroups as a resource of change

The subgroups, already mentioned above, are of crucial importance for the phenomenon of the large group and its interactions. In the context of the Tavistock Leicester Research Project, A. K. Rice examined subgroups and their intergroup dynamics. He reported his findings in *Leadership and Group* (1973). Obholzer and Glouberman (2000) demanded that 'not only should the processes in these sub-structures be understood, but it should also be considered what will, or is likely to, flow back from these subgroups to the large group' (p.63). In her definition of the large group, Hanna Zapp (2000) emphasizes the aspect of subgroups and says that, more or less significantly, large groups split up regularly, both formally and informally, into smaller groups, and interact as such.

A large number of subgroups are represented in institutions, e.g. clinics (Schmidts 1997). They are not identical in number with the groups officially named in many psychotherapeutic institutions, e.g. the various verbal and nonverbal therapeutic groups. In addition, there are usually just as many groups in the institution's public area whose importance is linked to various clinical departments and functions. However, the most important ones, in terms of dynamics, are larger and smaller coalitions of patients who hide in the subcultural spaces of the institution and are among those who determine the atmosphere of the entire organization for a long time.

There are, for instance, coalitions of individuals who put up resistance and cross boundaries, of those who are like-minded, or like protesting, secret informers, rumor-producers, grumblers, stubborn arguers and couples who, as lovers, have become immune to therapy.

In 1964 T. H. Mills pointed out that all people are members of various small groups and that the number of groups is much larger than the number of individuals. They are so important, because they constantly eliminate boundaries – thus, in the best of cases, entirely preventing the sclerosis that threatens all institutions, and consequently bringing about change. They create public awareness of the fact that integration is inadequate, which shows in the structure of the entire clinic group and its functional processes.

For instance, a psychotherapy group whose work may, temporarily, not have been analytical enough becomes conspicuous, because the large group develops in a way typical of small groups. If organizational problems are discussed with exhausting insistence, the reason is probably a lack of integration in clinical function areas. This is not always easily recognized, as the following episode shows. When the head physician came back from his vacation, the atmosphere was good and the head physician was pleased to have the large group report, with satisfied complacency, on work done in recent weeks, and to discharge some patients and welcome newcomers. This done, a natural break seemed to indicate the end of the session.

At this point, a young, extremely jealous patient with ADHD began to pull faces and belch excessively. Attempts not to respond to his provocation led to an emotional outburst. An experienced female member of staff thought she had to 'save' the situation. She started to acknowledge the successfully completed project of her milieu group in the usual festive manner, emphasizing the constructive contributions the young patient had made, but at the same time managing to show up the leadership completely.

Both patient and therapist reacted furiously when the leadership expressed its misgivings about inviting guests from other institutions to the celebration prepared for the end of the project, without asking for everyone's agreement and without preparing the event. What obviously mattered to the entire group as well as its protagonist was that boundaries were being blurred. A constructive change occurred once the large group had elected a planning group for the celebration, carefully balanced in its membership between patients and staff.

Exemplary for such results is the process in which, from the twilight of the institution, semi-anarchistic impulses surface from within the subcultural sphere and change, almost of their own accord, into group structures which are authorized by the large group in the context of the large group process. The authorization process itself is part of a therapeutic process. Understanding and accepting are crucial to putting things right; instead of exercising social control and ascribing a judgement of unworthiness, the valuable and meaningful experience of one's own person and the group as a whole become possible, and the confidence that conflicts can be communicated opens up a personal experience of justice.

The large group is, therefore – along with its hitherto emphasized multi-dimensionality and its continuum of space, time, meaning, experience, topics, identity, relationships and thought – an ethical and law-enforcing structure that substantiates a therapeutic culture and makes the experience of relationships possible by integrating and individualizing.

References

Ammon, G. (1959) *Theoretical Aspects of Milieu Therapy*. Topeka: The Menninger Clinic and School of Psychiatry.

Ammon, G. (ed) (1976) *Analytische Gruppendynamik*. Hamburg: Hoffmann & Campe.

Ammon, G. (1982) 'Das sozialenergetische Prinzip in der Dynamischen Psychiatrie.' In G. Ammon (ed) *Handbuch der Dynamischen Psychiatrie Band 2.* Mü nchen,Basel: Ernst Reinhardt.

Ammon, G. (1986) *Der mehrdimensionale Mensch.* M ünchen: Pinel.

Bion, W. R. (1971) *Erfahrungen in Gruppen und andere Schriften.* Stuttgart: Klett. (First published as *Experiences in Groups and Other Papers.* New York: Basic Books, 1961.)

Burbiel, I. (1997) 'Das Humanstrukturmodell.' *Dynamische Psychiatrie 30,* 162–165, 145–153.

Foulkes, S. H. (1968) 'Some autobiographical notes.' *Group Analysis, International Panel and Correspondence 1,* 2, 117–122.

Foulkes, S. H. (1969) 'Kongreß- und andere Nachrichten.' *Dynamische Psychiatrie 2,* 3, 194–200.

Foulkes, S. H. (1990) 'Concerning criticism of inner-object theory.' In S. H. Foulkes (ed) *Selected Papers.* London: Karnac Books. (First published 1975.)

Hopper, E. and Weyman, A. (1977) 'Große Gruppen aus soziologischer Sicht.' In L. Kreeger (ed) *Die Großgruppe.* Stuttgart: Klett. (First published as 'A sociological view of large groups.' In L. Kreeger (ed) *The Large Group.* London: Constable, 1975.)

Janssen, P. L. (1987) *Psychoanalytische Therapie in der Klinik.* Stuttgart: Klett-Cotta.(First published as *Psychoanalytic Therapy in the Hospital Setting.* London: Routledge, 1994.)

Kris, E. (1952) *Psychoanalytic Explorations in Art.* New York: International Universities Press.

Lohmer, M. (2000) 'Das Unbewusste in Unternehmen: Konzepte und Praxis psychodynamischer Organisationsberatung.' In M. Lohmer (ed) *Psychodynamische Organisationsberatung. Konflikte und Potentiale in Veränderungsprozessen.* Stuttgart: Klett-Cotta.

Main, T. F. (1946) 'The hospital as a therapeutic institution.' *Bull Menninger Clinic 10, 66,* 32–37.

Maré, P. de (1977) 'Die Politik großer Gruppen.' In L. Kreeger (ed) *Die Großgruppe.* Stuttgart: Klett. (First published as 'The politics of large groups.' In L. Kreeger (ed) *The Large Group.* London: Constable, 1975.)

Mills, T. H. (1964) 'Authority and group emotions.' In W. G. Bennis, E. H. Schein, D. E. Berlew and F. L. Steel (eds) *Interpersonal Dynamics.* Homewood, Ill.: Dorsey.

Obholzer, A. and Glouberman, S. (2000) 'Bewusstes und Unbewusstes in Großgruppen.' In R. Königswieser and M. Keil (eds) *Das Feuer großäer Gruppen.* Stuttgart: Klett-Cotta.

Ohlmeier, D. (1975) 'Gruppenpsychotherapie und psychoanalytische Theorie.' In A. Uchtenhagen, R. Battegay and A. Friedmann (eds) *Gruppenpsychotherapie und soziale Umwelt.* Bern: Huber.

Pines, M. (2001) 'There is something more – some ways in which group analysis heals: Moments of meeting.' *Dynamische Psychiatrie 34,* 188/89, 155–165.

Redl, F. (1976) 'Gruppenemotion und Fü hrerschaft.' In G. Ammon (ed) *Analytische Gruppendynamik.* Hamburg: Hoffmann und Campe.

Rice, A. K. (1973) *Fü hrungund Gruppe.* Stuttgart: Klett.

Schindler, R. (1957) 'Grundprinzipien der Psychodynamik in der Gruppe.' *Psyche 11*, 5, 308–314.

Schindler, R. (1960) Über den wechselseitigen Einfluß von Gesprächsinhalt, Gruppenposition und Ichgestalt in der analytischen Gruppentherapie.' *Psyche 6*, 382–392.

Schmidts, R. (1996) 'Die Großgruppe in der Dynamischen Psychiatrie.' *Dynamische Psychiatrie 29*, 1–2, 10–17.

Schmidts, R. (1997) 'Die Integration von Untergruppen in die Kultur der Großgruppe der Dynamisch-Psychiatrischen Klinik Menterschwaige.' *Dynamische Psychiatrie 30*, 1–4, 183–193.

Schmidts, R. (1999) 'Das sozialenergetische Prinzip Ammons, Rollendifferenzierung und Austauschprozesse in der klinischen Großgruppenpsychotherapie und anderen Großgruppen. Teil 1: Energetische Prozesse in der Gruppe-Anmerkungen zur Geschichte eines wissenschaftlichen Diskurses.' *Dynamische Psychiatrie 32*, 3–6, 174–182.

Schmidts, R. and Sandermann, G. (2001) 'Mythen, Erzählungen und Geschichten im großgruppen-dynamischen Prozess einer Klausurtagung – zur Integration von Untergruppen.' *Dynamische Psychiatrie 34*, 3–4, 221–238.

Schwarz, C. (1994) 'Kollektiver Narzißmus.' In R. Haubl and F. Lamott (eds) *Handbuch der Gruppenanalyse.* Berlin-Mü nchen: Quintessenz.

Springmann, R. (1977) 'Psychotherapie in der großen Gruppe.' In L. Kreeger (ed) *Die Großgruppe.* Stuttgart: Klett. (First published as 'Psychotherapy in the large group.' In L. Kreeger (ed) *The Large Group.* London: Constable, 1975.)

Turquet, P. (1977) 'Bedrohung der Indentität in der großen Gruppe.' In L. Kreeger (ed) *Die Großgruppe.* Stuttgart: Klett. (First published as 'Threats to identity in the large group.' In L. Kreeger (ed) *The Large Group.* London: Constable, 1975.)

Whiteley, J. S. (1978) 'Die heikle Position des Leiters in therapeutischer Gemeinschaft und Großgruppe.' In H. Hilpert, R. Schwarz and F. Beese (eds) *Psychotherapie in der Klinik.* Berlin, Heidelberg, New York: Springer.

Zapp, H. (2000) 'Rituale und Systeme fü rGroßgruppen in der kirchlichen Tradition.' In R. Königswieser and M. Keil (eds) *Das Feuer großer Gruppen.* Stuttgart: Klett-Cotta.

CHAPTER 12

The Large Group
in a Virtual Environment

Haim Weinberg

Until recently, the common uses of Large Groups in therapeutic settings were in mental hospitals and therapeutic communities, group analytic training studies, conferences, and organizational consultation. In the last ten years, since the Internet has spread out around the world, a new version of the Large Group has emerged: The Large Group in cyberspace. Do these groups present the same phenomena as face-to-face Large Groups? What unique features do these 'virtual' Large Groups acquire? What can we learn from Large Groups in cyberspace about Large Groups in general? The present chapter discusses these interesting and other related questions.

The Internet Large Group

One of the main uses of the Internet is as a medium for communication for people around the world. People 'talk' by sending email, exchanging ideas on discussion lists, forums, and virtual communities or participating in online chats. The difference between chat and other multi-participant modes of communication mentioned above is its synchrony. In chatrooms people must be online at the same time in order to communicate. In discussion lists, forums, and virtual communities, they can send email and retrieve the others' responses at their own convenience. To join a discussion list one just sends a subscription command to the server and is automatically subscribed. From that moment on until signing off, all the messages distributed to list members reach the subscriber's email-box. Discussion lists can contain an unlimited number of participants. This means that theoretically hundreds or even thousands of people can participate in the discussion. Numerically, this makes the list a Large Group.

A practical-structural definition of the Large Group can be, 'any group with such a large number of participants they cannot be encompassed in a single glance'. This makes Internet groups Large Groups by definition because people cannot see one another at all, so the real number of registered members is not important. This definition stresses the importance of seeing everyone in a group. Seeing everyone is essential in order to have the intimacy typical in small group dynamics. Strange enough, this means that any email exchange on the Internet, even between two people, involves some Large Group dynamics. It is possible that when people cannot see all the details, fertile ground for imagination and projection is found.

Before going any further, I want to clarify that I confine my analysis to Internet discussion lists of mental health professionals (especially the group-psychotherapy discussion list based in www.group-psychotherapy.com), and to unmoderated and unstructured Large Groups ('unmoderated', on the Internet, means that no-one controls the flux of information; 'unstructured' means that the group does not have a dictated set of rules). Large Groups can be an important instrument for studying social forces and inter-group relations in society at large. As Pat de Maré (1975) put it, 'the large group…offers us a context and a possible tool for exploring the interface between the polarised and split areas of psychotherapy and sociotherapy. This is the area of the inter-group and of the transdisciplinary, where a crossfire between distinct hierarchical structures…can occur' (p.146). He recommends exploration of 'meetings of the same members over a considerable time, and not simply a sudden short burst of meetings, however "marathon"', as is usually done in conferences or plenary meetings. Discussion lists on the Internet provide such an opportunity. People 'meet' for a prolonged period of time (as long as they are subscribed to the list), exchange ideas, communicate around their field of interest and engage in social interaction. Although these meetings lack the rigorous group-analytic setting, and are not meant to be therapeutic (but neither are Large Groups), we can still learn a lot from them about the dynamics of Large Groups, inter-group interactions, and social conflicts.

The social insight and elucidation of current unconscious social assumptions that de Maré (1975) mentions as developing in Large Groups shows itself clearly in virtual reality.

Belonging to an ongoing Large Group makes a member a citizen of a community. According to many writers (e.g. de Maré *et al.* 1991) developing a sense of citizenship is one of the main tasks of participants of the Large Group. There may be active or passive members of the Large Group, but they all feel a sense of belonging to the group. The degree of involvement in the group, identifying itself by the volume of messages a member sends to the list, changes through time. Sometimes activity level is related to the issue discussed, which might interest certain members but not others. This is a natural result of ongoing groups, whether online or outside the virtual environment. On the other hand, in a Large Group meeting outside cyberspace, people do not have the same competition from external forces i.e. life, since everyone is committed to being in the room and distractions can only be internal. Other causes for changed involvement over time might be the person's priorities. Life commitments compete with members' participation, as it takes time to read and answer the letters. For those reasons we can observe periods of time when certain members lead the discussion, while at other times some of those whose contributions have been prominent in the past, become silent and others take the lead. Some members' contributions are remembered for a long time, even though their silence is long-standing. They might even sign off the list without anyone noticing, because in contrast to face-to-face Large Groups where leaving the room cannot remain unnoticed, a member can leave the virtual group without anyone paying attention.

Van Vliet and Burgers (1987) argue that communities contain the following elements: social interaction, a shared value system, and a shared symbolic system. Communities in cyberspace attain these three elements. Even if they are very task-oriented (e.g. forums focused on technical help for personal data assistant users), participants are involved in many types of social interaction: thanking one another, empathizing with others' difficulties, etc. The depth of interactions attained in discussion lists with a psychological component will be illustrated later. The shared value system of participants in Internet communities is evident in different layers, both conscious and unconscious. For example, there is a shared belief in freedom of speech and respecting the others' expression of ideas. We can see additional unconscious values in lists of mental health professionals. Anger, hostility and frustration expressed directly or covertly are also part of such a community. The shared symbolic system can be seen in its simplest version by the different icons developed in order to convey feelings across the Internet, and by the use of Internet special abbreviations.

As Internet groups progress, new members join and others sign off. When too many departures and entrances occur in a group, its stability is severely shaken. In small groups, too much rotation in group membership can evoke a feeling of fragmentation, endanger the conditions needed for the group to become a safe environment, and affect the openness of group members and their self-disclosure. Trust develops with stable objects. Does this mean that Internet groups become unsafe and that people cannot be open in their cyberspace interactions? Not necessarily. Two factors work in favour of creating an illusion of safety in the Large Group in the virtual environment. The first is the anonymity of the members, which reduces the risks of ridicule or rejection of people disclosing personal information. Online interaction is similar to the 'stranger in the train' interaction. As McKenna *et al.* (2002) found out, relationships develop closeness and intimacy significantly faster over the Internet than offline. Anonymity has its impact on the presentation of identities on the Internet too, but this is beyond the scope of this chapter to discuss. The second factor is the creation and development of a core group that carries on group norms of tolerance and openness, and an atmosphere of cohesion, 'we-ness', and belonging. The core group consists of members that are more involved in the exchange of messages, post more often and become more salient and important in this Large Group. The newcomer might sometimes have the notion that the group is dominated by this subgroup, and this might at first restrict the participation of new members. However, once the newcomer is ready to respect the group norms and its veterans, he or she can be included in that core group. New people who join the group cannot differentiate between actively involved members who joined the group a few months ago, and those who were there from the beginning.

Time perception in Internet groups is very subjective and different from common time reference in everyday life. Many responses to one's email bring the impression of short time-lags. Time perception also has its impact on the emotional tone of the Internet Large Group. There are no auditory or visual cues in cyberspace, so it seems as if a person's emotions can only be judged from the content of their posts. However, the perception of the emotion in a post is often influenced by the surrounding climate. The group emotional climate is also highly determined by changes and contrasts in content over time. For example, if messages on a list change suddenly from openness and interpersonal empathy to angry and annoyed posts, it will be perceived as an outburst of uncontrolled affect parallel to what can be observed in a face-to-face Large Group.

The psychodynamics of Large Groups in virtual reality

Large Groups tend to generate strong emotions in its members, such as annihilation anxiety, feeling one's identity is threatened, envy, aggression, and sometimes also compassion. They also tend to restrict, or even temporarily block, clear thinking within its participants and conductors. De Maré (1975) claimed that the powerful emotions could easily become uncontrollable and uncontainable. Many other theoreticians who studied Large Group processes (e.g. Anzieu 1984; Main 1975; Turquet 1975) focused on these destructive, powerful forces and saw them as a result of unconscious psychological defense mechanisms such as projection, splitting, displacement, and projective identification.

Cyberspace provides an inevitable source for such psychological processes. Its incomprehensibly boundless vastness evokes anxiety, and its lack of other than textual cues encourages projections to fill in the incomplete picture and only partial information that the reader receives. Just as in the psychoanalytic setting, when the patient lying on the couch projects an array of feelings onto the psychoanalyst because the information provided is limited, the computer screen is almost a perfect 'blank screen', devoid even of the voice components of the analyst. Small wonder, then, that Internet communication can become a source for a lot of misunderstandings, and that strong emotions develop in a discussion. Projections on the Internet seem more massive than in individual therapy or in a small group, and resemble the quick changes of emotional discharge that can be seen in Large Groups. A calm and intellectual exchange of ideas can swiftly become an uncontrollable interchange of angry feelings, a process known in cyberspace language as 'flame wars'. Suspicion, impulsivity, inability to listen to the other, rage and high anxiety govern the scene, reminiscent of similar vignettes from face-to-face Large Groups.

Understanding and predicting the events in the Internet Large Group is quite complex. Linear causality no longer prevails in these circumstances, and instead we should use nonlinear theories, especially complexity theory (Rubenfeld 2001). There is no way of anticipating when a 'flame war' is going to burst, or which email receives a volume of responses and which will be totally ignored. Chaos theory and non-linear determinism explain better the course of the Large Group, especially in the virtual environment. The bigger systems are, the more difficult it is to predict their processes. Social processes are unpredictable unless we take into consideration the chaos that creates unpredictable waves in a seemingly quiet lake.

The Large Group is full of negative feelings, expressed in anger and aggression. The frustration of not being heard or mirrored, the alienation one feels in the crowd, the bombarding by stimuli that blocks cognitive functions, the tendency to find some refuge from losing one's identity in the mob by clinging to subgroups and attacking other subgroups, all these and much more lead to a hostile atmosphere bursting sometimes into angry interactions. These phenomena help us understand better the psychology of the mob and how it can be so easily incited. The 'flame wars' of the group in the virtual environment serve the same purposes of discharging the frustrations that result from being unheard, unrecognized and misunderstood, and also bring forth the image of the restless crowd. But, in contrast to the intensive negative feelings expressed in a face-to-face Large Group, Large Groups in cyberspace act more like Janus, the double-faced god in Greek mythology. Sometimes they show their ugly and aggressive face, looking like the angry and hateful mob, but sometimes they can show compassion, care, mutual help and altruistic behaviour.

It seems that cyberspace provides a wider containing ability than is anticipated. The anonymity, which can have the negative effects of de-individuation and alienation, can have positive effects too. McKenna and Green (2002) mention that anonymity on the Internet helps members to express how they really feel and think, and encourages the emergence of healthy group norms. Simple leadership interventions, even administrative ones such as taking care of the technical details, give the group members a feeling of safety and decrease the alienation typical of Large Groups.

Foulkes (1964) and Pines (1984) saw mirroring as an important 'group-specific phenomenon'. Group members see themselves reflected through the others' reactions. In a small group, mirroring starts with looking the other in the eyes. In a Large Group, where 'participants cannot be encompassed in a single glance', such a mirroring is impossible. In fact, instead of seeing the other's eyes, sometimes all one can see is the other's back. Small wonder that the Large Group arouses paranoid feelings. Mirroring in the virtual Large Group seems, at first, even more impossible. Instead of looking into the other's eyes, one looks at one's own reflection on the screen. In order for an individual to feel that the others really see him, the Large Group in cyberspace should develop other modes of mirroring. This is not an easy task to accomplish, and requires a lot of sensitivity and attunement from the members and the leader.

The fact that the screen reflects one's image might explain why people relate to the computer as a self-object, expecting it always to function properly, as if it is part of their body, and becoming frustrated (even slightly depressed) when it crashes. Self/other relationships are more fluidly shifting or differently constituted in the absence of fewer contextual cues, so that in this imaginary Large Group one might write to/for oneself as much as another, or might treat other(s) as an extension of oneself with less immediate reality principle contradiction. When you look at your screen, what do you see? Yourself. This phenomenon reminds us of Winnicott's sentences (1971) in 'Mirror-role of mother and family in child development': 'What does the baby see when he or she looks at the mother's face? I am assuming that ordinarily, what the baby sees is himself or herself' (p. 131). Unconsciously, the computer screen makes the writer regress to archaic developmental stages.

As time progresses and the Large Group in cyberspace advances, some participants become consistently and extensively involved in every discussion. Their contributions are obvious, they write frequently to the forum, respond to upcoming threads, and introject the discussion list as part of their professional (and sometimes personal) life. They become a core group, which develops private jokes, unique kinds of humour, and hidden norms. These participants create a sense of cohesion in the Large Group, relate to one another as old friends (and sometimes develop real friendship in and out of cyberspace). They carry the tradition of the forum and its norms over time, and those who later join the list have the feeling that they are entering a close group. This core group is responsible for the illusion of a small group, because they counteract the feeling of alienation and become more open and self-disclosing over time. When one of these frequent contributors fails to write to the forum for a period of time, it is felt like a missed presence.

The functions of the group leader

Holding is the main function of the leader in the 'virtual' Large Group. Usually the functions of the leader in a small group are holding, containing and interpreting. Holding or containing mean something different in cyberspace, given that their origins presuppose particular notions of embodiment that rely on co-presence or proximity that do not apply, or apply differently, in cyberspace. This is a much broader question for further investigation. Given the scope of this chapter I will only say that the holding function is most important in cyberspace because this space is far from being a holding environment by its basic characteristics. Cyberspace is perceived as a huge, endless space with no boundaries and no limitations. One can surf the Internet, from websites physically situated in the surfer's area to those that are thousands of miles away, with a click of the mouse. This fact can arouse the illusion of a boundless space. The ease of communication with people from faraway countries feels as if 'the world is at the tip of my finger' on one hand, but also creates some anxiety of getting lost in those interactions. People are worried about becoming addicted to the Internet, or spending too much time surfing the web and writing emails. The fear of drifting away and becoming immersed in that huge environment is very common. The leader's holding functions as an anchor to stabilize participants and reduce their anxieties so they feel safe enough to interact.

Holding can be achieved by very simple measures. In small groups the holding function is similar to the function of the blue-collar worker. The leader provides the basic conditions for making the environment convenient. The group members should be free of worries about the physical environment in order to be able to work on their psychological issues. Holding the group starts with very simple actions such as taking care of the arrangements of chairs in a circle. Providing holding also has to do with clear boundaries. Setting the rules or taking care of the boundaries of time and space can achieve this function. In Large Groups the boundaries are looser (space is bigger and the individual feels less commitment to the group), so the need to clarify them becomes stronger. As stated above, the Large Group in cyberspace has even vaguer boundaries. The space is imaginary and can contain an unlimited number of members. In asynchronic discussion lists, time boundaries are erased completely.

Most of the forums on the Internet are not process groups. They focus on a subject that interests its members and is specified in the forum title (e.g. parenting, French films, addictions, etc.). What does this imply about the leader's interventions? In task (content–process) groups, the leader should interpret the process only when a serious interruption erupts, blocking the group from working on its task. As long as the working group prevails, there is no need for interpretation. The same applies to the Large Group on the Internet. There is no need for the leader to interpret the process, unless some crisis occurs or the group is severely distracted from achieving its goals. For example, when the group is in danger of turning a member into a scapegoat, a leader intervention is necessary, preferably by an interpretation first.

Transference

Contrary to what happens in face-to-face Large Groups, the main transference towards the leader identified in the Large Group in the virtual environment is idealization. This phenomenon does not subside even after a long period the group has existed for. This phenomenon is in sharp contrast to Anzieu's arguement, that the collective transference generally appears as negative transference in non-directive Large Groups (Anzieu 1984, Chapter 4, p.84). It can be argued that this strong negative transference is an artifact of the approach that focuses on authority and leadership, such as the Tavistock approach. Indeed, some writers in this book do hold this position. This approach might increase alienation between the group and its leaders.

The lack of cues other than textual ones on the Internet can lead to two different situations. One is the projection of aggressive feelings, and interpreting ambiguities in a negative way. This was described earlier as leading to the sudden, intensive development of 'flame wars'. But another possibility is that people tend to 'fill in the blanks' with idealization instead of suspicion. Bargh, McKenna, and Fitzsimons (2002) concluded that different interpersonal goals of the interaction partners caused projection of the idealized, hoped-for qualities of a best friend onto the partner. We can conclude that Internet group members project the qualities of the good-enough conductor and idealize the function of the manager because they need a safe object in this vast anxiety-provoking environment. All the conductor has to do is to provide the participants with adequate holding in order to maintain this idealization for a long time.

Idealization of the Internet Large Group leader is enhanced by virtue of the medium. When the participants are not very computer-sophisticated (and let me remind you that I am talking specifically about mental health lists, and that most mental health professionals are computer beginners) they start their Internet discussion list experience with some inferiority feelings and anxiety evoked by the unknown situation. So they can easily project wisdom and computer-wizardry onto the leader. Talking specifically about the group psychotherapy discussion list, the fact that each member entered this list with a welcome and netiquette message from the leader might contribute to idealization. This modelled a relationship between individuals that might mitigate some of the more terrorizing aspects of the Large Group dynamics.

In asynchronic discussion lists, the list leader has enough time to consider responses and not act them out, even when the list is very stormy. In face-to-face Large Groups, the group exerts a lot of pressure on the group leader to intervene when the process seems to get out of control. It is difficult for the leader to stay in an observing mode and plan the intervention calmly when regressive dynamics take over and the group uses projective identification mechanisms. But on the Internet, in the absence of time pressures, the virtual Large Group leader can even consult a colleague when a difficult situation arises. This makes the leader's intervention more optimal. So the idealization of the leader, and by the leader, have some basis in reality.

Unfortunately, idealization is a double-edged sword. It fosters unrealistic expectations of the group leader, and when these expectations are not met, the group becomes furious. For example, on one forum the members changed from admiring the leader to being very disappointed and turning against her, when they found out that one member of the group was an imposter and had made up a false crisis in his life. They were angry that the group leader did not detect sooner that this member was an imposter.

Idealization creates an intensive counter-transference reaction of the leader. It is very easy to fall into the trap and believe that the leader is really the best Large Group leader that there ever was. Such counter-transference might blind the leader to the real dynamics of the Large Group and the need to be prepared that for the possibility that de-idealization will be necessary.

The Internet unconscious

Large Groups can be effective in exploring the Social Unconscious. The idea of the social unconscious construct is twofold. On the one hand it reflects the social and cultural arrangements of which individuals are unconscious (Hopper 1996) and on the other it means the representation of social forces and power relations in the psyche (Dalal 2001). The Large Group, with its tendency to mobilize strong emotions in its participants, gives an opportunity to study the Social Unconscious by analysing the events from a broader point of view through using parallel process concepts.

In the same way we can argue that processes in the Internet Large Group reveal the Social Unconscious too. But which society does this unconscious reflect? Members of Internet communities and forums come from different countries and cultures. Weinberg (2002) postulated a community unconscious in a discussion list of group psychotherapists, which portrayed itself in stressing empathy and acceptance while avoiding anger and conflicts among therapists. Professional identity might play a role in the (self) regulation of members in such groups. They invest in presenting themselves as competent, efficient, integrated, knowledgeable, etc. – and so less likely to exhibit the kinds of inconsistencies, fluidities or open-ness to new radical changes that characterize other people's behaviour in cyberspace. So one possibility is that the social unconscious on the Internet reflects the unconscious of the community of people who share a common field of interest. Another possibility is that it represents the unconscious of society at large, not of a specific culture (thus becoming close to Jung's concept of the collective unconscious). But there is a third option, where we can relate to a specific concept that we can label 'the Internet Unconscious'.

The Internet is supposed to be the ultimate free-democratic society. No one governs or controls it, any participant has the right to express his/her ideas with no restrictions, it is the most egalitarian society because social status does not pertain to it and there is no differentiation between young and old, men or women, expert and novice. In fact it was hoped that the Internet would facilitate the spread of democracy and become ubiquitous and widely available around the world. This illusion continues to rule, even though connection to the Internet is still rare in poor countries. The Internet unconscious contains an illusory belief that ultimate freedom of speech is achieved in cyberspace and that forum members always show respect and tolerance to different opinions.

Implications of virtual large groups for face-to-face Large Groups

The most salient difference between groups in reality and in the virtual environment is the ability to develop norms of tolerance and even intimacy in cyberspace. This warm atmosphere is in sharp contrast to the usually alienated climate in face-to-face Large Groups. Can we learn from Internet Large Groups how to make groups in reality less alienated?

Part of the answer might reside in the holding functions of the leader that can sooth the anxiety evoked in the alienated and strange situation. As stated above, we rarely have the opportunity of exploring the dynamics of long-term Large Groups. Cyberspace provides this opportunity. What this valuable opportunity reveals is that, after some time, members who contin-ually contribute to the group create a core group that develops an illusion of a small group with norms of intimacy and self-disclosure. Continuing the process of the Large Group, even when it seems hopeless and violent, with the wise interventions of a holding leader might eventually lead to dialogue.

References

Anzieu, D. (1984) *The Group and the Unconscious.* London: Routledge and Kegan Paul.

Bargh, J. A., McKenna, K. Y. A. and Fitzsimons, G. M. (2002) 'Can you see the real me? Activation and expression of the true self on the Internet.' *Journal of Social Issues 58*, 1, 33–48.

Dalal, F. (2001) 'The Social Unconscious: A post-Foulksian perspective.' *Group Analysis 34*, 4, 539–555.

de Maré, P. (1975) 'The politics of large groups.' In L. Kreeger (ed) *The Large Group: Dynamics and Therapy.* London: Karnac Books.

de Maré, P., Piper, R. and Thompson, S. (1991) *Koinonia: From Hate, through Dialogue, to Culture in Large Group.* London: Karnac Books.

Foulkes, S. H. (1964) *Therapeutic Group Analysis.* London: George Allen and Unwin.

Hopper, E. (1996) 'The social unconscious in clinical work.' *Group 20*, 1, 7–42.

McKenna, K. Y. A. and Green, A. S. (2002) 'Virtual group dynamics.' *Group Dynamics 6*, 1, 116–127.

McKenna, K. Y. A., Green, A. S. and Gleason, M. E. J. (2002) 'Relationship formation on the Internet: What's the big attraction?' *Journal of Social Issues 58*, 1, 9–31.

Main, T. (1975) 'Some psychodynamics of large groups.' In L. Kreeger (ed) *The Large Group: Dynamics and Therapy.* London: Karnac Books.

Pines, M. (1984) 'Reflections on mirroring.' *International Review of Psycho-Analysis 11*, 27–42.

Rubenfeld, S. (2001) 'Group therapy and complexity theory.' *International Journal of Group Psychotherapy 51*, 4, 449–471.

Turquet, P. (1975) 'Threats to identity in the large group.' In L. Kreeger (ed) *The Large Group: Dynamics and Therapy.* London: Karnac Books.

Van Vliet, W. and Burgers, J. (1987) 'Communities in transition: From the industrial to the postindustrial era.' In I. Altman and A. Wandersman (eds) *Neighborhood and Community Environments.* New York: Plenum Press.

Weinberg, H. (2002) 'Community unconscious on the Internet.' *Group Analysis 35*, 1, 165–183.

Winnicott, D. W. (1971) *Playing and Reality.* London: Pelican Books.

CHAPTER 13

The Large Group and Leadership Challenges in a Group Analytic Training Community

Thor Kristian Island

In this chapter I will describe the large group experience at the Norwegian Training Program in Group Analysis in Oslo, and I will discuss different modalities of running large groups with a special focus on leadership issues.

Towards the end of the Fifties a growing interest in the systematic study of large group processes took place. Under the sponsorship of the Tavistock Institute of Human Relations a tradition evolved of arranging conferences with the major purpose of studying the large group *per se* – to study the typical large group processes and dynamics, the self-acquisition of insights through experience in the here and now (Turquet 1975). At the Tavistock Conferences the participants get a more comprehensive understanding of the dynamics in groups and among groups within social systems and organizations. There is a particular focus on hidden and unconscious processes which influence the interplay between individuals and organizations, e.g. processes which promote or inhibit leadership and cooperation within an organization – the hospital ward, the treatment unit, the community meeting, etc. In these large groups the study of the unconscious has precedence. Reality on the surface level plays a subordinate role. In these large groups incidents, statements, actions are interpreted as expressions of unconscious forces.

For many years the large group has been an element at group analytic conferences, symposia and meetings, though the rationale of the large group in these contexts has not always been more obvious than the exciting experience of being part of such a group for a few sessions.

In many group analytic training programs today the large group is institutionalized as a core element of the training program.

The Norwegian Training Program in Group Analysis is a block-training program with the traditional elements of self-experiential small therapy groups, supervision groups and theory lectures. The daily large group is a core element in this training. The training started in 1984, and at present 81 participants and 11 staff members meet for five extended weekends a year for these varieties of settings, as well as the encounters during the breaks and meals. The training program consists of three levels: a one-year introductory course, a two-year intermediate course, and finally a two-year qualifying course, for a total of five years. The large group has been run continually since 1984. Members have participated for one to five years, and some staff members have participated since the beginning. This large group has a long history, and the participants become actors in this history through their individual contributions and histories in the large group. Through personal and group development significant experiences are accumulated over time. These experiences contribute to the configuration of the large group as cultural manifestation of the 'training community' of which it is an integral component.

The purpose of the large group in this context is multifaceted. One aspect is to study the typical large group processes and dynamics in the 'here and now' in order to experience and understand that such events, statements and incidents have unconscious roots. Another aspect is the integrating function as the training community's 'City Square,' where a continuous analysis of personal, cultural, professional and political training course dynamics takes place. Here the affective implications of being a citizen of this training community can be explored. The participants meet in a variety of settings, and each setting has its distinct task. Hearst and Sharpe (1991) and others (Island 1996) have pointed to the implications of being a part of a challenging project, which requires rapid adaptation to different modes of relating. These modes include regressed patient role in the therapy group, peer–supervisor in the supervision group, intellectually and cognitively present in theory lectures, and even confused, frightened and identity-threatened in the large group, where confirming and consolidating responses from others cannot be taken for granted.

The training program itself is a complex integrated whole, where the evolvement of a rich matrix promotes an open and self-exploring communication. The large group reflects themes from the small therapy groups as well as 'political' issues related to the training (Island 1992, 1993; Lorentzen 1990). One important task of the large group is to help integrate affects connected to the various aspects of the training program as such, on a personal, group and inter-group level. If there is an overflow of strong emotions from one context to another, the large group can contain these emotions and channel them to the appropriate setting. When the large group is not converted to a 'parliament' for decision-making, or starts discussing practical or organizational issues to avoid the exploration of underlying affects, the large group has the potential to be an arena where destructive emotions can evolve, be exposed, highlighted, explored, understood and transformed. Thus the participants' comprehension of unconscious dynamic processes may be promoted. In the large group there is a shared endeavor to explore the dynamics between 'surface' and underlying unconscious forces within the group.

Context

The large group described here takes place within the specific context of a group analytic training community. Every large group takes place within a certain context, and the process will always be influenced by that context. At the same time, the large group will influence the context, the surrounding environment. The large group should be understood within its cultural and historical context, though this view seems to be underestimated or even ignored by some large group convenors and authors.

At the International Association of Group Psychotherapy (IAGP) international conference of group psychotherapy in Jerusalem in 2000 there were two parallel daily large groups. I found it remarkable that the large group I attended barely commented upon the historical and tense political situation that surrounded the conference. There seemed to be a collective denial of the surrounding, very present reality, and a collective resistance against addressing these issues. A hidden collusion seemed to take place between the members of the large group and the convenors, where these sensitive and tense issues were toned down. The large group was managed as if it took place in a contextual void.

Leadership

Relatively little has been written about leadership of large groups. Wilke (1998) argues that too little has been written about the role and style of the large group convenors. He says that most authors operate within the Freudian and Kleinian paradigm, which rests on pre-Foulkesian theory, when they write about large groups. Within this paradigm the leader maintains an analytic stance toward the group. He keeps a dyadic relationship to the group. His role is to interpret unconscious processes with special emphasis on transference material towards the leader. Little or no attention is paid to non-transference material. Shaked (1997) argues that the large group conductor should limit his interventions mainly to the interpretations of transference and resistance reactions of the large group. He maintains that all interactions in the large group should be considered as distorted expressions of unconscious impulses or defense mechanisms against these. Then the complicated social network of the large group will be connected to its unconscious roots.

There are several problems related to this stance. It presupposes that the convenor is in a privileged, 'knowing' position towards the large group, and that he/she knows in advance the meaning of the unfolding process. In my view, this monolithic position, which promotes and reinforces the vertical transference, has a strong impact on the process to be explored. It is not a 'neutral' position. This attitude might force the large group process towards a predictable development that circles around the monolithic position of the leader. Thereby a free-floating associative dialogue could be discouraged. This strong attention to leadership is not an inherent quality of the large group *per se*, but more a result of the theory-laden preconceptions of the convenor. If the leader ignores his contribution to the intersubjective context in which the phenomena arise, and attributes all events in the large group to its members as an expression of unconscious impulses or resistance, his interpretations might alienate the members and create confusion and impoverished ability to engage in dialogue and reflection. It is not possible for one or two or even a team of convenors to fully grasp what is going on at the unconscious level in a large group, not least due to the fact that the convenors themselves are an integral part of the process, both influencing and being influenced by it. As Segalla pointed out, 'the group provides an intense experience for the leader(s) in that, while attempting to maintain their individual cognitive and emotional capacities in order to study the large group, they are also, at every moment, a part of the large group experience, shaping their interpretations from within that context' (Segalla 1996, p.268). She emphasizes the danger of being snared by the group's regression (Kohut 1976), losing the very perspective needed to understand the group, and even the same danger of loss of cohesion for the large group therapist as occurs for the member.

P. de Maré focuses on the cultural aspects of the large group when he says that 'the large group has societal parameters, it cannot adequately be understood via psychoanalysis and small group analysis models' (de Maré 1989, p.186). He argues that we need to understand the phenomena of the large group in its own terms as a developing and self-regulatory system. Trying to comprehend the rich matrix and complex processes that unfold in the large group through pre-Foulkesian psychoanalytic theory and concepts must inevitably be reductionistic. Psychoanalytic interpretations might easily be stereotypic, clichéd and presumptuous.

Multiple leadership

Foulkes seemed to have an ambivalent attitude towards large groups. Nevertheless, he suggested that a team of conductors for the large group would be preferable (Foulkes 1975).

At the Norwegian Group Analytic Training Program we have decided upon a collective or multiple leadership where all staff members – the small group conductors, supervisors, theory lecturers (11 persons) – are present in the large group as convenors. But this role is multifaceted. Each staff member is a nodal point (Foulkes 1948) in the staff/leadership matrix, as well as the matrix of the large group as-a-whole. He/she is present as an individual member of the large group, in the role of consultant and in the capacity of trainer/teacher at the training program, being influenced by and influencing the large group process. The staff members have to manage rapid shifts of functioning during the training

weekends – small group conductor, supervisor, theory lecturer, administrator, assessor – and all these roles are closely connected to the staff
members' role and presence in the large group. We have placed the large
group in the midst of the training community, and we find it an important
prerequisite that all citizens of this community should be present during
the large group sessions.

The function of the convenors is to engender the development of a
culture where experience, exploration and self-reflective dialogue have
priority. The large group convenors contribute to the process in the form of
enabling comments, voicing some of one's own thoughts and feelings,
contributing to the imagery or symbolization in the group in order to
facilitate the process and enable a free and associative dialogue to develop
and expand. An important role of the staff members is to secure the
boundaries around the large group; one member of the staff is designated
to keep the time boundaries.

In such a large group the communication moves in various directions
and on different levels simultaneously, with the focus on individuals,
subgroups, large group-as-a-whole, the surrounding society and
foundation matrix. Though present and visible, the large group convenors
try to limit their own activity during the sessions. They must, however, be
attentive and not negligent to the process. Interventions, clarifications, and
even interpretations might be needed to address defensive maneuvers and
resistance in order to generate or re-establish the dialogue when the communication process comes to a halt. From a self psychological point of
view, resistance is a self-protective maneuver. In the large group one might
experience a lack of nurturing and confirming selfobject responses. The
unfamiliar situation, the difficulty of grasping the task and nature of the
group, people sitting behind, out of visual control, what is said often being
ignored or responded to in very strange ways – all these are existential
here-and-now realities, which undermine the cohesion of the self
(Karterud 1999). Segalla (1996) has pointed to the fear of re-experiencing
earlier trauma in large group settings, like school, religious, cultural,
political and ethnic groups. These are some of the reasons why members
might resist participating in the large group process, becoming silent or
withdrawn, or actively attack the large group project as such. Staff interventions, when needed, should address these resistances through empathic

understanding of the anxious feelings and experiences, and not by con-fronting interpretation of resistance.

The convenors should attempt to keep an intersubjective perspective in mind, acknowledging that the staff cannot have access to a full compre-hension of what is taking place in the large group. Individual or even group interpretations are easily experienced as persecuting in the large group, particularly when they come from the staff members. In fact, interpreta-tions can be punitive and attacking when the convenors have been exposed to criticism or feel overwhelmed by negative projections. In a large group of professionals, interpretations might even impose professional defensive maneuvers towards intellectualization and psychologizing, and distract the attention from experiential aspects.

In this large group, the members try to 'tease out' who is the 'real leader.' They will try to understand and define the process of the large group within well-established analytic categories, categories too narrow to fully grasp the complexity of the large group process. When they finally accept the multiple, collective leadership as a functional fact, exploration of the multifaceted elements of leadership beyond the stereotype clichés becomes possible. Shaked (1997) notes that attack on leadership is a prominent feature in the large group, and this is comprehended as symbolized parenticide. In our large groups attacks on leadership are not so prominent, with less fear of destroying the 'leader' or 'leaders.'

Challenges to leadership

In a large group there is a continuous interplay between the exposure to the primitive processes and the cultivating aspects of the group. The large group convenors should attentively monitor their interventions in order to maintain this perspective, being considerate to the individual members, the large group and the training program as such.

A collective leadership does not imply that the staff speaks with one voice. Within the intersubjective context of the large group each of the staff members participates with their individual style, personality, theoret-ical orientation and meta-psychological frame of reference. Skynner (1975) has previously underlined the importance of making room for normal expression of disagreement among the leaders rather than avoidance of conflict by formation of a 'monolithic block' around a theoretical model. He states, 'honest and open disagreement between leaders provides the most powerful stimulus of all towards individuation of other participants' (Skynner 1975, p.251).

Though no staff member has a different or more prominent position in the large group than the others, there are differences in experience, therapeutic style, ability to convey personal contributions or formulate interventions, etc. These differences have to be dealt with within the staff group. After the large group session, the staff members meet for a brief review of the meeting. This gives us the possibility to discuss the diversity of perspectives and forms of interventions, be it focus on empathy and selfobject failures or confrontations and interpretations. Diversities and disagreements can be explored. In addition to the brief reviews after the large group meeting we have decided upon a more process-oriented staff group every block weekend, in order to maintain a necessary perpetual self-analysis within the staff group, to comprehend what is going on internally and to counteract destructive processes within the staff group.

Sometimes the members of the large group have a tendency to idealize one of the convenors. This need for idealization seems to be necessary and more in the foreground during critical phases of the group process. Any personal expression from the idealized leader might then be understood as the utmost wisdom with some hidden, secret meanings. He/she provides mirroring and worth, someone to lean on. He/she will necessarily be affected by a stimulation of his/her grandiose self. However, within a collective leadership the danger of an idealized leader being engulfed in the process and acting out his or her narcissistic need for mirroring is reduced. The group of convenors has potential for a comprehensive understanding of what is played out and to manage their envy and narcissism and deal with this dynamic material without destructive rivalry.

However, this is a difficult matter, since idealization might be accompanied by devaluation, e.g. when splitting dominates the scene. The devaluation of some of the staff members might be less obvious, more implicit and unspoken, while the idealization is more prominent. Nevertheless, the devaluated staff members may collude with these destructive projections, lose their capacity for self-reflection and behave in destructive ways. Another possibility is that the idealization is a manifestation of selfobject transferences and not primarily a part of the defense mechanism of

splitting. In that case idealization is not necessarily accompanied by devaluation. Even then it might evoke envy in other members of the staff.

We believe that the ability to reflect upon these matters among the staff
group is a precondition for the large group to develop a more integrated
culture. Most large groups, in particular occasional groups at conferences,
do not reach any development beyond the formative phase. Thus large
group theory has been over-focused on the primitive defense mechanisms
of denial, splitting and projective identification. The art of constructively
dealing with rather stable selfobject transferences in large groups has been
ignored.

A clinical vignette

The large group had been preoccupied with one of the staff members for
some sessions. He was a well-regarded professor of psychiatry in
Norway, and also internationally acknowledged for his research on
group analysis and group psychotherapy. He had written several books,
and recently published a textbook in Group Analysis. Many of the participants expressed pride in belonging to the training program where he
was a teacher and trainer. In the large group every comment or remark
from him became very important, loaded with deeper meaning. Sitting
next to him in the large group became an issue for several of the
members. They felt nourished by his presence.

One of the members told a dream in the large group:

He was at a party, like a large group. Food was served, but the tables
were too small, and there was not food enough for everyone. He could
not reach the table to get the food. Dr A., the idealized leader, was there
too. He forced his way to the table and got what he wanted. The
candidate had mixed feelings about that. He admired A's ability to get
what he wanted and needed, and he also felt envious that he did not get
his share... But in the end he put the whole party and A in a matchbox,
and put it in his pocket...

Another member of the large group remembered when he was
young:

The young kids caught bumblebees, which they put in matchboxes.
They put holes in the boxes so the bees could live. The kids lay in the
green grass, looking at the sun peacefully, holding the matchbox close to
their ears, and listening to the buzzing from the matchbox. It was the
'discman' of the Sixties, he said. If they put two bumblebees in one box

the buzzing became stronger. But if there were two from different hives, they would fight till one was killed. It had to be two from the same hive…

In the afternoon, when they went home for dinner, they forgot about the bumblebees in the boxes. Next morning when they opened the boxes, the bees were in bad shape though they had been supplied with sugar and air. He went to the windowsill in his room on the second floor, opened the window, and placed the bumblebee on the sill. Then he snapped the bee out of the window. Would it fly or not…?

After this story the large group sat in thoughtful silence. The way he told the story had moved the group.

After a while the group started working on topics related to the staff members and especially the idealized leader. They realized how their idealization of a staff member might deplete the group of its own vitality and creativity. But they also pointed out how restricted the staff might feel being put in narrow roles like idealization. Eventually mixed and ambivalent feelings were articulated. The wish to be nourished by the idealized leader, and the wish to restrict and control. Childhood memories were shared, not least the absence of someone to idealize in childhood.

These images unveiled many individual themes for the participants — themes they could work further on in their small therapy groups.

The trainers (staff) did not say anything for a long time. No interpretations were given. The group did the important work itself. The main challenge for the staff was to manage their own feeling of envy or relief at not being subject to the idealization. A comment from the staff could easily become a cliché.

Of course there are disagreements about the 'correct' understanding of the large group process. We have learned, in our collective of competent convenors, that there are different ways of comprehending the group process. But our setting has enabled us to discuss these diversities and thereby enriched our knowledge. Maybe, as a single large group convenor, one might maintain the illusion that one has access to an authoritative comprehension of the large group process.

Important issues are conflicts and controversies within the staff group. The large group can be very focused on fantasies about rivalry within the large group. Perceived conflicts could be projections from the large group. The large group may attribute conflicts and controversies within the individual member or fraction of the large group to the leadership collective, but *de facto* conflicts within the staff should not be mystified as projections. I have elsewhere (Island 1992, 1996) discussed the important role of the large group in dealing with the complex material of irrationality, strong affects, mistrust and conflicts within the training community when Norwegian trainers would substitute trainers from IGA, London, and when the Norwegian Institute of Group Analysis took over full responsibility for the training program. Strong doubts as to whether the Norwegians could provide proper training were voiced among the trainees. Skepticism concerning the competence and skills of the new trainers were expressed. And there was also a strong fantasy about power-struggle and rivalry within the Norwegian staff group. Concerns about the future of the training program were also in the foreground. The large group became an important arena for exploration of the affective aspects of this process: what were irrationality and envious projections? What were real difficulties and problems? What were appropriate concerns? What belonged to the large group *per se*, and what belonged within the staff group? Having the large group as an arena for open exploration of these multifaceted emotional issues made the organizational and political process and decisions outside the large group less complicated.

Conclusion

The large group in the context of our training program has a history of almost 20 years. It is a 'very slow open group' and some of the convenors have participated from the beginning. We have emphasized the role of the large group as the 'City Square' of the training community, where the continuous, public, free and exploratory dialogue has precedence over interpretations.

Over the years the large group in this context has developed a culture where the vitalizing and creative potentials of the large group have become more evident. We have experienced how the large group could work meaningfully on personal matters concerning one or several members of the group – issues that could not be handled in the small therapy groups. The capacity of the group to cope with tragic and dramatic material with empathy and concern is striking. During these instances the large group is perceived as a nurturing, affect-validating self-object milieu, where attuned responses provide both a sense of communality, of belonging, and possibility for necessary self-demarcation. The large group convenor should be a responsible citizen of this community. The large group serves as the City Square that offers citizenship, but at the same time the individuality of each citizen is secured. It is my strong conviction that this citizenship also contributes to the devoted commitment to the group analytic community after the training is finished.

Acknowledgement

I wish to thank the members of the large group for generously allowing the dream and the associated story in my clinical vignette to be published.

References

de Maré, P. (1989) 'The history of large group phenomena in relation to group analytic psychotherapy: The history of the median group.' *Group 13*, 173–197.

Foulkes, S. H. (1948) *Introduction to Group-Analytic Psychotherapy.* London: Wm Heinemann Medical Books.

Foulkes, S. H. (1975) 'Problems of the large group from a group-analytic point of view.' In L. Kreeger (ed) *The Large Group.* London: Constable.

Hearst, L. and Sharpe, M. (1991) 'Training for and trainees in Group Analysis.' In J. Roberts and M. Pines (eds) *The Practice of Group Analysis.* London/New York: Tavistock/Routledge.

Island, T. K. (1992) 'From peers to parents – from trainee to trainer.' *I.G.A.R. Conference Bulletin.* (Warsaw) 22–34.

Island, T.K. (1993) 'Sitting at the trainer's table': Boundaries and barriers within a block training community. In W. Knauss and U. Keller (eds) Proceedings from 9th European Symposium in Group Analysis. Heidelberg: Mattes Verlag.

Island, T. K. (1996) 'Distortions, echoes, reflections: the role of the large group in group analytic training community.' In F. Peternel (ed) *Median and Large Groups in Group Analytic Training.* Ljubljana: University Psychiatric Hospital.

Karterud, S. (1999) *Gruppeanalyse og psykodynamisk gruppepsykoterapi* (Group Analysis and Psychodynamic Group Psychotherapy.) Oslo: Pax Forlag.

Kohut, H. (1976) 'Creativeness, charisma, group psychology.' In J. E. Gedo and G. H. Pollock (eds) *Freud: The Fusion of Science and Humanism.* New York: International Universities Press.

Lorentzen, S. (1990) 'Block training in Oslo: The experience of being both organizer and participant.' *Group Analysis 23*, 361–366.

Segalla, R. A. (1996) 'The unbearable embeddedness of being: Self psychology, intersubjectivity and large group experiences.' *Group 20*, 4, 257–271.

Shaked, J. (1997) 'Den psykoanalytiske storgruppe.' (The Psychoanalytic Large Group.) *Matrix 13*, 4, 282–291.

Skynner, A. C. R. (1975) 'The large group in training.' In L. Kreeger (ed) *The Large Group.* London: Constable.

Turquet, P. (1975) 'Threats to identity in the large group.' In L. Kreeger (ed) *The Large Group.* London: Constable.

Wilke, G. (1998) 'Storgruppen og storgruppelederen.' (The Large Group and the Large Group Convenor.) *Matrix 15*, 2, 69–98.

The Larger Group as a Meeting of Minds

A Philosophical Understanding

Patrick de Maré and Roberto Schöllberger

The Median Group, as a Larger Group, is discussed in terms of the meeting of minds. Patrick de Maré, after 65 years of experience as a therapist, has come to realise that it is the mind which takes precedence over libidinal drives and which should be regarded as a primary entity in its own right; not an epiphenomenon.

In the Median Group all members have the opportunity to contribute since the Group is small enough for all to participate within a reasonable time and large enough to be experienced as sociocultural, as distinct from familio-tribal. Through discussion the inhibitions of infantile sexuality become lifted; this enables growth to an adult level, not as a sublimation, but as a complete metamorphosis analogous to a caterpillar becoming a butterfly, a total transformation. Not more of the same but a total metamorphosis constituting a totally different 'substance', a duality of two distinct categories of body and mind; it was Descartes who first established a philosophy of mind which he termed the First Philosophy. The Median Group is a primary face-to-face group which Charles Cooley (1902) envisaged as 'the nursery' of human nature in which dialogue takes on a role similar to free association.

Therapists have the privilege of exploring the mind to an extent that has never been done before, and by actually applying Plato's Supreme Art of Dialogue have established a third principle to Freud's two, pleasure–unpleasure and reality – that of meaning. The word 'mind' is derived from the Old Norse term meaning 'vote'.

Descartes made an amazing discovery when he recognised the certitude of mind. Mind is where growth occurs – infantile sexuality grows into the erotic mind of the adult, once it has been de-inhibited. Freed from being identified with things, Descartes concluded that the reflection of things by mind can never be the same as the thing reflected. This establishes mind as an individual entity which is crucial for therapists to take into account as of primary consideration, and also that empirical research, cost-effectiveness, statistics, numeracy and science are essentially materialistic and secondary and were originally created by the mind. When group analysis first started it was speculative, hypothetical and certainly not cost-effective.

Minding entails caring and addresses not the how of things but the why. The human race is endangered by confusing actual with abstract. An interesting example is the widespread confusion of cash with credit. The term 'cash' is derived from the Sanskrit word meaning 'precious metal'. So while cash is a concrete commodity, credit is an abstract of means of distribution. The creation of credit (debit and its repayment in cash) causes inflation and poverty in the midst of plenty.

Dualism is distinct from monism or one-dimensional singularism, which maintains that there is only one fundamental reality and which Russell terms 'neutral monism'. Dualism maintains that there are two substances, two entities, e.g. the sensible versus the intelligible of Plato, the *res extensa* and *res cogitans* of Descartes, the actual and potential of Leibnitz, the noumena and phenomena of Kant.

The monistic approach to the mind, that it is the highest neurophysiological extension of the brain, leads to a sterile, repetitive, mechanistic complexity which is distinct from the notion of antinomic reflexion by the mind, which produces a third dimension of creative dialogue and synthesising. Supporting this suggestion, Eccles (1953) accepts the mind as a genuine non-physical entity, where the problem was how to liaise. In 1954 Penfield accepted as an empirical fact the fundamental duality of mental and physical entities, between living matter and immaterial mind substance.

Freud was primarily concerned with the biology of sexuality. In the *Three Essays* (1905) he finished with the comment 'we know far too little about the biological processes constituting the essence of sexuality to be able to construct from our fragmentary information a theory adequate to the understanding alike of normal and pathological conditions' (p.243). In *The Future of an Illusion* (Freud 1927): 'It would be very nice if there were a God who created the world and there was a benevolent Providence, and if there were a moral order and an after-life...' (p.33), implying that he didn't believe this. Rather he saw myth, religion and morality as attempts to compensate for unsatisfied desire. For us the mind is in no way an illusion or false perception since it is abstract, certainly not a perception.

Whilst mind is immaterial and abstract, it is not a passive reflector like a mirror but plays an active role in establishing meaning, thinking, caring, choosing, deciding, healing, vision, aided by freedom in space and time. Like any good hypothesis it simplifies.

Freud used many terms which could be seen as referring to the mind – e.g. psyche, mental life, consciousness, ego, spiritual, psychic apparatus, Consciousness is an organ of the senses ('Sinnesorgan'). (See *The Interpretation of Dreams* (1900).) He makes a distinction between sensations and conscious perceptions. The fact of consciousness is a mental process which actually coincides with mental life to the exclusion of all else (Freud 1940).

In initiating the Median Group it became evident that people had been practising all sorts of large groups indiscriminately whilst the Median Group itself was emerging in a specific direction of its own. It took some years for the Group Analytic Society to recognise this and to agree to a Median Group section. The term itself, 'Median', indicated that it is in the middle, between small and large; the term was introduced by de Maré in *Koinonia* in 1991, when dialogue was referred to as distinct from free or group association; this implied that it was meaning which took priority over deterministic libidinal forces. Median groups bridge the gap between familio-tribal and society; large groups that between median group and global.

When the logic of physio-chemical numeration becomes confused with the logos of word and meaning, chaos ensues. It is the function of mind to cultivate their distinction in the form of deduction by science and

induction by the mind. It is not only chemistry which facilitates the trans-
mission of impulses across the neuronal synapses, but thinking. The mind
is bifocal: multitudinous things and the humanising of social issues on the
one hand, related to self; and the totalising of a unified wholeness of the
universe of cosmic consciousness with the humanising of the divine on the
other, related to soul.

It is fashionable today for group analysts to stress the importance of
empirical research and cost-effectiveness for the survival of group analysis.
In fact, funding only becomes necessary in a bankrupt economic system
which is itself failing, and this failure has first to be recognised by the
understanding generated not by economics but by thinking. Matter and
mind are not mutually exclusive but each is essential to the other, with the
proviso that mind takes the initiative. As we have mentioned, when group
therapy was first launched it made history and was not initially political,
scientific or cost-effective. Shakespeare commented that the brain is
female to the mind.

It is interesting that it was Anaxagoras (500 BC) who first made
references to the mind (*nous*), as the primary cause of physical change and
motion, when everything but mind, was limited by nothing, was
self-ruling (self-generative) and infinite.

Later Plato followed this line of thought believing in the spiritual view
of life. Plato and Aristotle battled with each other. They are still regarded
as the greatest of all philosophers. Aristotle postulated that it was the
senses which constitute the source of all knowledge, i.e. knowledge is of
bodily origin, whilst Plato postulated that it was ideas (forms) which were
primary. Aristotle regarded the soul as an extension of the body
(hylomorphism).

We would prefer to use the term 'scientific' as distinct from 'empirical'
research, which is evidently contradictory, oxymoronic, as are other terms
such as 'ego instincts', 'unconscious mind', 'psychic apparatus', 'dialectical
materialism'. There is no discussion, no conversation in the primary
process such as in dreams which to that extent is mindless. Collective
unconscious is collective mindlessness. Schopenhauer wrote that we forfeit
three-quarters of our minds in order to be like other people. In consum-
erism people are free to consume but not to think. In Nazism thinking is
the prerogative of the dictator, in communism of the proletariat, in
economics of the bankers, for Chomsky language, for Freud libido.

Another example of contradiction is that of Wittgenstein, who was to produce a dichotomised Wittgenstein I which was repudiated by Wittgenstein II. In *Tractatus Logico-philosophicus* (1921) he described his propositions of Logic; in *Philosophical Investigations* (1953) he dismantled his logic and attributed primacy to human beings.

The radical *res cogitans* of Descartes was the only substance to which Descartes attributed indubitality. By acknowledging this primacy of mind, much of the verbiage of modern-day thinking becomes clearer; instead of identifying with the sheer quantity of information it becomes unified by the simple reflection by a single mind.

It is in contemplation of the cosmic consciousness of the universe that personal meaning is experienced, rather like the holographic fragments reflecting the whole plate. It is a matter of choice as distinct from invasion by the repetitive machinery of materialism.

The cultivation of the Median Group constitutes a major development in revisiting the Large Group. This development marks a radical opposition, from the concrete familio-tribal approach of Freud to the psychosocial abstraction of the mind.

The introduction of the Median Group into prisons and armed forces is proving remarkably successful. In prisons, for instance, small groups have failed, since they merely stir things up by infantilisation.

The Median Group, in addressing social issues, brings about a welcome relief from tribalism. It is hoped that this unique innovation will act as an incentive for addressing other institutions such as education and group analysis itself. It is the creative inspiration of ideas which is primary for the survival of group analysis, not money.

Middle-class culture is inherently contradictory – basically the middle class consists of skilled working class – e.g. professionals, but in a mindless manner usually identified with capitalists, a viewpoint which is shared in this respect by the working class who envy the middle class, in favour of their own infantilisation, treating intelligence as 'cerebral', mutually disempowering. Revolutionaries are usually from a middle-class background. There is a similar discrepancy between capitalist owners of the means of production being disempowered by financiers, who take concrete possession of the credit system of the abstract means of distribution, presented as if it were a commodity. These are all examples of results of mindlessness and lead to confusion unless the elemental entity of mind can be included. Alas! mind is an abstraction and therefore usually disregarded in favour of mechanical, obsessional, counterphobic anality.

The Median Group is a sort of reflective think-tank which generates minding, caring, sharing, thinking, choice and decision-making. It marks a striking development in our revisiting of the Large Group initiated by Lionel Kreeger's publication in 1975. We are not concerned with the truth but with meaning. Truth is another aspect of the mind, another category, a different 'substance'. The mind is a reflecting centre. Mathematicians define 'centre' as a point so small as to be non-existent and without dimensions. Between the centre of the mind and its circumference is the circumference of reflection, so there are two circles, the reflection circle and the world circumference. Between the mind and the circumference lie the reflections, which are constituted by substances or categories: a triad of centre, circumference, and reflections which are categories.

Mind	Reflection categories	Circumference
mind	self	people
mind	thinking	thoughts
mind	soul	universe
mind	spirit	matter
mind	logos words	logic numbers
mind	caring	body
mind	fiction	facts
mind	abstraction	concrete

There are as many reflective substances or categories as there are reflected 'realities' in the circumference: two categories of self and soul.

Minding, caring, thoughtfulness are generated by the mind, which *ipso facto* creates a natural narcissism which constitutes the basic necessity for living and engenders a sense of meaning. Pausanius describes how Narcissus had a beautiful sister who reflected his own beauty – which presumably provoked the jealousy or punishment of the gods, so that she mysteriously disappeared and he wandered round the earth seeking for her, eventually locating her in the reflection of her face in a pool and drowning, so that narcissism started as a love for someone else as distinct self-love – in other words, the opposite of what is usually understood by the word, which is treated as reprehensible, causing guilt and shame.

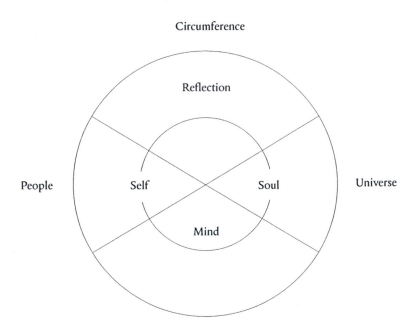

From the beginning natural, normal, healthy narcissism is given short shrift, is constantly being challenged, implying that self-love is unacceptable, like the little girl reprimanded for standing in front of a mirror declaring how beautiful she was. The net outcome of this attitude is that caring and minding and thoughtfulness cause hubris and puritanism from all sides. In therapy and the Median Group attempts are made to restore this imbalance, so that instead of good things being bad and bad things good, good is good and bad is bad; hanging on to the good reclaims the source of meaning of life, and recognition of what is patently bad becomes openly acknowledged, which is not an automatic process but a deliberate, active determination by the mind.

Shakespeare wrote: 'Self love, my liege, is not so vile a sin as self-neglecting' (Henry V).

Blackwell (2002) wrote: 'This closing down of political space effects a closing down of mental space. The currency of ideas and social discourse becomes increasingly one-dimensional and linear. In education the idea of developing a certain quality and flexibility of thought has become all but lost in a plethora of tests which measure little more than the capacity to give simple answers to trivial questions'.

Another quotation is from the Book of Wisdom, written probably about 200 BC and constituting part of the Apocrypha which is included in the Rheims-Douai version but not in the St James' version. We see wisdom as another term for mind:

> Wisdom is a spirit intelligent, holy, unique, manifold, subtle, active, incisive, unsullied, lucid, invaluable, benevolent, sharp, irresistible, beneficent, loving to man, steadfast, dependable, unperturbed, almighty, all-surveying, penetrating all, intelligent, pure and most subtle spirits; for wisdom is quicker to move than any motion; although alone she can do all.

Recapitulation

We have postulated the elemental primacy of the individual personal mind in the process of reflecting and thinking; it is the personal mind alone that singly and actually thinks; everything else, including other people's minds, are reflections of this one and only, unique mind.

From the early beginnings of Greek philosophy there has always been an interest in what in one guise or another refers to the mind, but never before have philosophers been in such a privileged position as psychotherapists in engaging in the study of the actual mind itself with the intensive consistency required for treating the mind which – is indeed their primary task. The very derivation of the word 'mind' is from the Old Norse meaning 'to vote', your personal vote. This conclusion leads one to the unique realisation that therapists have made a profound discovery of a new philosophy that must affect the entire field of philosophy generally.

As we have already pointed out, there have been many indications and references foretelling the praxis of mind. Socrates (through Plato) stated that it was 'the mission of philosophers to search into one's self and others'. Plato also wrote 'there is one kind of being which is always the same, uncreated and indestructible...invisible and imperceptible, and of which contemplation is granted to intelligence only'. He also referred to space as the third dimension of space, equivalent for us of the extensive nature of dialogue. There is a duality amongst the ancient Greeks between those who were primarily scientific, interested in acquiring knowledge and the diversity of facts, in logic and mathematics, and those who were interested in the revelations of religion, the soul, the air, the logos, mysticism. The Pythagorean view was that the empirical philosopher is a slave to his material world, whilst the mystic is a free creator of his world of beauty.

Many centuries later it was Edmund Husserl (1901) who, as a good Cartesian, reiterated Descartes' maxim (the '*cogito ergo sum*' *of res cogitas*) in the comment that there is one thing that is indubitably certain, and that is our own conscious awareness. Therefore, if we want to build our knowledge of reality on rock-solid foundations, that is the place to start. He held that the mind and nothing else has a directedness towards something outside itself, similar to Descartes' reflection, and related to Husserl's intentionality, a 'wunderbar phenomenon', the world of appearances, similar to the reflections of Descartes. Reflection precedes the reflected. This is a crucial issue for establishing an authentic philosophy of psychotherapy.

Husserl put it that to hammer his subject-object model, he had to have a hammer. The reflection is a primary, single centre to a secondary, multitudinous array of things reflected, the reflected circumference. It is the mind of reflectioning that psychotherapists address, which constitutes therapy, the source of all thinking. The machine, for instance, computes, but can never think. Since it is already programmed, is already a repetition, like obsessions, more of the same, whilst the living mind is ever new. Exercising the mind is the alternative to this mechanical repetitiveness and therefore has a healing quality, but has, like *Dasein*, to be discovered.

From a rather different stance, Karl Marx, in the opening passages of *Capital*, points out the striking dualities of stomach and imagination, the hunger of body and the appetite of mind, of consumption and production, of use value and exchange value, of actual things and their reflections, content and form – and introduces the third dimension: 'both are therefore equal to a third thing which in itself is neither one nor the other. Each of them so far as it is exchange value must be reducible to this third thing. But clearly the exchange relation of commodities is characterised precisely by its abstraction from their use values'. Money is human labour in abstract. Marx did not regard his work as scientific or economic, but 'my writings are an artistic whole'. The confusion which classical economists make between accumulation and consumption is disastrous. Of his own ill health Marx wrote that 'my sickness always originates in the mind'.

Finally it should be said that the Median Group proffers a stepping stone towards the greater understanding of Larger Groups, of which we know very little and which we would hope to explore more in the near future. Perhaps by convening several groups together.

References

Bawaroska, H. and Schick, H. (2000) 'Culture as group.' *Group Analysis 33*, *1*, 21–27.

Blackwell, D. (2002) 'The politization of group analysis.' *Group Analysis 35*, 105.

Brown, D. G. (1994) *The Psyche and the Social World.* London: Routledge.

Cooley, C. (1902) *Human Nature and the Social Order.* New York: Scribner.

de Maré, P. and Yannitsi, S. 'Phallus and kunta.' *Group Analysis 31*, 1, 121–123.

de Maré, P., Piper, R. and Thompson, S. (1991) *Koinonia: from Hate, Through Dialogue, to Culture in the Large Group.* London: Karnac Books.

Descartes, R. (1996) *Discourse on the Method and Meditations on First Philosophy.* Translated by Elizabeth Haldane and G.R.T. Ross. New Haven, CT: Yale University Press. (Ed. David Weissman)

Eccles, J. C. (1953) *The Neurophysiological Basis of Mind.* Oxford: Clarendon Press.

Freud, S. (1900) 'The Interpretation of Dreams.' *Standard Edition, 4–5.*

Freud, S.(1905) 'Three Essays on the Theory of Sexuality.' *Standard Edition 7.*

Freud, S. (1927) 'The Future of an Illusion.' *Standard Edition 21.*

Freud, S. (1940) 'Outline of Psychoanalysis.' *Standard Edition.*

Hass, D. (2001) 'Psychotherapy and research.' *Group Analysis 34*, 3, 357–393.

Husserl, E. (1901) *Logical Investigations.* The Hague: Cartesique Meditarious (1960). (Translated by Dorian Cairn.)

Kreeger, L. (1975) (ed) *The Large Group.* London: Constable.

Marx, K. (1976) *Capital.* London: Penguin Books. (First published 1867. This edition translated by Ben Fowkes, edited by Ernest Mandel.)

Parsons, D. (2000) 'Dialogue in prisons.' *Group Analysis 33*, 1, 91–96.

Penfield, W. (1950) *The Cerebral Content of Man.* London: Macmillan.

Pisani, R. (2000) 'The median group in clinical practice.' *Group Analysis 33*, 1, 77–90.

Russell, B. (1946) *History of Western Philosophy.* London: Allen and Unwin.

Wittgenstein, L. (1961) *Tractatus Logico-philosophicus.* London: Routledge and Kegan Paul. (First published 1921.)

Wittgenstein, L. (1967) *Philosophical Investigations.* Oxford: Basil Blackwell. (First published 1953.)

The Contributors

Joseph H. Berke is in private practice as an individual and family psychoanalytic psychotherapist in London, England; Fellow of the Royal Society of Medicine, Fellow and Diplomate of the American Board of Medical Psychotherapists and Psychodiagnosticians, and Registrant with the United Kingdom Council of Psychotherapy; co-founder and former Director of the Arbours Association, London, and founder and Director of the Arbours Crisis Centre. Author of many articles and books including *The Tyranny of Malice: Exploring the Dark Side of Character and Culture* (Simon & Schuster, 1988) and co-editor and contributor of *Even Paranoids Have Enemies: New Perspectives on Paranoia and Persecution* (Routledge, 1988). Currently working on a two volume study of *Psychoanalysis and Kabbalah* with Stanley Schneider.

Patrick de Maré worked with Bion, Rickman and Foulkes at Northfield Hospital. He later ran the 21st Army Exhaustion Centre during the European Campaign; in 1952, he co-founded with Foulkes the Group Analytic Society, and subsequently, with others, the Institute of Group Analysis and the Group Analytic practice; author of *Perspectives in Group Psychotherapy* (Allen & Unwin, 1972) and *Kononia: From Hate through Dialogue to Culture in the Large Group* (Karnac, 1991), in which he invented the term 'median group'.

Earl Hopper is a psychoanalyst and group analyst; Member of the British Psychoanalytical Society, the British Association of Psycho-therapists, the Group Analytic Society and the Institute of Group Analysis; Member of the National Registry of Certified Group Psychotherapists and Fellow of the American Group Psychotherapy Association; Past Chairman of the Group of Independent Psychoanalysts of the British Psychoanalytical Society, and Past President of the International Association of Group Psychotherapy; formerly Lecturer in Sociology at the London School of Economics, Cambridge University and the University of Leicester; member of the Faculty of the Post-Doctoral Program in Group Psychotherapy of Adelphi University.

Thor Kristian Island is a psychiatrist, psychotherapist, and group analyst; training group analyst and supervisor; Director of Institute of Group Analysis, Norway; committee member of European Group Analytic Training Institutions Network (EGATIN); Member of the Board of Directors, International Association of Group Psychotherapy (IAGP); past president of the Norwegian Association of Group Psychotherapy.

Lamis K. Jarrar is the Director of the Practicum and Externship Training Program, Howard University Counseling Service; Faculty, National Group Psychotherapy Institute and Advanced Psychotherapy Training Program, Washington School of Psychiatry; Faculty, Institute for Contemporary Psychotherapy and Psychoanalysis, Washington, DC; Associate, Washington-Baltimore Center, A. K. Rice Institute; and in private practice.

Otto F. Kernberg is Director, Personality Disorders Institute, New York-Presbyterian Hospital, Westchester Division; Professor of Psychiatry, Weill Medical College of Cornell University; Training and Supervising Analyst, Columbia University Center for Psychoanalytic Training and Research. Immediate past president, International Psycho-Analytical Association.

Robert M. Lipgar is a Clinical Professor, Department of Psychiatry at the University of Chicago Medical Center; Lecturer, Department of Psychiatry at the University of Illinois at Chicago College of Medicine; Diplomate in Group Psychology (American Board of Professional Psychology); Fellow of the A. K. Rice Institute; founding member and former president of the Chicago Center for the Study of Groups and Organizations of the A. K. Rice Institute; and in private practice.

Malcolm Pines is a Founder Member, Institute of Group Analysis, London; past president of the International Association of Group Psychotherapy; past president of the Group-Analytic Society; editor of the journal *Group Analysis*; editor of the *International Library of Group Analysis* series (Jessica Kingsley Publishers, London); former Consultant Psychotherapist, Tavistock Clinic, Maudsley Hospital, St George's Hospital, Cassel Hospital; former Member of the British Psychoanalytical Society.

Rolf Schmidts is a psychoanalyst; Member of the German Association of Psychoanalysis (DAP), German Group Psychotherapeutic Society (DGG), German Academy for Psychosomatic Medicine (DGPM), German Association for Dynamic Psychiatry (DGDP), German Association for Psychiatry, Psychotherapy and Neurology (DGPPN), and the General Medical Society for Psychotherapy (AÄGP); Medical Director of the Training Institute of the German Academy of Psychoanalysis (DAP); former Medical Director of the Dynamic-Psychiatric Hospital Menterschwaige.

Stanley Schneider is a psychoanalyst, training and supervising analyst and group analyst; Professor and Chairman of the Program for Advanced Studies in Integrative Psychotherapy, Hebrew University, Jerusalem; Professor and Chairman, Department of Guidance and Counseling, Michlalah, Jerusalem; Adjunct Professor, Wurzweiler School of Social Work, Yeshiva University, New York; co-founder and former Executive Director of the Summit Institute, Jerusalem; associate editor, *Psychoanalysis and History*; editorial board member, *Therapeutic Communities* and *Mikbatz: Journal of Israel Association of Group Therapy*; International Advisory Panel: *Group Analysis*.

Roberto Schöllberger is a training analyst and supervisor at the Institut f ür Psychoanalyse Zü rich-Kreuzlingen. He has worked with Psichiatria Democratica, the movement that helped to get asylums closed and made possible community psychiatry within the Mental Health Centers in Italy; supervisor of teamwork in clinical and social psychology; and leads training sessions in group therapy and group work.

Josef Shaked is a professor in applied psychoanalysis at the Institute of Psychology, Klagenfurt University. He is a psychiatrist, psychoanalyst and group analyst; training and supervising psychoanalyst and group analyst; Chairman of the Austrian Group Analytic Society; co-initiator of training courses in group analysis. He has written about, and worked extensively with, large groups in different countries.

Joseph Triest is a clinical psychologist, psychoanalyst and organizational consul- tant; Lecturer, Tel Aviv University (Department of Psychology, School of Psychotherapy, and Group Facilitators' Training Program); Board Member, OFEK, Israel; Faculty, Program in Organizational Consultation and Development: A systems Psychoanalytic Perspective (Israel); Director, Triest-Sarig Clinic.

Haim Weinberg is a clinical psychologist and group psychotherapist; Director of Tmourot Ve'Anashim Institute: Clinic for Individual and Group Therapy; Faculty, the Group Facilitators' Training Program at Tel-Aviv University and at Beit Berl College; President, Israel Association of Group Psychotherapy; Board Member, International Association of Group Psychotherapy (IAGP); Member, American Group Psychotherapy Association (AGPA) and Group Analytic Society (GAS); Moderator of the group psychotherapy discussion list on the Internet (http://www.group-psychotherapy.com).

Gerhard Wilke is a group analyst and social anthropologist working in private practice and independent consultancy. He is a Member of the Institute of Group Analysis (IGA), London; member of Board of Directors, International Association of Group Psychotherapy (IAGP); Member of the Group Analytic Society (GAS); and works in private practice.

Subject Index

Name Index

Printed in the United States
28013LVS00001B/111-118